ARTHUR YOUNG AND HIS TIMES

ARTHUR YOUNG
AND HIS TIMES

Edited by
G. E. MINGAY

Professor of Agrarian History
University of Kent at Canterbury

First published 1975 by
THE MACMILLAN PRESS LTD
London and Basingstoke
Associated companies in New York
Dublin Melbourne Johannesburg and Madras

SBN 333 15366 9

Printed in Great Britain by
WESTERN PRINTING SERVICES LTD
Bristol

Contents

List of Maps

Editor's Note

In editing the excerpts from Young's works for this volume a few archaic terms and the spelling of place-names have been modernised, and in the interest of clarity some slight amendments have been made to the original punctuation. The page references are those of the original works specified, except for the travels in France and Italy where it was thought advantageous to give the references to the most easily available modern editions.

G. E. M.

INTRODUCTION: ARTHUR YOUNG

Introduction: Arthur Young

To most of us Arthur Young is known only by a few hackneyed quotations in the standard works dealing with the eighteenth century – quotations, incidentally, often lifted quite out of context and not infrequently misinterpreted. These references are generally accompanied by a few disparaging comments referring to Young's failure as a practical farmer, and his unreliability as a contemporary observer. Even in the specialised works on agriculture, authors have been unkind to Young: Lord Ernle, who was well versed in Young's writings, gave currency to the view that 'as a practical farmer he failed, and the impression left by his writings is that he always would have done so. . . . Young was a man of strong prejudices. He was also wanting in power of generalisation.'[1] More recently, Dr Kerridge, in his *Agricultural Revolution* and other work, has indicated that Young's views are almost invariably in error, or even idiotic. Young, says Kerridge uncompromisingly, 'was a mountebank, a charlatan, and a scribbler' who 'led Ernle quite astray and helped to divert him from studying the one writer who might have put him on the right track' – his less well-known contemporary, William Marshall.[2]

Dr Fussell, too, accepted the criticism that Young was a total failure as a farmer. He held that much of Young's writing was slipshod, and that his great rival, Marshall, was a more reliable observer of the rural scene. Nevertheless, Fussell, in his article of some thirty years ago, took a more balanced view of Young than some more recent writers have done. He comments, for example, on Young's passion for precise facts and figures, his wide reading, his down-to-earth 'cash profit' approach to agricultural experiments, and his enormous enthusiasm in the cause of farming progress.[3] More, perhaps, might have been said on Young's side had his modern critics taken time to survey his many contributions to the *Annals of Agriculture*, or to examine the volumes of his correspondence and unpublished manuscripts long accessible in the British Museum.

I

Let me begin this brief discussion of Young, however, by recalling the main facts of his life.[4] He was born in 1741 of an old-established Suffolk family. His father, Dr Arthur Young, was Rector of Bradfield, near Bury St Edmunds; he was, in addition, Prebendary of Canterbury and chaplain to Speaker Onslow, and an author of religious works. As the second son Arthur did not go to university, unlike his elder brother – a fact which rankled all his life. Instead he was sent to Lavenham Grammar School, and subsequently was apprenticed for a short time to a merchant of King's Lynn. He began his career as a writer at the age of seventeen, his publishers paying in parcels of books for his precocious novels and political pamphlets. At the age of twenty Young was torn between following a literary career and farming, and at this time he turned down the opportunity of a commission in the army. It was in 1763 that he turned decisively towards agriculture, taking his first farm as tenant of 80 acres of his mother's estate at Bradfield. To this he added another farm, to a total of some 300 acres. Four years later, following a disagreement between his wife and his mother, Young moved to Sampford Hall in Essex where he had ambitions to try on his own a single farm of 300 acres. Unfortunately he was unable to raise the money with which to stock this farm, and within the year he was obliged to cut his losses and move to a smaller farm at South Mimms in Hertfordshire.

His first book of farming travels, the *Six Weeks' Tour through the Southern Counties*, was based on the excursions he made at this time to find himself a suitable farm, and this followed hard on the work which laid the foundation of his reputation, *The Farmer's Letters* of 1767. The *Northern Tour* and *Eastern Tour* rapidly succeeded, and by the time he was thirty Young had already produced seven large works on agriculture in addition to a number of lesser volumes and pamphlets. One of these works, however, was the *Course of Experimental Agriculture*. This was a rash venture which Young later admitted to be immature and unsound, and he did his best to suppress it by buying up and destroying all the copies he could lay hands on. At this period of his life he appears to have been exceptionally hard up, and while he was at South Mimms he combined farming with writing, and also held a job as Parliamentary reporter for the *Morning Post*, walking 17 miles home from Westminster every Saturday evening to spend Sunday with his family and farm. Further works rushed from his pen: *Observations on Waste Lands*, his well-known *Political Arithmetic*, and in 1780 *A Tour in Ireland*. This last was the result of his visits to that country as agent of Lord Kingsborough, and remains one of the most important works available on Ireland in the eighteenth century.

The end of the 1770s found Young in a mood of disappointment and frustration. His farm had lost money, and only his writing kept him afloat financially. And although his *Tours* and later works had brought him a very wide circle of friends among landowners and farmers, and had brought him the chairmanship of the agricultural committee of the Society of Arts, he felt that his efforts were not fully appreciated and his work had not received proper recognition. He failed to settle down in Ireland, owing to a disagreement with Lord Kingsborough; he thought of emigrating to America, but satisfied himself instead with writing on the advantages and disadvantages of living in Ohio. He applied for a professorship of Trade and Political Agriculture to be created by the Lord Mayor and aldermen of the City of London, but the scheme seems to have come to nothing.

The problem of his future eventually solved itself by the death in 1788 of his mother, leaving him the inheritance of the family estate at Bradfield. Here at last he had an adequate base for his farming experiments and for his work as the country's leading agricultural writer. A remarkably unproductive period, for him, was brought to a close by the launching of the *Annals* in 1784. He continued for thirty years editing and writing this great periodical work until at last old age and blindness forced him to give it up. In the later 1780s he toured extensively in France, Spain and Italy, but he still continued to keep the *Annals* going, led the opposition to the Wool Bill, and constantly argued in the *Annals* the advantages of a General Enclosure Act. Ill health delayed the publication of his *Travels in France* until 1792, and then followed his long period of service as Secretary to the Board of Agriculture. Throughout the war years he spent his winters in London on the business of the Board, overseeing its various activities and writing himself six of the county reports. In addition he found time to edit and contribute to the *Annals*, and published pamphlets on conditions in France, war-time scarcity, rural poverty, the need for a yeoman cavalry, manures, and other matters. The summers he spent at Bradfield, supervising his estate and farm, and working on his monumental, still unpublished, *Elements of Agriculture*. In 1811, after an unsuccessful operation for cataract, he became blind. Yet he continued his work with the aid of an amanuensis until his death in 1820 at the age of seventy-nine.

II

Over forty years elapsed between the first and last of Young's major farming works, *The Farmer's Letters* of 1767 and his *General View of Oxfordshire* of 1809. He practised farming for nearly sixty years. He spent the best part of three years in Ireland, and much of 1787–9 in France, Spain and Italy. He toured England and Wales extensively, and was especially familiar with East Anglia. He was in personal touch with the leading experimental landlords and farmers of his time, including particularly Robert Bakewell, John Ellman of Glynde, the Culleys, Thomas Coke of Holkham, Lord Townshend, Lord Egremont, the Marquis of Rockingham, Lord Sheffield, the Duke of Bedford and the Duke of Grafton. He was widely known on the continent and was in frequent communication with leading agriculturists in France, Switzerland, Italy, Russia and Poland. He had a personal correspondence with George Washington on the problems of American farming, and resisted Washington's invitation to go out to Virginia. A request from the Russian government to visit that country and make a report on its agriculture came in 1804 when he felt himself too old to undertake the rigours of the appointment, and his son, the Revd Arthur Young, went in his stead. He had pupils at Bradfield from all over Europe. He was consulted by the British government, and was chosen to guide as Secretary the first state-supported body for the improvement of agriculture. He was made a Fellow of the Royal Society, and an honorary member of countless agricultural societies in England and in Europe. He was awarded two gold medals by the Royal Society of Arts, and the Empress Catherine of Russia presented him with a gold snuffbox. In his career he published a score of major works and made over 400 contributions to the *Annals of Agriculture*, many of them very substantial accounts of tours, descriptions of experiments and implements, and other miscellaneous discussions. His books ran to second, third and fourth editions, and were published in a variety of foreign languages. The *Farmer's Kalendar*, indeed, went through ten editions in his lifetime. In 1801 the whole canon of his works was translated into French and published in twenty volumes in Paris by order of the Directory. Yet this is the man whom modern writers have characterised as an uncritical publicist, an unreliable reporter, a charlatan, a scribbler – and of course a total failure as a farmer. If they are right, how was it that Young's contemporaries were so misled? Why was he so widely regarded as the leading agricultural expert of the age? And why was he rewarded with honour after honour? Let us try to disentangle the facts and look at Young's career afresh.

First, there is the matter of his incompetence in practical farming. That he failed in Essex, and on his farm in Hertfordshire, Young freely admitted. The Essex failure, however, had nothing to do with Young's capacity as a farmer, only his incapacity of capital. It was a big farm of 300 acres and required a large sum – probably something between £1,600 and £2,000 – to stock it. In agreeing to take it Young had relied on a relation who was to lend him the necessary capital but, in the event, proved unable to find the sum required. Without his relation's capital Young was forced to abandon the farm immediately, and this he did, paying the succeeding tenant £100 to meet his unpaid bills as they came in – an action which modern commentators, for some reason, have interpreted as paying £100 to take the farm off his hands. After this fiasco, Young advertised for a farm of more moderate size. Eventually he settled on one of almost 100 acres, Bradmore Farm, at South Mimms in Hertfordshire. Here he did make a serious error, completely misjudging the true nature of the soil on seeing it in an unusually favourable season. He was not the only one taken in, however, for his Suffolk bailiff, who came along to advise him, fell into the same trap. Despite drainage, manuring, and conversion of much of it to grass, the South Mimms farm proved a disaster. 'I know not what epithet to give the soil', Young wrote later, 'sterility falls short of the idea. A hungry vitriolic gravel. I occupied for nine years the jaws of a wolf. A nabob's fortune would sink in the attempt to raise good arable crops upon any extent in such a country. My experience and knowledge increased from travelling and from practice; but all was lost when exerted on such a spot.'[5]

Young's 'failure' as a farmer, therefore, consisted of one unfortunate accident over the question of capital, and a costly mistake over the nature of the soil – a mistake that might charitably be put down to inexperience. He was twenty-seven and had been farming for only four years when he went to South Mimms. Subsequently, when he returned to Bradfield in 1778, he seems to have managed a substantial farm business without difficulty, if without financial success. It is very probable that his frequent absences, and his preoccupation with writing and the Board of Agriculture, detracted from the more efficient running of his farm. It seems, too, that careful management and profitable returns were sacrificed to his consuming interest in experiments. Certainly he remained heavily involved in the problems of practical farming, using his own land as a trial ground for a wide variety of new ideas. The gold medals awarded him by the Society of Arts were for his work on coleseed and the rearing of hogs. He also won the Society's silver medal for potatoes, and gained prizes for experiments with madder. He was interested, too, in sheep, and carried out trials with some of Bakewell's animals and other breeds. In addition he experimented with manures, and with grasses to find which varieties produced the best meadow sward; and he persevered for years with various fodder crops, including his speciality, chicory. He collected implements for purposes of comparison, and his own invention of a swing-plough was much admired and sought after.[6]

Had he been so hopeless a farmer as has been argued, it is unlikely that Bakewell would have asked him for his carrot seed, or sent him samples of wool and his own cabbage seed; or that he would have sent him some of his improved breeds of animals to try; or that the Society of Arts would have asked him to make special trials of their samples of wheat, and make experiments with gypsum as a manure; or that King George III would have made him a present of one of his specially imported Merino rams. His name was such that Jeremy Bentham consulted him on the returns obtained on investment in waste land as compared with returns on cultivated land, and wrote to suggest arguments that might be used in favour of a General Enclosure Bill. Correspondents from overseas wrote to ask his advice, and asked him to send out skilled English bailiffs and ploughmen, implements, and seed. Ivan Petrovitch-Belianin wrote from Kaluga in Russia to tell Young about his English ploughman, and to ask him to send out forty ploughs of Arbuthnot's construction, as well as sward cutters, cabbage and carrot seed, and 'a farmer's cart that does perform such a deal of work on your farm'.[7] George Washington, similarly, wrote from Mount Vernon for ploughs, and for cabbage, turnip, sainfoin, clover and rye-grass seed, and told him he had constructed a barn on Young's plans. The two exchanged views on the farming problems of Virginia, Washington telling Young that sheep were not very successful in America, though English rams had been imported and Bakewell's sheep were well known. In a comparison of labour costs, Young stated that in England a labourer could be kept for £8 in wages and a further £16 for board. In Pennsylvania, by contrast, white workers were paid £22 10s. and their keep, and 'eat and drink well, and if married keep a family on the wages'. A Negro slave, wrote Washington, cost £75 at twenty-five years of age, had an expectation of life of thirty years, and cost £12 5s. a year to keep, including interest and depreciation on his capital cost. But in comparison with a white man he 'does not perform quite as much work, nor with as much intelligence'.[8]

Again, leading landowners and progressive farmers made a point of visiting Bradfield, as did foreign visitors, who often asked Young to take their countrymen as pupils. Indeed, distinguished visitors, such as Lord Darlington and Prince Massalski, Bishop of Vilna, paid homage to Young even in his earlier days in Hertfordshire, going out of their way to see his 8 acres of experimental crops, his newly introduced Suffolk swing-plough and his collection of implements. According to a Scottish visitor who was there in 1770, 'his implements of husbandry are so many and various, & their several uses & perfections discrib'd with such Volubility of tongue, that I can say little about them'.[9] Among the foreign visitors at Bradfield was a young German, Theodor von Schön, who made his pilgrimage there in 1798. He recorded the event in his diary, excerpts from which read as follows:

22 October. To dinner at Mr Young's, where I got acquainted with his wife and a gentleman farmer from this neighbourhood, a Justice of the Peace. We debated the whole time we stood in his hall several subjects. . . . Mr Young . . . spoke extremely against A[dam] Smith, but could not bring any particular things against him, but that he had written against the plough. I objected that the whole book was written only for the plough

against the commercial system of England, and he must agree
with me in it. He declared then that A. Smith would have been
a bad farmer. I desired particular objections, and he declared
himself against the land tax, praised by A. Smith. . . . We sat
at table at Mr Young's from four o'clock till half past ten,
eating, drinking, and talking.[10]

Few of the English farmers' visits to Bradfield have left any
record, though there are three contrasting accounts on which we
can draw. George Culley, the well-known Northumberland expert
on livestock, wrote in a letter dated 23rd December 1784:

We breakfasted yesterday with Mr Young, who wishes much
to have the sending of my manuscripts into the world, but his
own writings and deeds are in such bad repute that Mr
B[akewell] will not allow me to trust it to him, saying that
everything that comes through Mr Y's hands will appear to
disadvantage. And indeed when we consider it is not to be
wondered at, people that devote their time to writing cannot
act or execute; his sheep are scabbed, his cattle ill chose and
worse managed, in short he exhibits a sad picture of mis-
management.

Again, William Mure, writing to George Culley in March 1793,
related that

at Mr Young's I did not see much worth attention, indeed
there my disappointment was great; in reading his Annals he
immediately discovers the smallest fault in any other person's
management, from that I imagined to find an example of the
Old *Arcadian* agriculture – instead of that I met with a
hodgepodge of everything without arrangement or system.

None the less, Culley, in recommending examples of English
farming practice worth studying, wrote in 1789 as follows:

If you wish him to see the Essex draining and Norfolk culture
be so kind as to say. I have no acquaintance in Essex. But am
personally acquainted with Mr Young and several of his
Farming Neighbours where I think cultivation is carried on in
a much better manner in my humble opinion than in Norfolk.[11]

John Boys, a well-known Kentish farmer who wrote the report
on Kent for the Board of Agriculture, visited Bradfield in 1792,
and again in 1793, in company with the celebrated Sussex

breeder, John Ellman. A note of disappointment can be detected in his account of these visits, but he still found much worth noticing. On the first visit Boys took particular note of Young's novel practice of stall-feeding cattle on chicory, and his great collection of ploughing implements. He noted also Young's cultivated grasses, and his sheep, which included the Spanish Merino ram presented to Young by the King, and his cross-breeding experiments with Southdowns, Norfolks and Bakewell's New Leicesters. On the second visit to Bradfield, wrote Boys, they joined such a gathering as 'was perhaps never before collected from so great a distance, most of the party coming more than a hundred miles, and one gentleman, Mr Colhoun, to wait upon Mr Young has travelled 170 miles'. The party walked round Young's farm before dinner, observing his Dishley rams and the 'collection of grasses in his experiment ground'. They noted, too, how Young used only a single pair of oxen driven by one man to turn a stiff soil, for which a Sussex or Weald of Kent farmer would have required at least eight oxen with perhaps a horse or two and two and two drivers, 'and not plough much more, in a given time, than Mr Young does with his man and pair of oxen'.[12]

So much, then, for Young as a farmer. It is clear he was an avid experimenter, and it seems likely that his farming profits were eaten up by unprofitable trials and innovations. In any event, if he was not himself efficient in farm management, this failing does not mean that he could not have been an accurate observer and shrewd assessor of other farmers' practices. Certainly he was no mere 'scribbler', but employed his keenly enquiring mind in collecting and appraising information on numerous practices from a wide variety of sources at home and abroad. At Bradfield he carried out a large number of experiments on soils, most of them as bizarre as they were unrewarding. The results he published in the *Annals*, as papers on 'Phlogiston as the Food of Animals', 'Experiments on Expelling Air from Soil', 'The Philosophical System of the Anti-Phlogistonists' and 'On the Effect of Electricity upon Plants'.[13] Isaac Milner, a chemistry don of Queens' College, Cambridge, communicated with him on his experiments with air,[14] and for a period Young was in close touch with Joseph Priestley about the effects of air and of water on the growth of plants. Priestley carried out some tests for him, and in one of his letters paid Young a remarkable tribute, saying: 'You alone have certainly done more to promote agriculture, and

especially to render it reputable in this country than all that have
gone before you.'[15]

III

Young's interests, however, ranged far beyond the problems of
practical farming. He was drawn into politics in connection with
the prohibition on the export of wool, the reform of tithes, and
the securing of a General Enclosure Act. He was interviewed by
ministers and politicians on the regulation of Irish trade, and was
regarded as the leading authority on what might be described as
the political economy of agriculture. Jeremy Bentham asked him
for information on the value of the country's land and capital,
while Young was able to tell him that the Suffolk justices had
been so impressed by Bentham's idea of the Panopticon that they
would not consider any plans for a new prison that were not based
on his principle.[16] Connected with Young's interest in the economy
was his long-standing concern with population. He was an early
advocate of a national census, and his *Proposals to the Legislature
for Numbering the People . . . . a Sketch of the Advantages that
would probably accrue from an exact Knowledge of its Present
State* appeared in 1771. One of his associates was the Revd John
Howlett, a leading investigator of population questions. Young
published some of his work in the *Annals* and corresponded with
him on matters of common interest. In 1787, for instance, we find
Howlett writing to Young for information about wages in farming
and details of the Poor Law in France.[17]

Young, of course, was much taken up in later years with the
growth of rural poverty. He considered its connection with
enclosure, and advocated the cultivation of waste lands and the
provision of cow-pastures as a means of relieving pauperism.
Numerous papers on the Poor Law appeared in the *Annals,*
including Bentham's lengthy 'Pauper Management Improved'.[18]
In the 1790s Young was increasingly concerned with the French
Revolution and its threat to Britain. His pamphlet on *The
Example of France, a Warning to Britain*, published in 1793,
quickly ran to four editions, and was translated into French,
German and Italian. He wrote also on the project for building
warships by county subscription, and he advocated the formation
of the yeoman cavalry and a kind of county Home Guard as a
protection against invasion. Lastly, although he always regarded
agriculture as by far the most important branch of the economy,

Young had a considerable interest in industry. He frequently remarked on industrial activities in his tours, and some of his descriptions are both graphic and valuable. He was particularly interested in comparing wages in industry with those in agriculture. Thus, when in the West Country in 1767, he noted that the staple industry of Gloucester was the manufacture of pins, 'which employs near 400 hands, of whom a great number are women and children: good hands at pointing and sticking earn from 10s. to 12s. and 15s. a week; children of 8, 10 and 11 years old earn 2d. and 3d. a day; but some journeymen do not get more than 7s., 8s. and 9s. a week: the wages in general are good'.[19] There is, in fact, an enormous body of material on wages scattered through Young's pages, that so far as I know has never been brought together and analysed.

Young was an advocate of more vocational forms of education, especially for the sons of landowners. When in 1789 the University of Edinburgh proposed to endow a new chair of agriculture, Young warmly supported the idea, asking: 'Why not a Professor of Agriculture in every University? ... What a scandal is it, to the good sense of the age, to see the education given to young men in England who are designed by inheritance or profession for a country residence!' Young held that a proper understanding of farming could be gained only by practical application. 'If any one imagines', he exclaimed, 'that a competent knowledge is to be gained while he is following a partridge or a fox, or from admitting a farmer to his table on a Sunday, he is egregiously mistaken. ...' A gentleman's son, he said, should be taken 'at the age of sixteen or seventeen from his school; where he ought, among other things not so essential to have learned to be very ready at figures, and to be well grounded in the first principles of geometry as to be enabled to continue that study afterwards. A knowledge of mechanics is too useful to a farmer for this to be neglected; not to speak of the more general application of mathematical studies to natural philosophy and every other art or science. ...' However, if the parents considered that an education was not complete without three or four years at the university, the student should concentrate on 'those branches of chemistry, botany and mineralogy that will afterwards be of use to him. But I must own I do not recommend the university at all; and for this plain reason, that among the great numbers of gentlemen I have known who were educated there, I scarcely know a single one that acquired any knowledge which is of the least use or application to the life and pursuits of a country gentleman.'

On leaving school, therefore, the gentleman's son should be placed 'with a considerable farmer, for board, lodging and instruction', by annual agreement for a period of ten years – a shorter span would hardly be sufficient to learn the business properly. As for location:

> I know few situations more advantageous than the neighbourhood of Bury; for, besides many very good practices within a few miles of that town, such as ploughing with two horses, without a driver, and doing it exceedingly well; hoeing turnips, and feeding them, both on the land, in stalls, and on meadows; a sprinkling of the cabbage husbandry, and sainfoin; folding sheep; hollow drainage; it is within a moderate distance of the Norfolk tillage, the carrot husbandry, and various other excellent practices by Woodbridge, and the Essex wet land management.[20]

Young's own son went up to Cambridge in 1789. Cambridge, emphasised the father, was only a prelude to earning his own living, which could best be done by achieving excellence in his studies. Young told him: 'For four years I shall continue the expense of £100 a year, after that period you must provide for yourself; my house and table will be always yours, but nothing more.' He emphasised the great importance of mathematics:

> It is the fashionable study at Cambridge and without it you will do nothing. Your tutor will explain the necessity relative to the university, I shall therefore mention only that algebraic and geometrical knowledge are applicable to all the sciences and are every day more and more applied to them, even where they seem least connected as in chemistry; and that these branches may be of essential use to you in your future destination. That destination deserves the most serious attention; a couple of wretched curacies or a lousy living will clothe you, but for God's sake have ambition to do better than that – and remember that the most ample knowledge and the most splendid attainments will not prevent your taking up with such a provision if you can do no better. Milner by chemistry is master of a College with £800 a year, Watson by the same is a Bishop; botany has made Martin and many others; mineralogy

has promoted some; and classics hundreds: there is no branch of useful science that has not conducted men to fortune provided there is excellence and superiority; but moderation and a common degree does nothing. . . .[21]

IV

Of all Young's works, it is, of course, the *Tours* that have been most consulted by historians as a source for farming conditions in the second half of the eighteenth century, and it is on the question of the reliability of his material that much of the criticism of Young as an observer has centred. It should be remarked that the three well-known *Tours* were early works, all published by 1771 when Young was only thirty. In later years he published in the *Annals* a number of shorter tours which are more mature and probably better-considered accounts, but oddly enough these have been little used. Fussell's criticism was that Young was merely a traveller, who relied on whatever titbits of information he could casually pick up, while Marshall lived in the areas he described and wrote from first-hand knowledge. Fussell's point, however, requires some qualification. In the first place Young was never a casual traveller. The method he adopted for his two major tours, those in the north and the east, as for later ones, was to advertise his journey in advance and collect letters of introduction and information about which estates and farms were worth visiting. At each stop he detailed notes of crops, livestock, practices, costs and profits, preferably direct from the landlord or farmer himself; these notes he printed almost verbatim, occasionally with criticisms of a severe kind. It is probably significant that after publication he received a number of letters from informants telling him how their practices had since developed, but few suggesting that he had got the details wrong. To judge from Bakewell's letters, however, Young's sharp criticisms were sometimes taken amiss. We can totally disregard, I think, Thomas Stone's gibe that Young depended on alehouse gossip and could be taken in by any tall story.[22] Stone had a grudge against Young, who had reviewed his *Essay on Agriculture* in the *Annals*, saying rather too frankly that it added nothing to the existing stock of knowledge and, moreover, was not free of errors.[23] Stone, furthermore, did not forgive Young for superseding him as the Board of Agriculture's reporter for Lincolnshire.

In fact, Young relied exclusively on personal information from the leading proprietors and farmers of the district; he had no faith in the wisdom of small farmers, whom he constantly characterised as ignorant and prejudiced. It is really a reflection on Stone himself that he viewed Young's progressive farmers as 'amateurs'. Innovators, he said, were considered by 'the common farmers' as men like Young himself, that is, 'book-learned, and in their vulgar conceptions are spending their money without any prospect of meeting with a return'.[24] This of course was precisely Young's point. Only wealthy landowners and farmers could afford to undertake costly experiments; the small farmers had no money to spare for the purpose, and in any case were too un-educated and conservative to see any advantage in them.

By the time of his later, more limited, tours, Young had gathered a wide acquaintance of leading farmers, many of whom became well known to him through the *Annals of Agriculture*. He knew exactly where to go in order to see the best example of particular practices, and when he travelled it was usually in company with other experts of the farming fraternity. Finally, in regard to the comparison with Marshall, it is worth pointing out that the two writers were not trying to do exactly the same thing. Marshall was concerned with describing the general practices of a particular region, adopting a highly systematic treatment in which his material was broken down under the headings of various crops, types of livestock, implements, and so on. Young never tried to describe the *general* system of any district, and made only occasional references to curious local practices and the general standards of husbandry, whether good, bad or indifferent. He was interested in finding out what the *leading* farmers of the district were doing, what new methods they were trying, and how successful they were. Marshall described the general practices; Young described the latest innovations and whether they were profitable. The distinction is an important one, and it will be seen that Young's method of collecting information was perfectly proper for his purpose, and was the only feasible way of going about it.

Young himself recognised that his original contribution lay in bringing to light the work of the progressive farmers: 'My Tours', he remarked twenty years after their publication, 'I believe were the first travelling enquiries into agriculture that have been made public.... To them I may, with a vanity perhaps somewhat excusable, assert that the agriculture of this kingdom owes much;

and that many of the improvements now practised with the greatest success may be dated from the publication of these journeys. . . .'[25] It has to be remembered that when Young began his writing the collection of precise information in a form that could be used for tabulation and comparison, and for the calculation of profit and loss, was quite novel. Hence the impact of the early *Tours* and the rapid rise of his reputation. The collection of material over so great an area was not the simplest of projects. In particular, Young had to deal with the problems of provincial terminology and local usage. As he said in the Preface to the *Northern Tour*:

For many hundred miles I had nothing but provincial weights and measures, totally unknown in the south. These were all reduced to the common standard; the intelligence I received in the most common points was conceived in such uncommon terms, and in such barbarous measures, that had I not gained numerous explanations my work would have been a volume of contradictions. A practical knowledge of agriculture is as requisite to such as plenty of patience. After abundance of explanations, I frequently had such intelligence as would have passed current with those who were inexperienced in husbandry, but which forced me to most uncommon attention to discover wherein was the mistake. My business was likewise so unusual, that some art was requisite to gain intelligence from many farmers, etc., who were startled at the first attack. I found that even a profusion of expense was often necessary to gain the ends I had in view: I was forced to make more than one honest farmer half drunk, before I could gain sober, unprejudiced intelligence. Nor were such my only difficulties; I met with some farmers who gave me accounts too improbable to credit; whether from ignorance or an intention to deceive, I know not; but I always repeated my enquiries upon those occasions, until I gained the truth.

Young probably regarded the *Annals* as his greatest achievement, and he was embittered by the smallness of its circulation. He wrote in 1791:

Before the publication of the *Annals*, where are you to find what is so often wanted to be consulted, the bills proposed in Parliament, the reports of committees, the registers of prices,

etc., etc., upon subjects intimately connected with agriculture?
You must seek them in, perhaps, £50 worth of books for the
half of fifty years. . . . It may be cited as proof of the culpable
inattention in country gentlemen, in clergy who farm, and in
opulent tenantry, that they do not give better encouragement to
such a work, which unquestionably contains much valuable
information; and which in price never yet arose to a guinea a
year . . . tell me if the *Annals* are not deserving of a better
regular sale than 350, at which number they stand at this
time![26]

An immense amount of labour was involved in editing so large
a periodical work, a task in which Young was ably assisted by his
old friend Dr Symonds of Bury, a keen agriculturist and Professor
of Modern History at Cambridge. The return on this labour was
in satisfaction rather than money, for the *Annals* was never a
profitable project. Young had difficulty, initially, in estimating
the likely circulation and the best number of copies to print, so
that he was left with many unsold copies on his hands. As he
remarked, it was 'a work greatly praised but not bought'. He
persevered with it, however, confident that it would 'convey to
posterity, so vast a magazine of information, and truly useful
experiments, that it is impossible it should fail to be of eminent
utility to the progressive improvement of the agriculture of these
kingdoms'.[27] He often reprinted a whole number for the sake of
selling a single complete set, but in 1795 he was obliged to
confess to his friend Dr Ruggles, the authority on the Poor Law,
that 'the *Annals* have not prospered of late. . . . I have thought
more than once of dropping the work entirely but the dead stock
of £3,000 in my warehouse prevents doing anything rashly. It is
a beggarly landed interest that cannot support one periodical
publication on that subject.'[28]

Throughout his life Young believed that agriculture did not
receive its due attention and was neglected both by the landed
interest and by Parliament. No issue favourable to farming,
exclaimed Young, could 'pass our manufacturing, trading, and
shop-keeping legislature. If the angel Gabriel from heaven
appeared with a proposal to promote agriculture, he would be
scouted.'[29] Young similarly considered that his own contribution
to agriculture had been underrated. In 1791, after the first thirty
years of his farming life, he reviewed his career to date:

I may say with confidence, because I say it with truth, that during that period I have hardly known what an idle hour has been. I have worked more like a coalheaver (though without his reward) than a man acting only from a predominant impulse. And for what all this restless activity – this eternal struggle! To serve the public (I am sure I have failed dreadfully if it was to serve myself) – a public, that if I were in the dungeon of a prison, would leave me to rot there.[30]

V

Certainly Young's work never made him a wealthy man. While at Bradmore Farm, his 100 acres of 'hungry vitriolic gravel' in Hertfordshire, he seems to have been in dire straits. A reckoning of his accounts at the end of 1771 showed his receipts at only £697 while his expenses amounted to £360 – 'I know not how', he commented. His wife, never the most complaisant person, it seems, 'detested' his experiments, maintaining 'I had ruined myself by them'. Fanny Burney found the couple 'at present reduced to a most distressful state. They seem to have almost ruined themselves, and to be quite ignorant in what manner to retrieve their affairs.'[31] A constant concern with money runs through Young's private correspondence. Returning from Ireland in October 1776 he wrote to his wife: 'My passage has cost me between £7 and £8 – which is the very devil, so that I shall come home without a shilling and the thought of coming full swing upon poverty again makes me miserable.'[32]

In 1776, of course, Young was still at an early stage of his career. But even ten years later, after succeeding to the Bradfield property, he was still anxious about expenses. In the spring of 1787 he was invited to accompany a group of French noblemen on a visit to the Pyrenees. Young was most enthusiastic about the trip but he would go, as he told them, only if the party did not travel post, which was expensive, but on their own horses. He was assured that the only expense would be for himself and his horse, and that the journey would lie 'mostly in a cheap part of the kingdom'.[33] The journey indeed proved interesting, but it irked Young that his companions wanted to spend time in conversation or playing cards when he wished to be out and looking at the farms. His next journey in France the following year he therefore made alone on horseback, 'my cloak-bag behind me; and I did not travel thus an hundred miles before my mare fell blind: I have

heard and read much of the pleasure of travelling; how it may be
with posting – avant couriers preparing apartments and repasts,
I know not; let those who enjoy such comforts pity me who made
1700 miles on a blind mare! and brought her (humanity would
not allow me to sell her) safe back to Bradfield'.[34] At Amiens he
almost ran into Charles James Fox, who travelled 'with a girl in
a post chaise . . . a waiting woman, and his valet in a cabriolet and
a French courier – the English at the Table d'hote said he
travelled in no style. It is however a plaguy style from mine, but
I have been doing all my life and he has been talking; and therefore my blind mare is but the world's justice, tho' not very
practical.'[35]

On his third journey to France and Italy in 1789 Young
travelled in a one-horse chaise, which was both more comfortable
and more convenient for carrying his specimens of remarkable
soils, samples of wool, and examples of manufactures. The horse
and chaise cost him 32 louis at Paris, and after carrying him
1,200 miles he was able to sell them again for 22 louis before
proceeding into Italy. 'It is much more comfortable', he confided,
'as I carry my baggage and regale with clean shirts which in a
hot climate is the first luxury.'[36] Nevertheless, he still practised
the strictest economy. He made the £100 he brought with him
last the whole first six months of this visit, and his expenses, it
may be noted, included the purchase of numerous books. In Italy
he was delighted by the cheapness of everything. He stayed in
Petrillo's, the first inn in Venice:

> . . . a clean comfortable room; excellent fine sheets; two
> windows that look out on to the Grand Canal and the Rialto,
> my breakfast of coffee and cakes $1\frac{1}{4}d$. Dinner: good soup, a
> whole fowl, a piece of beef, two small birds, brains, greens,
> ragout and two or three other things. Parmesan cheese, grapes,
> pears, etc., and a bottle of good wine 1s. 8d. Supper: a bottle
> of wine sealed, nutmeg, sugar, cheese and fruit 10d. Room 10d.
> Pit at the Opera 10d. My gondola and gondolier, equivalent
> to a coach everywhere else, the whole day 1s. 8d. In all 5s. 10d.
> a day, which is a common dinner at a London coffee house and
> not a dinner at the White Horse, Saxham [Saxmundham]:
> well attended by smart waiters who after five or six days will
> thank me for 2s. 6d. among them all. . . .[37]

Cheapness, he discovered, had its drawbacks, however. Writing in

November 1789, he told his daughter, Mary, that the journey from Venice to Bologna 'was the most disagreeable I ever made: all cheap things are alike. All expenses were paid for 30 livres or 18*s.*; but we laid on the floor, and eat steaks out of a snuffy, snotty handkerchief of the Courier, yet people in it above what you would think of.'[38]

Yet despite his search for economy Young was essentially a man of culture, mixing in the best society, visiting the theatre, and collecting a large private library. On his visit to Ireland Young reported on 'an ill-judged and unsuccessful attempt to establish the Italian Opera' in Dublin. 'Of course they could rise no higher than a comic one'; three pieces 'were repeatedly performed, or rather murdered . . .'. At Bordeaux in 1787 he described in a letter home the great quay, two miles long, with its hundreds of vessels, and went on:

> Besides this they are raising many new buildings, have a theatre far beyond London or Paris – it cost £270,000 English. Plays or operas every night in the year, Sundays not excepted; we went twice, as Larive, the first actor of Paris, is there, he has 25 guineas a night and two benefits. Dauberval and his wife are the chief dancers (she was the Theodora at London) – they have £1,500 a year. Sixty dancers, five or six capital, and everything established on the greatest scale. The luxury and expense of the place are great, and in consequence the merchants are bankrupts – some every year. They have some good inns also – but like all in France inconsistent: we were served on plate, and yet they had no necessary house that it was possible to go to.[39]

VI

Young was evidently a complex character, a man of enormous energy and great physical endurance, with a keen, inquisitive mind and deep intensity of feeling. The religious conversion which overtook him on the death of his favourite daughter greatly altered his life in later years. His married life was unhappy, and his wife appears to have been a difficult, un-cooperative, and ill-natured woman. A French visitor to Bradfield in 1784, François de La Rochefoucauld, did not enjoy the occasion for he found Young's table was 'the worst and dirtiest possible', while Mrs Young, looking 'exactly like a devil', 'hideously swarthy', and 'thoroughly evil', was reported as continuously tormenting her children and her servants, and frequently bad-tempered towards visitors. Young's writing must often have been done under very trying conditions, though he had a natural gift and his prose, at its best, was racy and vigorous, carrying the reader along with him; but when he tried to write impressively he became pompous and dull. It is true that one can easily find conflicting opinions expressed in his work (for example, on the effects of enclosure), but it must be remembered that his writing career spanned more than half a century in a period in which agricultural conditions were changing rapidly. It is not really surprising that an author who wrote so much – in his own opinion, too much – should reverse some early judgements when events proved them unsound or inapplicable in new conditions.

What did he achieve? His first biographer, writing soon after his death, listed among his achievements his success in bringing agricultural improvements to the public attention and his spreading of new ideas; the urging of enclosure and the cultivation of waste lands; his advocacy of the Board of Agriculture; his support for the census; his stand against the French Revolution and the successful suggestion of the yeoman cavalry. One might add to these the first-hand accounts of Ireland in the later 1770s and France in the later 1780s – both greatly used by historians. But I think his greatest work was undoubtedly the encouragement of innovation in farming and, despite the limited range of his readership, the spreading of a scientific, yet strictly commercial, attitude to progress in agriculture. In many ways this foreshadowed the work of Caird, Bennet Lawes, and all the innovators in the application of chemistry and machinery of the middle nineteenth century. Entering Suffolk in the course of his farming tour of 1850–1, Caird wrote as follows:

This country possesses a peculiar interest to the agriculturist as having been for many years the residence of Arthur Young. We had the good fortune to meet with Mr Biddell of Playford, himself an extensive farmer, who was acquainted with Arthur Young, and had frequently conversed with him on agricultural subjects. His ideas are represented to have been much in advance of the period in which he lived, and though they were ridiculed by the great body of the 'practical' men of his day, our informant has lived to see most of his recommendations carried into practice, and considers the county indebted to him for much of the progress that has been made in the cultivation of its soil and the economical application of labour.

Fifty years later Rider Haggard, the novelist, consciously modelled his own farming tour of a depressed rural England on Young's journeys of the 1770s. Like Young he announced his tour in advance, and accepted invitations to visit particular estates and farms with an eye to obtaining a good geographical coverage. He had also in common with Young the background of experience of practical farming and of belonging to a family of minor landed gentry.[40]

Young was no parochial enthusiast. His contacts, like his reading, were wide, and inded international, and he was a pioneer in the comparative study of farming systems. Through his books, his *Annals*, his knowledge of the progressive farmers and their practices, and his personal acquaintance with the leading men of the age – with Priestley, Davy, Bentham and Banks; Burke, Washington, Sheffield and Rose; Mansfield, Eldon and Cowper; Johnson, Wesley, Wilberforce, Reynolds, Burney, Sheridan and Nelson – he kept before the public eye his own profound belief in the primacy of agriculture, and above all the importance in agriculture of improvement.

Our last glimpse of Young, ageing and blind, is at Bradfield in the last of the Napoleonic years. He was still working away at the enormous *Elements of Agriculture* and had become an enthusiast for the steam engine, believing that agriculture would never be brought to perfection until every farm was designed in a circle with the steam engine in the centre to do all the work. He educated and clothed some thirty or forty poor children of the neighbourhood, and every Sunday a hundred tenants and villagers came to Bradfield Hall for prayers and an address from the aged agriculturist, whose ambition it was to make his little service a rival attraction to the alehouse. For much of this time his companion was young Marianne Francis, the granddaughter of Charles Burney, the musician. She spent a number of summers at Bradfield, helping Young with his schools and prayer meetings. In her letters she spoke about the delightful grounds and magnificent trees, 'beautifully laid out by Mr Young himself – the shade and the air – and the good library and a kind welcome. . . . You would like Arthur Young', she wrote. 'He admires you [Mrs

Piozzi] and Dr Johnson as much as the plough and the steam engine, which is saying a great deal for *him* .... and famous, *very* famous I believe he has been in his time – medals without end for his services: the King of England sending him rams, and the Empress of Russia snuffboxes for his labours. . . .'[41]

Finally, perhaps I may add one last point that may help restore Young in our favour – he was a devotee of economic history. This you will see if you look at his *Travels in France*:

> To a mind that has the least turn after philosophical enquiry, reading modern history is generally the most tormenting employment that a man can have: one is plagued with the actions of a detestable set of men, called conquerors, heroes, and great generals; and we wade through pages loaded with military details; but when you want to know the progress of agriculture, of commerce, and industry, their effect in different ages and nations of each other – the wealth that resulted – the division of that wealth – its employment – and the manners it produced – all is a blank![42]

NOTES

1. Lord Ernle, *English Farming Past and Present*, 6th ed. (1961) pp. 195–7.

2. Eric Kerridge, *The Agricultural Revolution* (1967) pp. 26, 38, 274, 309; 'The Agricultural Revolution Reconsidered', *Agricultural History*, XLIII (1969) 466.

3. G. E. Fussell, 'My impressions of Arthur Young', *Agricultural History*, XVII (1943) 135–44.

4. Since this introduction was first drafted, Dr Gazley's new and authoritative biography of Young has appeared: John G. Gazley, *The Life of Arthur Young, 1741–1820* (Philadelphia: American Philosophical Society, 1973). I have been able to draw on this work for some of the following details of Young's career.

5. *Annals of Agriculture*, xv (1791) 155–6.

6. B.M. Add. MSS. 35,127, ff. 127, 462; 35,128, ff. 1, 21.

7. Ibid., 35,127, ff. 292–3; 35,128, ff. 368, 372–3.

8. A. Young (ed.), *Letters from his Excellency General Washington to Arthur Young Esq., F.R.S.* . . . (1801) pp. 4, 19, 82–3, 86, 112–13, 141.

9. M. Tomkins, 'Arthur Young at Bradmore Farm', *Herts. Past and Present* (1970) pp. 15–20.

10. Journal of Theodor von Schön, Staatliches Archivelager Göttingen, Depositum von Brünneck 57.

11. Northumberland Record Office, ZCU 1, 18, 44. I owe these references to the kindness of Dr D. J. Rowe.

12. *Annals*, XIX (1793) 89–93; XXI (1793) 75–7.

13. Ibid., III (1785); VII (1786); XII (1789); XIV (1790).

14. B.M. Add. MSS. 35,126, f. 360 (1 Jan 1787).

15. Ibid., f. 225 (22 June 1783).

16. B.M. Add. MSS. 33,541, f. 609 (10 Oct 1794).

17. B.M. Add. MSS. 35,126 f. 409 (5 Nov 1787).

18. *Annals*, XXX, XXXI, XXXII (1798–9).

19. *Southern Tour* (1768) p. 109.

20. *Annals*, XI (1789) 367–8; XXI (1793) 235, 237–8, 240–1, 243, 253.

21. B.M. Add. MSS. 35,126, f. 478.

22. T. Stone, *A Review of the Agricultural Survey of Lincolnshire by Arthur Young*, 2nd ed. (1800) p. 71.

23. *Annals*, IV (1785) 353.

24. Stone, op. cit., p. 74.

25. *Annals*, XV (1791) 156–7.

26. Ibid., pp. 170–1.

27. Ibid., pp. 166–8.

28. Quoted by John G. Gazley, 'Arthur Young, Agriculturalist and Traveller, 1741–1820: Some Biographical Sources', *Bull. John Rylands Library*, XXXVII (1954–5) 423.

29. *Annals*, XIV (1790) 313.

30. Ibid., XV (1791) 177.

31. Tomkins, loc. cit.

32. B.M. Add. MSS. 35,126, f. 31.

33. *Annals*, XV (1791) 173.

34. Ibid., p. 174.

35. B.M. Add. MSS. 35,126, f. 426 (10 Aug 1788).

36. Ibid., f. 466 (9 July 1789).

37. Ibid., f. 490 (30 Oct 1789).

38. Ibid., f. 492 (18 Nov 1789).

39. *A Tour in Ireland* (1780) p. 4; B.M. Add. MSS. 35,126, f. 396 (2 Sept 1787).

40. James Caird, *English Agriculture in 1850–1851* (1852; new ed., 1967) p. 144; H. Rider Haggard, *The Days of my Life* (1926) II 136–7, 151–2.

41. Gazley, loc. cit., pp. 420–1.

42. *Travels in France* (1790) I 506.

SELECTIONS FROM THE WRITINGS
OF ARTHUR YOUNG

CHAPTER I

Farming Issues of the Period

I. THE PRIMACY OF AGRICULTURE

Young's interest in agricultural affairs ranged far beyond the technical details of practical farming which filled a great number of his pages. Each of his major *Tours* was completed by a lengthy section in which he brought together the information he had gathered on rents, prices, labour costs, size of farms, employment, and other matters. All these data were summarised for purposes of comparison and analysis with the object of throwing light on topical issues of the day, to support or refute, for example, the contentions which were made about the effects of large farms on output and employment, or the view that labour costs varied with distance from London. Young thus entered into the realm of what we would now call agricultural economics, but was then a branch of what was known as 'political arithmetic'. Young published a well-known volume devoted entirely to this subject, and he enjoyed a considerable reputation as a political arithmetician, Indeed, a reviewer of his *Travels in France* claimed that he wrote more effectively and knowledgeably on this topic than on anything else.

Throughout his life Young firmly believed in the overriding importance of agriculture. It was in his day by far the largest sector of the economy, and indeed it remained so for some decades after his death. Though Young lived in the age of the industrial revolution, and himself wrote on such of its manifestations as the Bridgewater Canal, the expansion of industrial Birmingham, and the proliferation of cotton factories, he nevertheless saw agriculture as the fundamental source of the country's wealth and employment. It has to be remembered that in the late 1760s and early 1770s, when Young was publishing his first books, agriculture employed directly something like two-fifths or perhaps rather more of the working population. Even in 1809, when he completed his last important work, it still employed about a third of a rapidly growing labour force, and in absolute numbers more people were working on the land than ever before. If one were to add in all those people who indirectly obtained their living from the soil – the landowners and their stewards and servants, professional men such as country attorneys and doctors, surveyors and enclosure commissioners, country-town tradesmen like the maltsters, millers and seedsmen, and craftsmen such as the blacksmiths, harness-makers, wheelwrights, and building workers engaged on repairing and rebuilding country houses and farmhouses, to say nothing of all those engaged in the transport and marketing of grain, livestock, cheese, hides and timber – then the figure would be far more impressive. When Young began his career it is probable that the land supported well over a half of the country's population.

Young was not mistaken, therefore, in emphasising the primary significance of agriculture. He was convinced that anything which helped to increase agricultural efficiency and output must be of importance, and must help to improve the welfare of the country at large. Equally, any government measure or traditional custom which he saw as obstructing agricultural progress was to be exposed for what it was, a hindrance to welfare, and pressure applied to get rid of it. Hence the violence of his attacks on the open fields, small farmers, and tithes, and his warm support for long leases, a General Enclosure Act, and the free export of wool. The basic principles of his views are well brought out in the following passage:

Both public and private wealth can arise only from three sources, *agriculture, manufactures,* and *commerce.* Hence the connection and importance of the present reflections must be sufficiently manifest. Agriculture much exceeds both the others; it is even the foundation of their principal branches.

In this view appears the vast importance to the state, of carrying the products of the earth to the highest pitch of which they are capable. Raising them, as I before observed, is increasing *general wealth,* and raising the *income* of all the ranks of the people; the public stock is therefore augmented; and as taxes are mostly laid on *consumption,* or *possession* (principally the former), an increase of riches and income infallibly increases taxes: since perhaps nine-tenths of income is, in some way or other, melted in the consumption of taxed commodities.

Northern Tour (1770) IV 525–6

2. YOUNG'S PRINCIPLES OF POPULATION

Young lived in a period when the population of England was rising at an unprecedented rate, after a century or more of near-stagnation. In England and Wales the population trebled to reach 18 million in the hundred years before 1850. Population was an aspect of political economy which always interested Young, and he was an early advocate of the desirability of carrying out a census in order to establish the precise size of the population, a step which was not taken until 1801. He ridiculed those who believed that numbers were actually falling, and confidently asserted the contrary. The rise in numbers, he thought, was associated with the increase in the demand for goods, and hence with higher levels of employment. Production, Young held, itself produced the numbers required to sustain it, because it provided the volume and regularity of employment which made it easy for parents to bring up families. His ideas are expressed with characteristic forcefulness in the next passage:

Increasing the demand for a manufacture does not raise the price of the labour, it increases the number of labourers in that manufacture, as a greater quantum or regularity of employment, gives that additional value to the supply, which creates the new hands. Why have the inhabitants of Birmingham increased from 23,000 in 1750, to 30,000 in 1770?[1] Certainly because a proportional increase of employment has taken place. Wherever there is a demand for hands, there they will abound: this demand is but another word for ease of subsistence, which operates in the same manner (the healthiness of one, and the unhealthiness of the other allowed for) as the plenty of land in the back country of America. Marriages abound there, because children are no burthen – they abound in Birmingham for the same reason, as every child as soon as it can use its hands, can maintain itself, and the father and mother need never to want employment, that is, income – land – support. Thus where employment increases (Birmingham), the people increase: and where employment does not increase (Colchester), the people do not increase. And if upon an average of the whole kingdom employment has for a century increased, most certainly the people have increased with it.

[1] Probably an underestimate: the modern figure for 1760 is 35,000 [Ed.].

Go to the shipping of the kingdom, it will be found the same; our sailors have increased. Why? Because their employment has increased. As long as the demand for seamen increases, that demand will be answered, let it rise as high as it will.

Nabobs from the Indies, planters from America, merchants from the exchange settle in the counties, they farm, garden, plant, improve – they want men, their demand is answered, and was it regular would around every great house found support a town.

Go to the villages, the same truth will everywhere be apparent: if husbandry improves, it will demand more labour – that demand is the encouragement of the production of the commodity demanded – and it will be supplied. Who supposes that a county of warrens, heaths, and farming slovens, converted to well-tilled fields, does not occasion an increased demand for hands? And was it ever known that such a demand existed without being supplied?

But the hands, it is said, leave certain villages and go to towns. Why? Because there is not employment in one case, and there is in another – their going to the town proves that they go to employment – they go to that very circumstance which is to increase their number. They go, because they are demanded; that demand it is true takes, but then it feeds them.

Let any person go to Glasgow and its neighbourhood, to Birmingham, to Sheffield, or to Manchester – according to some writers, every cause of depopulation has acted powerfully against such places: how then have they increased their people? Why, by emigrations from the country. It would be very difficult for any person to show me a depopulation in the country comparable to the increase of towns, not to speak of counter tracts in the country that have doubled and trebled their people. But why have not these emigrations been to other towns, to York, to Winchester, to Canterbury, &c.? Because employment does not abound in those places – and therefore they do not increase. Does not this prove that in every light you view it, it is employment which creates population? A position impossible to be disproved; and which, if allowed, throws the enquiry concerning the depopulation of the kingdom into an examination of the decline or increase of employment. . . .

What are the terms of complaint for depopulation in this kingdom? People scarce – labour dear; would you give a premium for population, could you express it in better terms? The commodity wanted is scarce, and the price raised; what is this but saying, that the value of MAN is raised. *Away! my boys – get children, they are worth more than ever they were.* What is the characteristic of a populous country? *Many people, but labour dear.* What is the mark of a country thinly peopled? *Few people, and labour cheap.* Labour is dearer in Holland than in any part of Europe, and therefore it is the most populous country in Europe.

Dr Price[1] says that for the last 80 years there has not been one great cause of depopulation which has not operated among us. What is the great encouragement of population? *Ease of acquiring income*: It is of no consequence whether that income arises from land, manufacture, or commerce; it is as powerful in the pay of a manufacturer, as in the wilds of America. What is the great obstacle to population? *Difficulty of acquiring income.* Here then we have a criterion, by which to judge of the population or depopulation of any period. If you view the country and see agriculture under such circumstances that the farmer's products will not pay his usual improvements, consequently he dismisses the hands he formerly kept. If the manufactures of the kingdom want a market, then the active industry exerted in them becomes languid, and decays. If commerce no longer supports the seamen she was wont to do – if private and public works, instead of entering into competition for hands with the manufacturer and the farmer, stand still amidst numbers who cry in vain for work – if these effects are seen, a WANT OF EMPLOYMENT will stare you in the face, and that want is the only cause of depopulation that can exist. Have these spectacles been common in the eyes of our people since the revolution? Are they common at present? Does not the great active cause, EMPLOYMENT, operate more powerfully than ever? Away then with these visionary ideas, the disgrace of an enlightened age – the reproach of this great and flourishing nation.

Political Arithmetic (1774) pp. 61–8

3. THE OPPOSITION TO REFORM

It greatly irked Young that, as he believed, so many improvements

[1] Dr Richard Price (1723–91), a well-known writer on financial and political questions [Ed.].

in farming were being held back by the conservatism of landlords
and farmers, the opposition of vested interests, and the apparent
indifference of Parliament. The effects of such attitudes could be
seen in the difficulty of securing a General Enclosure Act which
would reduce the cost of enclosing land, the hostility of the church
towards the idea of commuting tithes into allotments of land or
permanent cash payments, and the unwillingness of many landlords to assess their rents at a level which might induce more
activity among their tenants. Young was incensed that Parliament
rejected a Bill designed to enable proprietors anywhere to enclose
their commonable lands under the supervision of a jury of dis-
interested persons. This measure, had it been adopted, might
have reduced the harmful effects that some Enclosure Acts had
on small proprietors and cottagers. It might also have obviated
the need to obtain a separate private Act for each enclosure, and
so have avoided the Parliamentary and legal fees involved in
promoting a private Act in Parliament. To Young's chagrin, the
influence of those who drew an income from the fees, together
with the desire of Parliament to maintain a watch on the conditions under which land was enclosed, contributed to the defeat
of the Bill:

> The warmest wishes to serve the public, corrected by the
> coolest judgment to effectuate the means, could scarcely bring
> forward a proposition more unexceptionable than this.
>   A set of persons have shares in commonable lands, which they
> wish to be assigned them in severalty; instead of demanding a
> legislative act, to force others to conform to their desires, this
> bill enables them to demand their shares, without any control
> on the opinion of others. In the common acts of enclosure, the
> will of a part of the proprietors, by force, becomes binding on
> the whole, in spite of every opposition, however violent. In this
> proposition no man is forced to relinquish any right that belongs
> to him; and it secures nothing to any man but an exemption
> from being bound by the despotic will of another. He who
> refuses his assent to my having, in severalty, my legal, recog-
> nised, and decided share of a common, because he does not
> choose himself to have his own share, is a tyrant, whose will
> ought not to be a law. If one set of proprietors wish an
> enclosure, and another set wish the common to remain as it is,
> how can there be a more equitable method of settling the

question between them, than by assigning an enclosure to those who wish it, and leaving open lands to those who demand them?

It would only be taking up the reader's time vainly to suppose the objections to this plan – they are equally obvious and vague – and, in truth, there was not one argument advanced in the House of Commons against the bill that merited one moment's attention.

But it was lost. If the reader asks, why? he can only be answered, that it was a measure well calculated to favour the agriculture of this kingdom – and such measures never can pass our manufacturing, trading, and shop-keeping legislature.

If the angel Gabriel from heaven appeared with a proposal to promote agriculture, he would be scouted.

If an imp from somewhere else appeared with one to fetter it in favour of the loom or the counter, he would be heard with applause.

Annals of Agriculture, xiv (1790) 312–13

4. TAXATION AND AGRICULTURE

Young's review of British taxation in his *Political Arithmetic* indicated, as he said, that little of the tax burden fell on agriculture. The land tax, a tax originally introduced in 1692 in order to help meet the cost of William III's wars with France, was not prejudicial to agricultural production because it had become in effect a fixed levy, paid by landlords out of their rents and not by tenants out of their profits. (It is known, however, that some landlords attempted to pass the tax on to their tenants, though presumably at the expense of accepting a reduced rent.) A tax that was fixed in assessment (as it became), and did not vary with the volume of output, was clearly not an obstacle to agricultural improvement, Young argued.

The parish rates levied for the maintenance of the poor, repair of the roads, and upkeep of the church, were borne by the farmer, and he was assessed for these rates on the basis of the rent he paid. Rates, therefore, were likely to prove an obstacle to improvement since an increase in the productivity of land would result in due course in an increase in rent, and so in a higher assessment for rates. However, landlords were not in the habit of revising their rentals very frequently, and in periods of rising output and prices tenants enjoyed long periods in which rents and assessments lagged behind events. Moreover, the evidence collected by Young in the course of his early *Tours* showed the average rates in farming districts to be quite low. In the later years of the century and after, however, the level of rates was increased by inflation, the spread of industry into many villages, particularly in the Midlands and north, and the expense of supporting large numbers of pauperised labourers. In the southern counties which were most affected by underemployment and poverty among farm labourers, rates rose to burdensome figures, though there is little direct evidence that this, by itself, had much influence on the survival of small farmers, as has been argued. In any event, as Young rightly observed, a high level of rates was reflected in a reduced level of rents, since landlords had to keep their rents low enough to attract tenants in high-rated areas. Much of the increased weight of parish rates, therefore, fell on the landlord rather than the tenant.

The other taxes which were levied when Young wrote his *Political Arithmetic* were not particularly burdensome. Customs and excise did not bear heavily on agriculture, although the prohibition on the export of wool and leather tended to lower the prices of those commodities on the home market. The Corn Law of 1773 prohibited the export of wheat when it was at or above 44s. a quarter, and allowed in imports of wheat at a nominal duty of 6d. when it was at or above 48s. In the 1770s and 1780s the country was just at the stage of ceasing to be a substantial exporter of grain, and slowly becoming an importer; imports, however, were still very small in relation to the total supply, so at this point the Corn Law had little impact on price levels in the home market. Young was impressed by the fact that indirect taxes, such as customs and excise duties, were absorbed into the market price of commodities and were not very obvious to the consumer. He held that it would be advantageous for agriculture, and hence for the country at large, if the whole of government revenue was raised by indirect taxes so that the entire burden would fall on consumption rather than on landlords' rents and farmers' profits:

The public revenue of Britain is raised by such a mode of taxation that little of the weight falls on husbandry. The great division of our taxes is into: 1. Land; 2. Parish; 3. Windows; 4. Excises; 5. Customs. As to the smaller objects of stamps, licences, post-office, &c., none of them bear the least upon one set of men more than another, nor are they burthensome to any.

The land-tax is raised absolutely and totally upon the landlord, though paid by the tenant. In all cases it is the same thing to the farmer whether he pays his rent immediately to his landlord, or to the King in taxes; the latter are first carried to account, and the balance to his landlord is always proportioned to what he has already paid for land-tax. Whether it is one shilling or four in the pound, it is just the same to the farmer – the landlord is the only one concerned.

If he farms his own estate he pays it himself, which makes no other difference than the mere trouble of the payment.

An immense advantage is the amount of the tax being fixed: if I buy or inherit an estate consisting of waste or poorly cultivated tracts, which let only for an hundred pounds a year, and pay a tax of five pounds to the state; and if after by spirited exertions I advance the annual value of my estate to a thousand pounds a year, the tax remains just as it was before – no increase. This is an advantage, and an encouragement to improvements which no system can exceed. (Note: In one respect this is not so fully the case: the sums which parishes are assessed always remain the same, but the officers may vary the assessment on individuals; but then they must know at what rent a farm is let before they can raise any person's tax, and the person so raised may appeal if every other person in the parish is not equally taxed, which makes such alterations in the assessment rare.)

Several English writers have pleaded for a new and more equal land-tax, which might be perhaps a good measure if there was an absolute certainty of its then remaining unchangeable for at least a century; but as we cannot have such certainty, I must esteem it a most dangerous idea; for if the tax was by a general new assessment made an equal and fair one, then there would not be the same reason as at present for opposing alterations: a tax of so much in the pound, varying according to rent, would be at once a tithe, and the most pernicious system that could be invented because an improver would be TAXED IN PROPORTION TO HIS IMPROVEMENTS. Let therefore the tax remain upon its present footing: it is now perfectly innocent; if altered we know not where the alterations would stop.

Another circumstance which renders our land-tax so little burthensome to the agriculture of the kingdom is its being laid absolutely upon *rent*: the assessors cannot tax the landlord for any supposed or visible value; if a farm is ever so rich, or supports ever so many cattle, it is nothing to the assessor, he can tax the rent only; and if the landlord farms it himself he can only be taxed according to the rent the last time the farm was let, though an hundred years ago, and would at present let for quadruple the sum; if the old rent cannot be discovered the old assessment is continued, without enquiring on what foundation it was formed.

From this slight review of the land-tax of England it appears to be no burthen on agriculture: no system of taxing land could have been invented that would injure it so little.

It is not so with parish taxes: they are laid immediately on the farmer, and prove a burthen to him in proportion to their weight. They consist of the poor's rate, or the sums raised for the support of the chargeable poor; the church rate, for keeping in repair the parish church; the highway rate, raised by the surveyors for the repair of the roads. The latter is not general, as the statute duty of six days work with their teams is commonly more than sufficient; and in no case, by act of parliament, more than a rate of sixpence in the pound of rent can be laid in aid of the duty: this is the only resemblance we have in England of the Corvées of France and the monstrous personal service which is so destructive to the agriculture of Germany and Poland. The amount in England cannot be called burthensome since the six days work are performed only at a leisure time of the year, and may be generally compounded for at a fourth part of the real value.

With the poor's rate there is usually a few other small taxes thrown together, such as the constable's expenses, which however are trivial, and the county rate, being a county expense for certain bridges and other general expenses which concern the county at large; when divided among all the parishes it is a very small amount. The poor's tax, with these additions, including the church rate, are usually all thrown together and raised by a single rate, in which every occupier of lands or houses is charged in proportion to his rent. The

average of them in my *Northern Tour* came only to 1s. 1d. in
the pound; and in the *Eastern Tour* to 2s. 8d.; average of both
1s. 10½d. But in manufacturing, and many other particular
places, they rise much higher.

The reader will observe that this tax is entirely regulated by
the rent of the land, which is a circumstance that renders the
burthen comparatively light: if a man hires an hundred acres
of land for thirty pounds a year during a lease of forty years,
and by improvement raises the land to the annual value of an
hundred pounds, still he can be rated only at thirty pounds a
year as the value or goodness of the land, and the largeness of
the farmer's stock, have nothing to do in the account; he is not
to be taxed for them, but only in proportion to his rent.

Another observation I should make is that in parishes where
the rates run very high, as in some they do to 3, 4, 6, and even
10s. in the pound, in such, the tax is in fact on the landlord,
for no tenant will hire land in any parish without first enquiring
what the rates are; and when he finds them so high will give a
rent only in proportion to such certain expense; if the rates
were to be lowered from 10s. to 5s. in the pound, the landlord
at the expiration of his leases would be able to add 5s. in the
pound to his rents.

Upon the whole, though the poor's rate, &c., is a direct
burthen on the farmers yet the amount not being a matter of
great consideration, and being laid only on the certain rent, it
is not in any respect to be considered as checking the progress
and improvements of agriculture: the disputes. litigations and
lawsuits which arise from the quarrels between farmers on some
being rated higher or lower than others, and between parishes
concerning the settlement of their poor, are in some instances
a greater abuse and burthen than the total of what they pay
regularly in rates. This is an abuse of freedom, and rather
marks the lightness of the burthens laid on our farmers than
their weight.

The tax upon windows bears not particularly upon agriculture. The farmer pays something annually for each window
in his house, proportioned to the total number; it is a regular
tax and too inconsiderable to be esteemed a burthen, certainly
it has no ill consequences on our husbandry. Were it however,
as some authors have advised, to be the only tax by its
absorbing all others, it would be a deadly burthen to the whole

kingdom; since no man should pay to the amount of all taxes in proportion as he possesses but in proportion as he consumes; but of this more hereafter.

The two great branches of English taxes are the excises and the customs; their being burthensome to agriculture depends entirely on what objects they are laid, and to what extent they are carried; but in general I shall remark that they are much less detrimental than commonly imagined. Customs on the exportation of corn would be ruinous to agriculture; excises on wool and leather to such an amount as to lessen the consumption and sink the price in the hands of the farmer, would be evidently mischievous; such excises upon malt as would lessen the consumption of beer, and at the same time customs on the export of barley, would greatly hurt the culture of that crop; excises laid on butchers for all the beasts they killed, to such a height as to lessen the consumption of meat, would have the same effect. But these are cases of which we have no instances in England: our customs and excises are not prejudicial to our husbandry but in very few cases – the prohibitions, which is only another word for a very high custom, on the export of wool and raw leather are certainly heavy burthens laid on agriculture in favour of manufactures, the proof of which is the price of wool in England having fallen half since that policy was embraced, which has been a tax of near two shillings in the pound additional on land. Not that I would venture to plead in favour of the exportation of wool raw: I shall only refer the reader to the arguments of Mr Smith, in his *Memoirs of Wool* [1757], where he will find many extreme curious facts concerning wool and the woollen manufacture.

That customs and excises do not injure in the least the agriculture of Britain we have the clearest proof in their not lowering the prices of any of the farmer's commodities (wool, &c., excepted, as above); while they leave them at the price they found or raise them, certainly the farmer cannot be injured. When they are carried too far they lessen consumption, which in every circumstance is the great wound the farmer has most to fear, because his prices from that moment will fall. But in England the consumption of every commodity has increased under every burthen that has been laid on it: this has been uniformly the case with malt; nor have we an instance of either excises or customs lessening the consumption, and consequently the price of the farmer's products. The excellence of this species of taxation has been very ably explained by several writers, who have shown that by the tax being blended with the price the purchaser does not feel its weight, and never pays the tax but when he is best able to pay it, that is at the moment he makes the purchase. If all the taxes of England were consolidated into this general branch *on consumption* our system would be still more perfect. As to their raising prices, it is as I could easily show an advantage to every class in the state.

From this review of the system of taxation in Britain it is clear that the agriculture of the kingdom cannot suffer from any part of it without the amount being carried to a much greater height; but hitherto we have seen nothing like even the prospect of mischief to our husbandry from any of our taxes. This must arise in a great measure from their not being laid on improvements – from their being permanent and not varying – from the assessors, collectors, and receivers being armed with very moderate powers, and with none beyond the mere line of fraud against the tax – from their being no respecters of persons, dealing equally with the duke and his little tenant.

Political Arithmetic (1774) pp. 6–15

5. TITHES

The situation regarding payment of tithes in the eighteenth century was a complicated one. Because of the transfer into lay hands of church lands and livings at the Reformation, the tithe-holder was often a lay impropriator, frequently the principal landlord of the district. Where this was the case the tithes were usually commuted into an annual cash payment, or were absorbed into the rents, the lands being let at a higher rent tithe-free. When the tithes were still in the hands of the church they might be leased out to a local landowner at a fixed sum for a period of years. This saved the church the trouble of collecting the tithes, and the lessee might well again prefer to charge his tenants a cash payment or additional rent. However, some churchmen and lay impropriators still collected tithes in kind, a practice much condemned by the writers of the day as a deterrent to improvement, since the payment varied with the produce of the soil and was in effect a tax on output. More serious in practice, perhaps, were the frictions and disputes which frequently arose over the quantities of produce to be collected, and the difficulty of inducing good farmers to take land that was still subject to payment in kind. A leading object of a large proportion of Enclosure Acts was to secure the abolition of tithes by getting the tithe-holder to accept in lieu an allocation of land or alternatively an annual payment of a corn rent, a sum which varied with changes in the average price of wheat over the preceding few years. Tithe payments in kind finally disappeared following the Tithe Commutation Act of 1836.

The following passage shows not only Young's rooted antipathy to tithes as an obstacle to improvement, but also his tendency to exaggerate his point in order to drive it home to his readers:

TITHE

This is the greatest burthen that yet remains on the agriculture of this kingdom; and if it was universally taken in kind would be sufficient to damp all ideas of improvement. Fortunately the spirit of our clergy is too liberal in general to live in such a state of warfare with their parishioners, as pretty generally is the case where they submit to the trouble of gathering for the sake of the additional profit.

In many parishes, however, the tithes are gathered, and in them I will venture to pronounce no correct or spirited husbandry will ever be met with; and I may further remark that in the extensive journeys I have made through this kingdom for the purpose of examining its agriculture, I have never met with considerable improvements where the tithe was taken in kind; and a very little calculation would show the impossibility of it. The reason our husbandry has advanced upon the whole in so great a degree is such a large part of the kingdom not being tithed in kind, but a composition per acre or per pound being taken in lieu; and such a considerable portion of it being tithe-free, which is every day increasing by all the new enclosures. The great object at present of British agriculture is to obtain a general exemption from tithe by giving the clergy some settled income in lieu of it.

Political Arithmetic (1774) pp. 18–19

6. LEASES

Another example of Young's tendency to exaggerate in order to make his case the more forceful is provided by his statements on leases. According to Young, leases were essential for good farming because, he believed, tenants would not invest in improvements without the security provided by a lease. This was the view generally taken by the authorities of the period.[1] There has so far been little detailed investigation of leases by modern writers, but there appears to be general agreement that contemporaries made too much of the matter. Leases were not common for small farms, which were usually let on annual agreements; and when they were used in letting bigger farms it seems that the main object was to secure the landlord from possible loss by the tenant's damage to the buildings and neglect of the land. Leases which laid down in detail the system of cultivation to be followed seem not to have been common, and where they occurred it is difficult to know how far they were enforced, or indeed whether it was practicable to enforce them.

Young's main point, however, was that leases provided tenants with security. In practice, however, annual agreements or tenancies at will were rarely insecure. As he rather begrudgingly recognises in the second of the following extracts, tenants usually had confidence in their landlord and knew that they would not be turned out of their holdings without good cause. Equally, landowners had no wish to part with tenants who farmed reasonably well, were of respectable habits, and paid their rents regularly. As a result it happened that tenants without leases often stayed on their farms for longer periods than those with leases. When there was a lease there was an expectation on both sides that the rent would be revised at the end of the lease, and that a new tenant would follow. Leases were widely used, as Young indicates, to bring recently enclosed waste land into cultivation, and for this purpose they were probably essential because of the extraordinary effort and expenditure involved on the part of the tenant. The big price fluctuations of the French wars of 1793–1815 and their aftermath tended to make both landlords and tenants wary of entering into long-term rent agreements; and later in the nineteenth century there does not seem to have been much enthusiasm for leases on either side, despite the continued arguments in their favour put forward by leading agricultural writers such as Sir James Caird in his *English Agriculture in 1850–1851* (new ed., 1968):

[1] See, for example, Nathaniel Kent, *Hints to Gentlemen of Landed Property* (1775) pp. 270, 274, and William Marshall, *On Landed Property* (1804) pp. 362–5 [Ed.].

(1) The improvements which have been wrought in England have been almost totally owing to the custom of granting leases: in those districts where it is unusual to give them agriculture yet continues much inferior to what we find it where they are usual, nor can it flourish till this custom is adopted. If the mode and progress of country improvements is well considered, they will be found utterly inconsistent with an occupation without a lease. A farmer hires a tract of land in an unimproved or inferior state: he repairs the fences, deepens the ditches – clears away rubbish – purchases dung – forms composts – drains the wet fields – waters the meadows – adds to the buildings – digs for marl – gets the arable lands into good and clean order; these works take him three or four years, during which time he sacrifices his profits in hopes of being well paid. Now how can any person possibly suppose that such a system will be executed on his farms, if he will not or does not grant long leases? Is it to be expected that a tenant will lay a thousand pounds out upon improvements, and remain all the time at the mercy of his landlord, to be turned out of the farm as soon as the money is expended? The case is so self-evident that the necessity must be undeniable; no man of common sense will put such trust in another.

Nor is it sufficient that granting leases is a common custom, they must be so guarded by the laws as to give the tenant the most perfect security: he must be sure of his term, and also sure of being safe against any ill-designing, malevolent, or insidious attacks of a wealthy landlord, and be as independent while he adheres to the contracts of his lease as the landlord is of him; all this is the case with the majority of English farmers. It is true there are many tracts of country in which landlords will not grant leases, but then one of two circumstances must exist: either the land is of such a nature that no improvements are wanting – or, in consequence of no lease being given, the farms are let much under their value.

In some countries of Europe no leases are granted, in others they are very weak guarantees of the tenants' security, and in others the sale of the estate vacates the lease. These are all radical evils which must be cured, or husbandry can never flourish.

Political Arithmetic (1774) pp. 15–17

(2) Some landlords will not grant leases at all; others for only 3 or 7 years. This is a matter of small consequence to those tenants who purpose conducting their farm in a slovenly negligent manner, never to expend anything beyond absolute necessities, and always get from the land the utmost. To such, these maxims are very indifferent; for let them leave the farm when they will, they can lose nothing by former expenses, the land never owing them anything; but the case is surely different with a man who designs to expend considerable sums of money in bringing the land into perfect order; a three or a seven-years lease is to him much the same as none at all; and he would be an egregious fool to dispose of his money on any such uncertainties. If a man really means to be a good farmer it can never answer to him to enter a farm with a shorter than twenty-one years lease; nor can it ever be for the advantage of the landlord to let his farms on shorter. I am now speaking of rich countries: as to poor ones, to be enclosed, or marled, or chalked, &c., &c., it is once apparent that no man will hire them without a long lease.

But it may be said that farms are often very well managed by men that have no leases. This I readily grant; but then they have, probably, been bred up on their farms; they, as well as their family, may know their landlord; and several generations pass without a lease, and yet nothing unreasonable happen. But this is a peculiar case; I am supposing a landlord and tenant that are strangers coming together; in which case *caution* is at least requisite. Besides, we often see whole sets of old tenants trimmed up at once in their rents; not unreasonably indeed, but sufficiently to show that the farmer with a lease in his pocket is in a much more secure situation than another who has none.

The Farmer's Guide in Hiring and Stocking Farms (1770) I 74–5

7. LANDOWNERS AND RENTS

While Young launched fierce attacks upon tithes and the absence of leases as unnecessary obstacles to improving farmers, he was equally convinced that the rents charged by landowners were too low to impel somnolent tenants into greater activity. High rents, Young argued, meant good farming, for only an efficient,

progressive farmer could afford to pay high rents. Where landlords kept their rents low, bad farming was the result.

From modern investigations of landlords' rentals it does indeed
appear that at the time Young was putting this view forward
many estates were under-rented. Unenclosed arable land could
be found at 5s. or 6s. an acre; enclosed meadow, the most
valuable kind of land, as low as 10s. or 15s. In the previous
hundred years agricultural prices had tended to be low, and there
were long periods when rents were little changed or perhaps even
fell a little. Just at the time when Young was writing, however,
both prices and rents were on the rise, though rents usually lagged
some ten or twenty years behind prices. Between the 1750s and
the onset of high war-time prices after 1793 rents rose on average
some 40 per cent; during the war period they rose by a further
90–100 per cent, then to level out or decline somewhat in the
post-war depression.

Young ascribed the low level of rents of the middle eighteenth
century mainly to the landlords' hankering after popularity with
their tenants, or what he called a 'false magnificence'. This was
certainly an element in the situation, for the majority of English
landowners liked to be thought of as 'good landlords' who did
not oppress their tenants but presided benevolently over their
estates with paternal sympathies uppermost. There were other
considerations, however. Many landowners pursued political
interests and wished to preserve their political influence by
delivering the votes of their farmers to the candidate of their
choice. Low rents, 'good bargains' as they were called, were a
quid pro quo for the command of electoral power. Low rents
might also be a form of compensation for ravages to crops and
damage to fences caused by game and hunting, and this was a
period when systematic game preservation was becoming a feature of many estates. Again, where an estate had been neglected
for a long period, and the farmhouses were dilapidated and the
land in poor condition, easy rents might be necessary to attract
new tenants and retain existing ones. Many landowners felt it was
unjustified to raise rents except at very long intervals, or unless
major improvements had been made to the farms. Lastly, it is
relevant that in the 1770s the prices of agricultural commodities
had not long begun to rise after a lengthy period of depressed
conditions in the 1730s and 1740s.

The situation was thus more complicated than Young would

admit, and though rents did rise very substantially during the
next forty years, this was in response to the higher prices and
improved prosperity of farming, and as a result of enclosure of
common fields and pastures, rather than a general acceptance
of his arguments:

(1) It certainly must be a matter of vast consequence to keep
the property of the kingdom on the increase, which I take to
be the surest mark of a flourishing people. ... Agriculture
forms one of the grand pillars of the riches of the state;
improvements in it increase property, and consequently
income, and ought therefore to receive from politicians and
the great all possible encouragement. The rise of rent of 1s.
per acre increases the rental of the lands of England
£800,000 a year. Nor should it be considered as a *transfer*
of income from the farmer to the landlord but as a *creation*
of fresh income. There is scarcely a tract of country in the
kingdom in which a rise of rent (to a certain pitch, which,
by the way, is much higher than generally believed) is not
attended with a corresponding *increase of product*, but much
beyond the proportion. Instances are everywhere innumerable of farms low rented that have been occupied by none
but slovenly, poor, and ruined tenants; wheras the same
farms doubled or trebled in the rent become the fortunes of
succeeding occupiers. There is nothing in this difficult to be
accounted for: high rents are an undoubted spur to industry;
the farmer who pays much for his land knows that he must
be diligent or starve. Land of 20s. an acre *must* yield good
crops, or its occupier be ruined. Whatever be the nature of
the soil, that circumstance will make it yield them. In no part
of England where rents are low is there good husbandry.
Norfolk is not an exception; the waste parts of that county
were thrown into very large farms; the soil would yield
nothing without marling; consequently none hired it but men
who were either rich, or could command money. A first
expense of three or four pounds an acre is, considering the
value of ready money to a farmer, no low rent. Wherever
land is underlet twenty to one but the farmers are slovens
unless some such circumstance operates.

Hence let me remark that there is no evil more pernicious to the public than great families, through a false

magnificence, letting their estates be rented at low rates, from father to son, by a pack of slovens, rather than not have it to boast *that their rents have never been raised*; which is nothing more than saying, *My tenants are poor; their husbandry bad; and the state injured in wealth, revenue, and population.* A very patriotic boast! Universal experience justifies this assertion. There is no good husbandry without high rents; and the landlords who through a false pride will not raise, when they easily might, do an inconceivable prejudice to their country. I will venture to assert that the man who doubles his rental benefits the state more than himself.

Northern Tour (1770) IV 494–6

(2) [On large estates] the farmers are left to the care of stewards, the consequence of which is they are rarely so well managed as by the owners themselves. Estates so conducted are seldom let at their value, and no wonder; great men, in the first place, have county interests and popularity to keep up; and in the second, the influence and power of stewards sink very much when the tenant pays as much for his land as any other person would. Lands will rarely be well cultivated for which the tenant does not pay their value. I have seen so many instances of this in all parts of England that I almost lay it down as a maxim.

Observations on the Present State of the Waste Lands of Great Britain (1773) 41

8. FARM CAPITAL

In English farming there had developed by Young's time a fairly clear distinction between the landlord's capital and that of the farmer. The landlord provided the land, the farmhouse, barns, stables and other buildings, and paid for fences, embankments, access roads and other necessary facilities of a more or less permanent nature. The tenant provided the farm stock, the plough-team, livestock, implements, carts or wagons, and paid for seed, manure and farm labour. When landlords were letting their larger farms they or their stewards made a careful investigation of a prospective tenant's qualifications, particularly his experience of farming and the amount of capital at his disposal. It was recognised as dangerously imprudent to let a farm to a tenant who lacked sufficient capital to stock it and run it properly. With their smaller farms landlords seem to have been less careful, though it may merely be that the letting of small farms was done on a local, personal basis, leaving little or nothing in the way of records.

It was Young's contention that many tenants attempted to occupy larger farms than they had the capital to stock, and one of his earliest books, from which the first of the following excerpts is taken, was devoted to the subject of capital and the choice of farms. It seems very likely that both landlords and farmers accepted a lower ratio of capital to acreage than Young and his fellow-authorities advocated. Agricultural writers tended to argue for the ideal, while landlords and tenants had to face practical realities and make do with what was available. Nevertheless, the following two passages give a good indication of what was involved in taking on a farm in the 1770s and 1780s:

(1)   REMARKS ON THE CONDUCT OF COMMON
     FARMERS IN PROPORTIONING THEIR LAND TO
               THEIR MONEY

... It is universally known in every part of the kingdom that farms are every day hired with much smaller sums of money than the most considerate people would allot for the purpose. It is not gentlemen and landlords alone who think such sums too small; even farmers themselves will often own that a larger sum of money is really necessary than often possessed upon the hiring of a farm; and they will allow that it would be more advantageous to cultivate 200 acres completely than 300 indifferently for want of plenty of money. And the practices of the most enlightened ones prove the same thing as the sentiments of the rest, however contrary to their conduct; for we very often see very large sums applied to the culture of farms, and such as render a spirited practice necessary to pay the interest off.

The cause of such numerous deviations as we find from prudence, in this case, is the avarice of hiring a large quantity of land; their great ambition is not to farm *well*, but *much*. Nine out of ten had rather cultivate 500 acres in a slovenly manner, though constantly cramped for money, than 250 acres completely, though they would always have money in their pockets. And numerous are the instances in which they would be richer at the end of a lease of 200 acres than of 400. But from whatever source this error is derived, the fact that it is an error is indisputable.

Farms are sometimes hired with such small sums that many believe it to be almost impossible to carry them on: and yet the farmers of such do manage to go on after a manner to the end of the lease. Some explanation of this conduct is necessary.

Let us suppose a man to hire a farm of £200 a year, containing as many acres, 40 of them grass, and 160 arable. For how small a sum of money may a farmer hire such an one? *Answer*, for £422 – in this manner:

Implements

	£	s.	d.
These are all bought in second hand at low prices:			
2 Waggons	15	0	0
2 Carts	11	0	0
4 Ploughs	2	5	0
2 Pair of harrows	1	10	0
1 Roller	0	10	0
Screen, bushel, forks, rakes, shovels, etc.	2	10	0
20 Sacks	1	5	0
Harness for 8 horses, cart and plough	4	10	0
Dairy furniture	2	10	0
Household ditto	30	0	0
	£71	0	0

Live Stock

	£	s.	d.
8 Horses	£45	0	0
5 Cows	30	0	0
50 Sheep (old crones)	17	10	0
Swine	1	10	0
	94	0	0

Seed

	£	s.	d.
40 Acres of wheat	£24	0	0
40 of barley	20	0	0
10 of oats and clover	7	0	0
	51	0	0

Labour

Three servants (wages half a year) which, with himself or a son, makes one to each plough	£10	0	0
A labourer in harvest	2	0	0
A maid's wages (if he has not a daughter grown up)	1	10	0
	13	10	0
	£229	10	0

Sundry Articles

I suppose him to enter the farm at Michaelmas. His cows he will not buy till the winter is over: his horses he turns into a straw yard (his own if he has agreed with his predecessor for the straw of the last crop) but wherever it may be, at 1s. a week per horse, 5 months	£8	0	0
Corn and hay in spring sowing 2 months, at 3s. a week per horse	9	12	0
House-keeping a year (besides what the farm yields) that is, fat hogs and wheat	40	0	0
Half a year's rates, &c., at 3s. 6d. in the pound	17	10	0
Clothes and pocket money	10	0	0
	85	2	0
	£314	12	0

Thus we find that £314 12s. is necessary to carry him through the first half-year, and, in some articles, the whole year, consequently so much must at first be in hand; the further sum necessary will best appear from stating his expenses in half-year accounts.

Second half-year

	£	s.		£	s.
To half a year's wages	13	10	By product of 5 Cows	30	0
Ditto rates	17	10	Ditto of Sheep, the money doubled	35	0
Blacksmith and wheelwright a year	12	0	Balance (debit)	81	0
Half a year's rent	100	0			
Window lights	3	0			
	£146	0		£146	0

By this account we find a deficiency of £81 which must likewise be supplied by cash for stock at first.

Third half-year

	£	s.		£	s.
Wages	£13	10	By 40 acres of wheat at £4	£160	0
Rates	17	10	By 40 of barley at £3	120	0
Tithe at 3s. in the pound	30	0	20 Acres turnips sold	35	0
Blacksmith and wheelwright	10	0			
Rent	100	0			
Lights	3	0			
	£174	0		£315	0

	£	s.
Seed wheat, 40 acres	24	0
Ditto 40 of barley	20	0
Clover with it	3	0
Ditto 20 acres of beans	12	0
20 of oats	10	0
80 Sheep	28	0
Sundry small articles	10	0
	281	0
Balance (credit)	34	0
	£315	0

	£	s.
	£315	0

This half-year nothing is reckoned for house-keeping. A farmer, when once his land begins to produce, lives off his farm; I mean such an one as takes a farm as large as possible; the swine furnish him with meat; the screenings of his wheat with bread, and poultry and other small articles with malt, and the few things he wants besides.

Fourth half-year

Rent	£100 0	By cows	£30	0
Wages and labour	15 0	Sheep	56	0
Rates	17 10	Balance of last		
Wear and tear	14 0	half-year		
		(credit)	34	0
		Balance		
		(debit)	26	10
	£146 10		£146	10

In this half-year we find another deficiency of £26 10s. which, like the former, must be carried to the first account of stock.

Fifth half-year

Rent	£100 0	By 40 acres of		
Labour	15 0	wheat	£160	0
Rates	17 10	40 of barley	120	0
Wear and tear	15 0	20 of beans	50	0
Lights	3 0	10 of clover, hay		
Tithe	30 0	and feed	30	0
Seed for 50 acres		Balance		
of wheat	25 0	(credit)	129	10
30 Barley	15 0			
20 Oats	10 0			
	£230 10		£230	10

Sixth half-year

Rent	£100 0	By Cows	£30	0
Labour	20 0	Sheep this year		
Rates	17 10	for stock to		
Wear and tear	20 0	increase		
Balance	2 0	Balance of last		
		half-year		
		(credit)	129	10
	£159 10		£159	10

We are now come to the point when it appears that our farmer may get up the hill with luck, but yet he continues in such a situation that any unforeseen accident or failure of crop will sit very heavy on him. His general yearly account will now stand as under:

Expenses	£	s.	Product	£	s.
Rent	200	0	Wheat	160	0
Tithe	30	0	Barley	120	0
Wages and labour	40	0	Beans	50	0
Rates	35	0	10 Acres of clover,		
Wear and tear	35	0	or turnips	20	0
Lights	3	0	Sheep	100	0
Seed for 40 Acres			10 Cows (increased		
of wheat	20	0	to this number)	60	0
To Barley	20	0			
To Oats and beans	20	0			
Sheep	50	0			
Balance	57	0			
	£510	0		£510	0

The balance of £57 is, for all his private expenses, his profit, the interest of his money, and the chance of accidents, very inadequate to these demands; but in a term of years will increase, from the expenditure of itself in part on the farm, and from the gradual increase of stock by breeding, as he has besides the article of sheep charged £56 worth for breeding, either in kind or cash. Now if we go over these accounts, the sums wherewith the farm was stocked will appear to be as follows:

	£	s.	d.
The first expense	314	12	0
The first wrong balance	81	0	0
The second ditto	26	10	0
Total	£422	2	0

Which is little more than two rents.

This sketch, in which a minute accuracy was not necessary, will serve to show the management whereby farmers sometimes, with very small sums of money, get into large farms; and it proves, at the same time (notwithstanding the possibility of succeeding in such attempts), that the managing in this manner is very hazardous to the farmer, and pernicious to the farm.

If a bad year comes, or any accidents happen to his stock, he is ruined; with good years he can afford to do nothing in the way of improvement; and he is so weak in cattle and labour that in a few years his fields must inevitably be out of order for want of requisite tillage; and better horses must be bought, and more men employed, or all will go to ruin. His implements bought in with an eye to cheapness alone will soon be done with and fresh supplies demanded. All expenses will multiply.

In such a state how is it possible he should turn his land to the best advantage? A vein of the finest marl may be under his fields; he can have nothing to say to it. He may be within 3 or 4 miles of a town, where dung and ashes are to be had on very reasonable terms; but how is he to afford the purchase? Nothing can be clearer than the infinite disadvantages of such a confined situation.

The Farmer's Guide in Hiring and Stocking
Farms (1770) 1 97–107

This excerpt refers to an account given by Lord Shelburne of farming round his seat at Bowood, near Calne in Wiltshire:

(2)   In stocking a farm of £300 a year, 200 acres, 120 grass and 80 arable, they calculate as follows:

	£	s.	d.
6 Horses, at £15.	90	0	0
25 Cows, at £10.	250	0	0
50 Sheep	50	0	0
Swine	6	0	0
Harness	10	0	0
2 Waggons	42	0	0
2 Carts	20	0	0
2 Ploughs	1	10	0
3 Harrows	1	1	0
1 Roller	4	0	0
Dairy utensils	5	0	0
Sundry small implements	2	10	0
Rent	300	0	0
Tithe	25	0	0
Rates	75	0	0
Wages, one man	7	7	0
Ditto, a boy	4	0	0
A Dairy-maid	5	0	0
2 Labourers	35	0	0
Seed Wheat, 20 acres	16	0	0
Oats, 20, 5 bushels at 2s.	10	0	0
Barley, 20, 4 ditto, at 2s. 6d.	10	0	0
Beans, 20, 3 ditto, at 3s. 6d.	10	10	0
Wear and tear a year	5	0	0
	£984	18	0

Annals of Agriculture, VIII (1787) 64–5

CHAPTER II

The Agricultural Revolution

I. THE NORFOLK HUSBANDRY

The 'Norfolk system', despite its fame, was only one of the types of improved farming to be found in eighteenth-century England, though certainly one of the most striking and best-known. Its home was in the light sandy soils of northern and north-western Norfolk, and it could be introduced in other areas where the conditions were suitable. The essence of the system was its function in making these naturally rather poor soils profitable by a rotation which combined the production of wheat and barley as cash crops with the cultivation of fodder crops – turnips, clover and rye grass. These fodder crops supported sheep and other livestock, and the manure of the flocks helped to improve soil fertility. In addition, the clover had the effect of fixing nitrogen in the soil, an additional aid to fertility. The combination of grain and fodder crops made bare fallows – the resting of the soil from cultivation – unnecessary, and the hoeing of the turnips had the incidental effect of destroying weeds, which was one of the objects of a periodical bare fallow. Moreover, the feeding of the sheep feeding on the turnips helped to consolidate the loose, blowing sand, as did the binding effects of the clover roots.

Young lived most of his life in west Suffolk, not a great many miles from this area of Norfolk, and he was a frequent visitor to the famous Norfolk estates of the Walpoles at Houghton, the Cokes at Holkham, and the Townshends at Raynham, and so was thoroughly familiar with its farming from an early date. His first farming tour, *A Six Weeks' Tour through the Southern Counties of England and Wales*, written in 1768, began with an account of the Norfolk husbandry, and he visited the same area again in his *Eastern Tour* of 1771, from which the second description included here is drawn. In both accounts he emphasises that the farms were enclosed ones, and were of great size, running from several hundred to three, four or even more than five thousand acres. The farmers, he pointed out, were men of capital; and indeed they had to be, for success depended on investment in large numbers of livestock and willingness to spend money on adding marl to the soil as a dressing to enrich it and to prevent the manure from leaching away with the surface water. As a mixture of clay and calcium carbonate, marl tended to correct any deficiency of calcium and helped to free for plant growth nutrients such as phophates and trace elements. By Young's time Norfolk farmers were also manuring with oil cake imported across the North Sea from Holland. Long leases and low rents encouraged the farmers to undertake these costly expenditures. All the elements of the Norfolk system – the rotation, the enclosed, large farms, the capitalistic farmers operating under long leases and low rents – were all interdependent and all essential to the success of the system.

Though much admired, the Norfolk husbandry was not without its drawbacks. Young points out some of these at the close of the second description, and elsewhere in his *Southern Tour*. He stated also that the yields of wheat and barley, while very great for this type of soil, were not remarkable when compared with those obtainable on better land. Already in 1768 he noted the prevalence of soil problems arising from too frequent cultivation of turnips and clover: the turnips suffered from 'finger and toe' disease, and land became 'clover-sick', refusing to grow good crops unless longer intervals between sowings of clover were allowed. The solution to these difficulties, it was shown, lay in using a wider variety of fodder crops and more flexible rotations.

Incidentally, Young was in error in supposing that the Norfolk system had been introduced in the early decades of the eighteenth century. Research into estate records shows that it went back considerably further. Field cultivation of turnips was already in practice in Norfolk in the second half of the seventeenth century, and the Norfolk four-course rotation can be traced on the Coke estates to at least as early as the 1720s, and on the estates of the Walpoles to 1673. William Marshall, who seems to have possessed a stronger historical sense than Young, observed in his *Rural Economy of Norfolk of* 1787 that the farms of north-east Norfolk 'have been kept invariably, for at least a century past, under the following course of cultivation: wheat, barley, turnips, barley, clover, rye grass'. But here he was referring to an area where the soils were generally better than the 'good sands' of north-west Norfolk, the district where the turnip and clover husbandry produced its most remarkable effects.

As we have said, the Norfolk system was only one of the improved modes of cultivation which characterised the early stages of the 'agricultural revolution'. There were many other ways in which roots and grasses could be combined with cash crops to achieve the objects of reducing bare fallows, improving soil fertility, and carrying larger numbers of livestock. Difficulties relating to the survival of common fields, the existence of large areas of poorly drained clay soils unsuited to root crops, and the susceptibility of the turnip to damage from weather, held up the spread of the new husbandry. In the Midlands and north a succession of grain crops was alternated with a ley of legumes and cultivated grasses, the ley lasting for a period of years and so supporting livestock, while helping to prepare the soil for another succession of grain crops. As time went by, systems tended to become more flexible and less dependent on crops like clover and turnips as a wider variety of fodder crops were introduced and new sources of fertilisers and humus were found. Nevertheless, as Young remarked, the Norfolk husbandry was evidence of 'the spirit of improvement' which in its day helped solve the age-old problems of fertility and made inferior land more bountiful:

(1) All the country from Holkham to Houghton was a wild sheepwalk before the spirit of improvement seized the inhabitants, and this glorious spirit has wrought amazing effects: for instead of boundless wilds and uncultivated wastes inhabited by scarce anything but sheep, the country is all cut into enclosures, cultivated in a most husbandlike manner, richly manured, well peopled, and yielding a hundred times the produce than it did in its former state. What has wrought these vast improvements is the marling, for under the whole country run veins of a very rich soapy kind which they dig up and spread upon the old sheep-walks, and then by means of enclosing they throw their farms into a regular course of crops and gain immensely by the improvement.

The farms are all large, and the rents low, for the farmers having been at a great expense in improvements they could not afford them without very long leases, so that most of the farms are let at the present at rents much under their value; add to this a considerable part of the country belongs to landlords who have a vanity in not raising their rents, and others are supposed to have taken moderate fines; all together the farmers have managed to raise considerable fortunes, and to bid fair for being the *possessors* of the whole county.

The farms run from £300 to £900 a year, for which sums they have a great quantity of land. It is very difficult to discover the rents among such large farmers, who all make a great secret of it; but I have very good reasons for believing that they are in general from 2s. 6d. to 6s. per acre. Many farms under a modern let are rented at 10s. and more per acre, but they are not very common. I speak of a large tract of country stretching from Holkham to the sea westward, and south to Swaffham.

The principal farms (at least those that are most commonly mentioned) are Mr Curtis's of Summerfield, 2,500 acres, Mr Mallet's of Dunton, as much, Mr Barton's of Rougham, 3,000, Messrs Glover's of Creake and Barwick, Messrs Savery's of Syderstone, each 1,100 acres. Cultivation in all its branches is carried on by these men, and many others, in a very complete manner. But marling is the great foundation of their wealth.

They lay about 100 loads on an acre, which costs them for digging from £1 5s. to £1 10s., and they reckon the expenses of the team, and other labour, to be as much more. The improvement lasts in great vigour above twenty years, and the land is always the better for it. Their course of crops is: 1. marl, and break up for wheat; 2. turnips; 3. barley; 4. laid down with clover and rye grass for three years, or sometimes only two. They dung or fold for all their winter corn, and reckon two nights fold equal to a dunging; the quantity of the latter they lay upon an acre is 12 loads. For some years after the marling they reap, on a medium, four quarters of wheat per acre, and five of barley; and 15 or 18 years after marling, three quarters of wheat, and four and a half of soft corn.

The general economy of their farms will appear from the following sketch of one of 1,100 acres. The farmer generally has:

100 acres of winter corn
250 ,,   ,, barley and oats
50   ,,   ,, peas
200 ,,   ,, turnips
400 ,,   ,, grasses
100 ,,   ,, sheepwalk

——

1,100

He keeps: 6 servants
6 labourers
30 horses
20 cows
900 sheep
5 ploughs

and in harvest time has in all about forty people in the field.

The culture of turnips is here carried on in a most extensive manner, Norfolk being more famous for this vegetable than any county in the kingdom; but I have seen much larger turnips grown in Suffolk in gravelly loams than ever I saw in Norfolk. The use to which they apply their vast fields of turnips is the feeding their flocks, and expending the surplus in fatting Scotch cattle, which they do both in the stall-feeding method, in bins in their farmyards, others in pasture fields; and others again hurdle them on the turnips as they grow, in the same manner as they do their sheep. By stall-feeding they make their crop go much the furthest, but the beasts so fed are apt to founder on the road to London, the expense of it are great, and the soil loses the urine: but all these methods are yet in use. When the marl begins to wear out of the soil many of the great farmers have latterly got into a method of manuring with oil cakes for their winter corn, which they import from Holland, and spread on their fields at the expense of about 15*s.* per acre.

Southern Tour (1768) pp. 21–6

(2) From 40 to 60 years ago all the northern and western and a part of the eastern tracts of the county were sheepwalks, let so low as from 6*d.* to 1*s.* 6*d.* and 2*s.* an acre. Much of it was in this condition only 30 years ago. The great improvements

have been made by means of the following circumstances.

First. By enclosing without assistance of parliament.
Second. By a spirited use of marl and clay.
Third. By the introduction of an excellent course of crops.
Fourth. By the culture of turnips well hand-hoed.
Fifth. By the culture of clover and rye grass.
Sixth. By landlords granting long leases.
Seventh. By the country being divided chiefly into large farms.

In this recapitulation I have inserted no article that is included in another. Take any one from the seven and the improvement of Norfolk would never have existed. The importance of them all will appear sufficiently from a short examination.

THE ENCLOSURE

Provided open lands are enclosed, it is not of very great consequence by what means it was effected; but the fact is that parliamentary enclosures are scarcely ever so complete and general as in Norfolk; and how should they be, when numbers are to agree to the same measure? Had the enclosure of this county been by acts of parliament much *might have been* done, but on no comparison with what *is* done. The great difficulty and attention *then* would have been to enclose: now the works of improvement enjoy the immediate attention. And undoubtedly many of the finest loams on the richest marls would at this day have been sheepwalks, had there been any right of commonage on them. A parliamentary enclosure is also (through the knavery of commissioners and attorneys) so very expensive, compared with a private one, that it would have damped the succeeding undertakings in taking too large a portion of the money requisite for the great work in a mere preparation for it.

These circumstances are to be seen more or less in most of the districts enclosed by parliament.

MARLING

It is the great felicity of the sandy part of this county that, dig where you will, you find an exceeding fine marl or clay. The marl is generally white, with veins of yellow and red; sometimes only tinged with those colours. If dropped in fair water it falls, and bubbles to the top; if it is very good it has an effervescence. All effervesce strongly in vinegar if dropped in it in a lump, and some will at once make the glass, though half-full, boil over in a froth. But most will do this if the marl is powdered before it is put in. The clay has none of these qualities. The best marl is that which falls the quickest in water, for such will always have the greatest effervescence in acids.

It is common in this county to hear of the *salts* of marl. As well as they understand the use of it, they know little of its nature; no salts are to be extracted from marl, though a little oil is to be gained. It may produce salt when spread on the land by its absorbent and alkaline quality attracting the vitriolic acid, and converting it into a neutral salt; and this quality is probably one of its greatest advantages. It likewise not only attracts oil from the air, but dissolves and fits it for the purpose of vegetation.

I have not met with any persons that have been curious enough to form a series of small experiments on marl for the discovery of the proper quantities for use in proportion to the given *qualities* of it.

The farmers on the first use of marl spread it in larger quantities than others have done since: 100 loads were common, and few used less than 80. But land is now marled for the first time in some places with not more than from 40 to 60 loads. The reason given me for this change was principally a view to future marlings: if 80 or 100 are laid on at first they do not think a repetition of 20 or 30 at the end of 20 or 25 years will answer so well as if the first quantity had been smaller.

It is yet an opinion among some farmers that their land will not pay for a second marling. But the best husbandmen in the county are clearly of a different way of thinking. When the first manuring is wearing out pretty fast, which generally happens in about 20 years, they (on the renewal of their lease) replenish the ground with an addition of from 20 to 35 loads an acre more. And several tracts of country have been marled with success for the third time.

But it is not the marl or clay alone that has worked the great effects we have seen in Norfolk. It must be spread on a suitable soil: this is a light *sandy loam* or *loamy sand* – not a sand; in some places a *gravelly loam*, but not a gravel. What they call their *woodcock* loams are free from gravel, and rather so from sand; they are more inclinable to a dry friable clay, but at the same time sound and dry enough for turnips. These are their best soils.

Some tracts of pure sand have been marled, and with success, though not so great; but clay, from its superior tenacity, is reckoned better for them than marl.

The reader is not to suppose that the Norfolk men have depended on these manures alone; on the contrary, they have been very attentive to others. Folding sheep, through both winter and summer, is nowhere more practised or better understood. Winter fatting beasts on turnips in the farm-yards, confining the cows to those yards, and keeping in them very large stocks of swine, convert their plenty of straw into manure, which they make good use of. Oil cake they lay on their wheat at an expense of 40s. or two guineas an acre. All these manures they use to far greater profit than if their land had not been marled – that foundation of their husbandry is a preparative for all successive manurings; they take the greater effect from following an absorbent earth, and last (it is asserted) the longer: but that I should doubt.

THE COURSE OF CROPS

After the best-managed enclosure, and the most spirited conduct in marling, still the whole success of the undertaking depends on this point: no fortune will be made in Norfolk by farming unless a judicious course of crops be pursued. That which has been chiefly adopted by the Norfolk farmers is:

1. turnips
2. barley
3. clover or clover and rye grass
4. wheat

Some of them, depending on their soils being richer than their neighbours (for instance, all the way from Holt by Aylsham down through the Fleg hundreds), will steal a crop of peas or barley after the wheat; but it is bad husbandry, and has not been followed by those men who have made fortunes. In the above course the turnips are (if possible) manured for, and much of the wheat the same. This is a noble system which keeps the soil rich; only one exhausting crop is taken to a cleansing and ameliorating one. The land cannot possibly in such management be either poor or foul.

The only variations are in the duration of the clover, which extends from one year to three or four. On the first improvement rye grass was generally sown with it, and it was left on the ground three or four years: but latterly they sow no more rye grass than merely sufficient for their flocks, and leave it two years on the ground. The rest of their clover crop is sown alone and left but one year. Opinions are not clear on these variations. Some think the modern method an improvement; others that the old one was better.

If I may be allowed to hazard an idea on this point, I should venture to condemn the ploughing up the clover the first year, and for these reasons. It is exhausting the land more: two crops of corn in four years exhaust much more than two in five years; hence appears to me the *modern* necessity of buying oil cake at two guineas an acre. The marl is lost sooner in this method, for that subsides in exact proportion to the quantity of tillage in a given time. It does not sink while the land is at rest, but while it is pulverizing by the plough. Lastly, the stock of cattle is less, consequently the quantity of dung inferior: instead of folding 25 acres only 20 are done. They do not pretend that the wheat after a ley of *two* years is worse than after that of *one* – but they say it is not so clean. I admit that there will be more trouble in clearing the turnip fallow of twitch [couch]; but let that trouble be carried to account, and it will not balance the counter-advantages.

Besides the best farmers agree that if the turnip fallow is well executed, the plants twice well hoed, and the land stirred thrice for barley, that then the clover lying two years will not give a foul crop of wheat. Twitch generally comes from some neglect.

TURNIPS

Every link of the chain of Norfolk husbandry has so intimate a connection and dependence that the destruction of a single one ruins the whole. Everything depends not only on turnips, but on turnips well hoed; an assertion that will receive but little credit in various parts of the kingdom. Turnips on well-manured land, thoroughly hoed, are the only fallow in the Norfolk course; it is therefore absolutely necessary to make it as complete as possible. They cannot be changed for a mere fallow because the stock of sheep kept for folding and eating of the clover and rye grass, and farmyard cattle, would then all starve; and add to this, that the tillage during the latter part of the summer, &c., which must be substituted instead of them, would pulverize the sands too much, which are greatly improved by the treading of the cattle that eat the crop off. In a word, the improved culture of this plant is so important to the Norfolk husbandry that no other vegetable could be substituted that a common farmer would cultivate.

CLOVER AND RYE GRASS

This also is another article that could not possibly be dispensed with. The light parts of the county have neither meadows nor pastures; their flocks of sheep, dairies of cows, their fatting beasts in the spring, and their horses all depend on these grasses and could subsist by nothing else; nor could they raise any wheat without this assistance. Their soil is too light for that grain before it is well bound and matted together by the roots of the clover, which are at the same time a rich manure for the wheat: a fallow instead of clover would be worse than nothing, it would render the land much too light. For these reasons, which certainly are decisive, nothing could be done here without clover.

LEASES

It is a custom growing pretty common in several parts of the kingdom to grant no leases: this will do very well where no improvements are carried on; where a tenant can never lose anything by being turned out of his farm; but it is absurdity itself to expect that a man will begin his husbandry on your land by expending 3, 4, or £5 an acre while he is liable to be turned out at a year's notice. I shall not take up more of your time on a point which is self-evident. Had the Norfolk landlords conducted themselves on such narrow principles their estates, which are raised, five, six, and tenfold, would yet have been sheeepwalks.

LARGE FARMS

If the preceding articles are properly reviewed, it will at once be apparent that no small farmers could effect such great things as have been done in Norfolk. Enclosing, marling, and keeping a flock of sheep large enough for folding belong absolutely and exclusively to great farmers. None of them could be effected by small ones – or such as are called middling ones in other counties. Nor should it be forgotten that the best husbandry in Norfolk is that of the largest farmers. You must go to a Curtis, a Mallet, a Barton, a Glover, a Carr, to see Norfolk husbandry. You will not among them find the stolen crops that are too often met with among the little occupiers of an hundred a year in the eastern part of the county. Great farms have been the soul of the Norfolk culture: split them into tenures of an hundred pounds a year, you will find nothing but beggars and weeds in the whole county. The rich man keeps his land rich and clean.

These are the principles of Norfolk husbandry, which have advanced the agriculture of the greatest part of that county to a much greater height than is anywhere to be met with over an equal extent of country. I shall in the next place venture slightly to mention a few particulars in which the Norfolk farmers are deficient.

1. Peas are never hand-hoed.
2. Wheat, though weedy, the same.
3. Beans the same everywhere, except in marshland.
4. No regular chopping of stubbles for littering the farm-yards: it is very incompletely practised.
5. Meadows and natural pastures managed in as slovenly a manner as in any part of the kingdom.
6. The breed of sheep contemptible.
7. That of horses very indifferent.
8. Vast tracts of land admirably fitted for carrots, but none cultivated except a very few near Norwich.
9. All their hedges managed on the old sad system of cutting off live wood and supplying the place with dead: no plashing.

These circumstances, however, are by no means a balance
to the merit of the good husbandry before stated; I hint them
only as matters deserving the attention of farmers who have
shown in general such enlightened views.

Eastern Tour (1771) II 150–63

2. IMPROVEMENT OF LIVESTOCK

The improvement of livestock in the eighteenth century is invariably associated with the name of Robert Bakewell, the
celebrated pioneer stockbreeder of Dishley in Leicestershire. It is
not always realised, however, that the modern history of selective
breeding goes back some fifty years before Bakewell's time, and
that since the Middle Ages attempts had been made by crossing
animals to obtain a larger sheep and a longer wool staple. In the
same part of the Midlands in which Bakewell had his farm some
little-known predecessors, like Webster of Canley and Joseph
Allom, had already achieved advances in cattle and sheep in the
earlier eighteenth century; and in Bakewell's heyday his contemporary, William Marshall, could name some fifteen or twenty
breeders who were doing similar work.

That Bakewell is so well known arises partly from the fact that
he specialised solely as a breeder rather than breeder-cum-grazier,
as was the case with his fellow-breeders, and that he was successful in producing a new breed of rapidly fattening sheep, his
famous New Leicesters, as well as improved cattle, horses and
other animals. He helped to popularise the practice of letting out
individual rams and bulls for hire, and his renowned beasts, his
methods of breeding, and the management of his farm generally,
were all publicised by Young. Dishley was visited several times
by Young over a period of years, and the two agriculturists were
on good terms, went on agricultural tours together, and exchanged
information and samples: Bakewell sent Young some of his
animals to try, and bags of seed went to and fro between Dishley
and Bradfield. It appears from some of Bakewell's surviving
correspondence that, in private, he was inclined to think Young
subject to hastiness of judgement and prone to an excess of
candour in his published statements, but nevertheless a close
relationship subsisted between them over a long period of time.

Bakewell played a part in the evolution of both the modern
sheep and the shire horse, but his experiments with cattle were not
very successful. His New Longhorns rapidly accumulated fat in

preparation for the butcher but failed to preserve the good milk and the fecundity of the original stock. Other breeders demonstrated that improvement could best be achieved with shorthorns rather than longhorns. Similarly, his New Leicesters, though fattening quickly, produced less wool and were less fertile than the old stock with which Bakewell began. Their meat, too, tended to fatness, and the flesh of the full-grown animals was derisively described as 'coal-heavers' mutton'. However, Bakewell did succeed in his major objective of producing animals that could be fattened for market in much shorter periods than was the rule hitherto, and though his New Leicesters soon disappeared as a distinct breed they played a major part in the improvement of other breeds, particularly the Border Leicester, Wensleydale, and the improved Leicesters.

Bakewell was one, but only one, of the 'intelligent and spirited breeders' of his day. Others, then and subsequently, developed his work, such as Ellman and Webb who improved the Southdown sheep, the Culleys of Northumberland, and the Colling brothers, the Booths and Thomas Bates, who laid the foundations of an important industry concerned with breeding and exporting pedigree cattle. The following excerpt from one of Young's several accounts of Bakewell's methods possesses an additional interest in showing the great breeder as involved in other matters, particularly the watering of meadows to secure earlier and richer bites of grass, and in determining the relative advantages of rye grass and a mixture of clovers and rye grass as fodder. Bakewell was very much in the tradition of the gentlemen-experimenters on whose patient investigations by trial and error the contemporary progress in agriculture was founded:

> To Dishley, where I found the enterprising Mr Bakewell amidst improvements that will reflect a lasting honour to his name.
>
> The fifteen years that have passed since I had seen Mr Bakewell's cattle have not elapsed without his gaining considerable experience and carrying every part of his stock much nearer perfection.
>
> The time alone is sufficient to explain the reason of some difference that will be found between the present minutes and those taken here before.

GENERAL PRINCIPLE

To explain the principles which have guided him in breeding a beast or sheep (for the same rules are applicable to both) for the butcher, will at the same time explain his own stock which are in the highest perfection when examined with an eye to those principles.

The leading idea, then, which has governed all his exertions is to procure that breed which on a given food will give the most profitable meat; that in which the proportion of the useful meat to the quantity of offal is the greatest; also in which the proportion of the best to the inferior joints is likewise the greatest.

The propriety of the rule is obvious, and at one stroke cuts off many common notions that will not stand the test of that critical examination which may on this principle be instituted. Thus the short leg, when the result of a great heaviness in the belly and the shoulders, indicates no more than the weight of the beast being in the worst joints. Some are at present fond of a great dewlap, with Vergil, *Et crurum tenus a mento palearia pendent.* But, as it is mere offal, yet undoubtedly demands that nourishment which might go to a better place, it is to be rejected as an absurdity and classed with the folly of a Norfolk sheep-master who admires a ram's horn three feet long and nine inches in circumference. (Mr Bakewell, when in Suffolk, measured the horns of one of Mr Macro's rams of those dimensions.) For the same reason a thick hide, a great head, or in a word any part of the animal being heavier than ordinary, except those joints which are the most valuable, are to be considered as breeding offal, not meat; and, on the contrary, those best joints cannot be too heavy; under which idea Mr Bakewell has bred some beasts to be so exceedingly fat on the rump as to appear monstrous to the eye. Of this sort was the ox shown at Mr Tattersall's, and he has many bulls and cows of the same kind. The experiment is very remarkable and shows to what perfection skill and attention will carry breeding.

POINTS OF A BEAST

On this plan the points to attend to in a beast are those where the valuable joints lie: the rump, the hip, the back, the ribs, and after these the flank, that is to say, the backward upper quarters; but the belly, shoulder, neck, legs, and head should be light; for if a beast has a disposition to fatten or be heavy in these it will be found a deduction from the more valuable points. It has been said, but improperly, that a barrel on four short sticks would represent the true form; but that shape swells at the top and bottom, whereas the back of a beast should be square, straight, and flat; or, if any rising, it should be from a disposition to fatten and swell about the rump and hip-bones. And the belly should likewise be quite straight; for if it swell, it shows weight in a bad point. Again, the shortness of the leg is what Mr Bakewell calls a non-essential; under which title he classes all those points which fashion, custom, or prejudice have, at different times and in different places, called attention to, but improperly. Head, neck, horn, leg, skin, colour, &c., have all been considered as important (thick hides, however, are generally to be esteemed worse thriving beasts than thin; and pale colours, as white, yellow, &c., Mr Bakewell thinks are indications of finer meat than darker ones); but in fact none of them are so; for let every one of these circumstances be condemned in a beast, he should, notwithstanding that, prefer him, if his carcass was well made and showed a disposition to fatten in the valuable points.

This doctrine is new and of very great importance to graziers. As far as reason will permit one to judge, the principles on which it is founded are just, and whoever has the pleasure of viewing Mr Bakewell's cattle will see them powerfully exemplified in actual practice with a success that cannot permit many to remain infidels. . . .

SHEEP

The points in which to examine a sheep and the general form of his carcass are the same as in an ox: the fatness and breadth of back, a spreading barrel carcase, with *flat* bellies and by no means curved and hanging, with such a disposition to fatten as is indicated in the bulls and cows.

A very great error has been spread by some persons which seems to connect Mr Bakewell's breed with the Lincoln, but in fact it is not more distinct from the Norfolk. The Lincoln has been entirely spoiled by breeding for quantity of wool only; which however it might answer when wool was at a high price, could not but be attended with bad consequences when prices fell.

The non-essential points in sheep are the short legs so much valued in some counties, the white faces of Wiltshire, the black faces and legs of Norfolk, the horns of various sorts that are so much valued, &c., &c., carcass all, and a disposition to fatten on the carcass, and perhaps to have the least tallow on the inside.

A considerable illustration will be thrown on this doctrine by some observations Mr Bakewell made in Norfolk and Suffolk, where he examined all the best flocks; because there can scarcely be two animals of the same species more different than a Dishley and a Norfolk sheep. If the Norfolks are good sheep, Mr Bakewell is in a cruel error and all his principles are worthless. The characteristics are these: the back is narrow instead of being broad, and ridged in the middle instead of being flat; there is no disposition to be fat in the rump, back, or ribs, but they die better than they feel, as they tallow well, which is a fault when gained as in this breed it is at the expense of the fat which should be better placed; when killed in hot weather it will not keep sweet so long, by twenty-four hours, as the meat of the Southdown breed; the flavour of the mutton is excellent, a circumstance not uncommon in lean venison; the gravy of the meat is unusually plentiful, and remarkably high-coloured.

There are several circumstances in this description that deserve considerable attention. The fact of the breed not keeping when killed so long as another, which I had from Mr Bakewell, he received from an authority perfectly competent to ascertain it, the butcher of Eton College. The joints in demand for the foundation make it necessary for him chiefly to kill Norfolks and Southdowns; and as he has both in plenty, and often hanging up together, he has repeatedly observed this remarkable fact.

It appears to me so singular that I got an application to be made to Mr Vyse, the butcher, for a confirmation of it, and also for his opinion of the two breeds. He appears to be a very clear and intelligent man; I shall therefore give his opinion in his own words:

The Norfolk mutton certainly will taint sooner than any in very hot weather; neither is there any sort (that I know) of a worse flavour at that time, though inferior to none in cool weather. Many very fine and fat Norfolks do not please on the table; the fat often runs away in roasting if they are laid to a hot fire, and they rarely are so sweet as the Southdowns. The latter are in hot weather worth a halfpenny a pound more than the Norfolks.

When both are *completely* fatted it is hard to say (supposing the season cool) which, upon an average, are fattest. The flavour, too, in such a season I think is equal; and as to coarse meat, there is none in either sort. But if they are killed in cool weather before they are very fat the preference must be given to the Norfolks, because the meat will in that case eat better and there is a probability of much more fat within.

With respect to profit to the feeder, if they are fed entirely with grass and upon good land, my opinion is decidedly in favour of Southdowns; or if they eat turnips in the winter, and after that are kept two or three months upon grass in the spring, it is the same. But if they are half fat against winter, and are to be completed at turnips, I believe no sheep are more profitable than Norfolks, perhaps none so much so. But both sorts should be kept where there is both turnip and grass land.

JOHN VYSE, Butcher,
Eton College.

... Mr Bakewell, who has not only viewed but made experiments on most of the breeds of sheep in the kingdom, thinks there is no comparison between the Norfolks and Southdowns; that the latter are much better for any kind of food, for folding, or for any purpose, than the former, except the flavour of the mutton. Their shape is an illustration of his principles: that of the Norfolk is already described; the Southdowns have flatter backs, more spreading, rounded carcasses, a much greater disposition to fatten, a point infallibly attending (in a well-made animal) the deficiency of tallow within, and less *offal*. By which term is to be understood not only the skin, tallow, head, and pluck [heart, liver and lungs], but the horns, hoofs, and bones of every joint. It is remarkable that the last are very small in those breeds that have a true disposition to fatten. They are much less in the Southdowns than in the Norfolks. Mr Bakewell when last in that county ate a neck of mutton at an inn which afforded him a bone, which he considered as a curiosity and kept it. It was full twice the size of that of one of his own sheep, which had four inches of fat on it. He made enquiries of the butcher where the sheep came from, thinking it might be a Lincoln, but it was clearly ascertained to be bred a true Norfolk black-face, bought, if not bred, at Massingham. This circumstance of bone is not simply of consequence to the consumer in his buying meat instead of bone, but it implies a breed without a right tendency to be fat; since in all animals whatever the largest-boned are the leanest, and the smallest bones covered with most fat.

Good as the Southdowns are on comparison with the Norfolks, Mr Bakewell's own breed far exceeds them; their form is truer, their back much flatter, their carcasses heavier in proportion, and they have so much greater a disposition to fatten beyond all other sheep as to make a parallel absurd. (This is evident by the prices Mr Culley and others let their rams for that have been bred from this stock, for many years past.) Mr Bakewell has the part of a neck of mutton in pickle which is at present four inches and a half thick with fat on the bone. (He has also a piece of rump of beef that has been in pickle a year and three-quarters, four inches thick of fat. I may here add that on the 6th of December last a three-shear [thrice-shorn] wether, got by a tup of Mr George Culley's from Mr Bakewell's breed, was killed at Darlington by Mr Colin of Skarlingham, which weighed 46 lb. a quarter. It cut six inches thick of fat between the tail and loin, and from thence along the back and shoulders to the neck three inches thick; and at the division of the quarters through the ribs six inches and a quarter thick in fat.) His observation on this is perfectly just. It is no question whether a man would wish to have such mutton on his table, but the breed that has such a disposition to fatten will in any given circumstances be the fattest. Gentlemen who are curious in their meat, and think a great plenty of claret-coloured gravy an excellence, may breed for it, as they do deer in their parks; but the great mass of mutton-eaters, which are in the manufacturing towns, will for ever choose the fattest meat and give the greatest price for it. His own and the similar breeds, well fatted, sell at 5*d.* per lb. in markets where a Norfolk sheep would be considered not so good. Let any man put a Dishley wether or one of this kind to fatten with a

Norfolk, a Southdown, a Lincoln, a Dorset, &c., &c., and try by every effort to make them all equally fat, he will find this kind superior to all; and when killed, and the offal (including the bones scraped clean) weighed, the proportion of it to the gross weight will show a second superiority.

If it is contended that Mr Bakewell's sheep, being long-woolled, must be kept, as all long-woolled sheep are, on very rich land, he denies the conclusion and asserts that the same disposition to be fat will, in a moderate-sized sheep (and it is to be remembered that the Dishley sheep are small on comparison with the Teeswater, but heavier than any other) prevail, let the food be what it may. The worse-formed the carcass, and the less tendency to fatten, the worse must the animal thrive or do on any food. This is to be seen in all sorts of animals. Some will be lean in spite of every attention to make them fat; and others will be fat on better keeping than those that are lean: this plainly appears by a collection of different sorts he has now in his possession which he has procured for this purpose, and wishes may be carefully examined by any person desirous of having information on this subject. Mr Bakewell has gradually formed his breed by a selection made with constant attention to this circumstance. . . .

I was witness at Dishley to a very interesting experiment on different breeds of sheep. He has a sheep-house in which six rams were tied up and stalled on turnips: one of his own breed, one Norfolk, one Teeswater, one Wiltshire, one from Ross in Herefordshire, and one from Charnwood Forest. They were weighed alive when put to turnips, their food weighed to them, and weighed alive again at the end of the trial. The following [table] is the result of the experiment. It was conducted entirely by a young Russian, resident at Dishley, to whom Mr Bakewell entrusted it, as it was not a trial on a scale to which he could attend himself; nothing therefore, could be fairer than the manner in which it was conducted.

. . . A circumstance which seems very clearly to ascertain the superiority of Mr Bakewell's breed is that his principal market of late years has been in Lincolnshire, Warwickshire, and other counties where those breeders, who once were his rivals, now establish the superiority of his breed by that most incontestable of all methods, becoming purchasers of it.

That the breed has improved in estimation, as well as beauty, appears from the prices of his tups rising much higher than ever was attained before.

	Weight of the Sheep	Food from March 19th to April 2nd, 1786
	lb.	lb.
Durham ram	290	498
Wiltshire	173	313
Norfolk	162	298
Dishley	158	174
Charnwood Forester	131	304
Herefordshire	115	202

If I am asked, as I have often been in conversation, whether this breed is adapted to all sorts of soils and circumstances, I must reply in the negative; but that the principles which have produced it are certainly so applicable. Norfolk, Southdown, and Mountain mutton are beyond all question finer flavoured; and if I kept a stock of Mr Bakewell's sheep I should at the same time have some others, as a man keeps deer for his table without an idea of any profit attending them. Upon rich soils there can be no doubt of the matter; and on poor ones the same breed would in a few generations adapt its size to the nature of the pastures, for on such soils the necessity of having the best form and tendency to fatten is there the most apparent. In respect to folding, and especially where there is a long drive, and the flock, to use a common expression, is worked hard, I have many and great doubts which experiment only can remove. I think the lightness and agility necessary to a sheep in that circumstance quite inconsistent with the disposition to fatten, which is the great merit of Mr Bakewell's breed, in the same manner as no art or effort can make a fat fellow walk like a thin one. The Norfolks work admirably at the fold because they have almost as great a disposition to be lean as Mr Bakewell's to be fat. I speak this, however, as theory, for I do not know that any experiment has been made by setting Mr Bakewell's on long legs and then trying them at the fold. . . .

BULLS AND COWS

The improvements Mr Bakewell has made in his cattle since I was before at Dishley are, I think, considerable. He had not then attempted to produce any protuberances of fat, but only to render the beast heavy in the hind quarters and to perfect his shape. He has now, in addition to the true form of the carcass, produced a remarkable disposition to fatten in the rump and on the hip-bone. The ox which he showed two or three years ago at Mr Tattersall's appeared in those parts to be a monster of fat. Many of the kind I saw at Dishley: I measured the hip-bones of one, buried in a mound of fat 14 inches in diameter, with perfect hillocks of fat on her rump and along the back-bone; and, with all this fat, she has a calf every year.

His bulls are admirably fine. D of 7 years old is the most capital animal of the kind I have seen; but he has many of them of all ages that are of the most perfect form to be imagined. They have all, however, horns, and not small, which upon his own principles are offal and ought to be excluded.

While we had the pleasure of being with him he sold one three-year-old bull, one two-year old, and two yearlings, all bulls, for a very high price, to go to a gentleman in Jamaica, who having purchased one in 1777 now in perfect health and vigour notwithstanding the change of climate, found the breed to answer so well that, eight years after, he came again to replenish a stock which experience had convinced him was superior to all others.

We found the bulls, cows, calves, and in general all the stock tied up in houses and sheds, nearly in the manner I have described in the *Farmer's Tour*. The troughs out of which they eat their hay or turnips are two feet and a half wide at top, in a space of three feet allowed in the building. Their standing, at a full growth, 6 feet, then a step of 5 or 6 inches down to a space for the dung being taken up and thrown through holes in the wall on to the dunghill. Three feet in breadth are allowed for a cow, and four for a bull.

When I was before at Dishley Mr Bakewell used no litter whatever. He has changed his practice and now litters with straw; the beasts are cleaned once a day and driven to water twice. This littering is with a view to making dung, not the good of the cattle; they were as clean, I think cleaner, without litter than they are with. In a farmyard in the higher part of his farm he has 45 tied up that are taken care of and fed by a man and a boy.

In breeding his bulls and cows (and it is the same with his

sheep) he entirely sets at naught the old ideas of the necessity of variation from crosses; on the contrary, the sons cover the dams, and the sires their daughters, and their progeny equally good with no attention whatever to vary the race. The old systems in this respect he thinks erroneous and founded in opinion only, without attending either to reason or experience; and he asks anyone to point out a stock of beasts or sheep, now in high credit, that have not originated from this stock and been bred in this way. Is not this the practice with the pigeon-fanciers and cockbreeders? and probably would hold equally good in horses and dogs, were they to persevere in the same practice: but when anything happens contrary to their expectations it is attributed to the want of a proper cross in blood, and they immediately decline this mode. But ask whether anything has ever happened in this way that they have not experienced in the common way of breeding; then why condemn the practice till further proof has been made by reversing every one of those maxims?

HORSES

Mr Bakewell's breed of horses is the great heavy black, and his stallions are by far the finest I have seen of that breed. Nothing can be more compactly formed.

For all those farmers, but especially for those carriers and others whose teams must draw great weights, and who, in consequence, think it necessary to have a horse of great weight, there cannot be a better breed than this. And the same observation may be applicable to heavy cavalry. The great black horse is in high estimation in this kingdom; it is, therefore, of very considerable importance to carry the breed to the highest perfection. Mr Bakewell's exertions appear to be as successful in this line as in any other. Whether it is likely to be of equal national advantage is with me questionable. I am no friend to the horse at all. For the use of farmers if they want great strength to be applied a large ox I hold to be a much better animal; and if they want activity mingled with a certain portion of strength, more nimbleness than oxen are capable of, then a lighter and a smaller horse will be more applicable. But for carriers, &c., this observation may not hold.

WATERED MEADOWS

The importance of watering is nowhere seen to more advantage than on Mr Bakewell's farm: 80 acres he improved in this manner long ago, and he has lately hired a water-mill which, giving him a command of the river so much higher, has enabled him to plan out an irrigation of 40 acres more by cutting a large carrier trench, near a mile long, as high up the slope of his fields as the levels will admit. He has made a great progress in this work, and executes every part of it with that intelligence and precision that seem to animate all his exertions.

The banks of the river being constantly raised, little breaches sometimes happen, and rats make leaks that require attention. In stopping them he makes use of the very ingenious Mr Brindley's method of *puddling*, which is very well known in all those counties where modern navigations have been cut but is rarely applied in others; yet there never was a simpler or more useful invention. If a stank or dam is to be made or repaired which is to keep out water, the method is to keep a narrow open trench in the centre of the bank as it rises, into which water can be let at pleasure. As the bank rises, let in water, and throw in molds [loose earth] enough to turn the water into mud, which is to be done by working the water and molds well together till it comes to be quite thick, and being afterwards left to settle it becomes a thin wall of a mud plaster in the middle of the earth bank. This method is infallible in stopping water, and it is not a tenth part of the expense of the old way of ramming clay.

More satisfactory experiments could never be made on the benefits of irrigation than those which Mr Bakewell calls his *proof pieces*. They are small squares in most of his meadows, over which the water is prevented coming by drains cut around them. Most of them are in low, boggy, miserable spots, where these drains must alone be of use; but notwithstanding that advantage, they are perfectly contemptible in comparison with the immediately contiguous spots over which the water is conducted. The difference is so great as to bring complete conviction to the mind of every person who views them.

To describe the whole operation of watering would be tedious; and since Mr Boswell[1] has written so well upon the

1 G. Boswell, *Treatise on Watering Meadows* (*1779*) [Ed.].

subject is not necessary. Mr Bakewell varies from his plans, however, in more than one circumstance, particularly in cutting his carriers and main drains together with only a small space between for a bank so that they form a fence in the subdivision of a meadow; and by an ingenious contrivance, a bridge with hinges can be turned up and forms a gate. In conducting his water under roads, &c., where arches are necessary he builds them of bricks made on purpose for an arch, without mortar, by one side being thinner than the other.

There is one use to which Mr Bakewell applies water in which he is perfectly original: it is that of making roads. He lets it into a short one that leads down to his house, and by washing cleans and improves it. Upon this subject he has a favourite theory. It is that all roads should instead of being convex be made concave, with a view to mending them by waterings which he contends is much better than any other way, and in which a shilling will do as much as five; that there are many new roads taken out of hollow ways and raised on high grounds, at a very great expense, when a proper conducting of the water that flows in such hollows would preserve the road in perpetual repair; that in the very worst roads good spots are found where every water has a free spreading course; for washing away the loam or clay leaves the sand, stone or gravel bare, and forms as good a road as art can effect. This theory has certainly many facts for its support, and beyond all doubt deserves considerable attention in numerous ways where materials are scarce and money scarcer.

LAYING LAND TO GRASS

Mr Bakewell has tried some experiments in laying arable to grass which merit attention, and especially as he has repeated them in various seasons, and from the mass of his experience has drawn decided conclusions. He has a field in divisions; one laid with rye grass alone, another red clover alone, a third white clover alone, a fourth white clover mixed with red, a fifth red clover mixed with rye grass; and in the feeding the field with various sorts of cattle and sheep, as well as mowing for hay, he finds the last the best. And his general conclusion is that the best method of laying down is to sow 10 lb. an acre of common red clover and 2 pecks of good clean rye grass.

To this I must add that his soil is a mellow, rich, friable

sandy loam which runs naturally to white clover and other valuable plants. Upon various soils rye grass and red clover would become a field of rye grass and weeds....

3. DRAINAGE

Drainage was one of several agricultural problems that were only partially solved in Young's time. From a very early period farmers had attempted to make the heavy clay soils of the Midlands a little drier and easier to work by means of ridge and furrow, a practice in which, through ploughing in a certain manner, oval ridges were raised at regular intervals across the fields; the rain water drained off these ridges into the intervening furrows or 'lands', and so ran off to a ditch or watercourse on lower ground. Ridge and furrow, however, was of only limited advantage on low-lying, level, or excessively heavy land. Experiments with under-drainage involved the digging of trenches across the field and lining them with stones, tree branches, broom or furze before replacing the soil. Much skill was required to estimate correctly the required depth and frequency of the trenches, and gradually methods were improved, particularly under the influence of the well-known expert, Joseph Elkington.

The drainage of the heavy Midland clays, however, remained imperfect until the introduction in the 1840s of machines for making cheaply the many thousands of clay pipes or tiles required to under-drain a farm, and there followed a period of heavy investment in the under-drainage of these soils during the middle decades of the nineteenth century.

The following passage is taken from one of Young's last works, a lecture which he delivered to the Board of Agriculture. The lecture dealt with three of Young's distinguished contemporaries, and this excerpt comes from his discussion of one of these, John Arbuthnot of Mitcham, Surrey. In addition to experimenting with the drainage and cultivation of clay soils, Arbuthnot also invented his own swing-plough, and made use of a crop of beans to abolish summer fallows and clean the soil of weeds:

.'... Having examined the husbandry of Flanders with a farmer's eye, and compared their broad lands with the high ridges of our central counties, he [Arbuthnot] was convinced of the excellency of the system as conducted in the Netherlands and the horrible deficiencies of the English imitation; and in order to examine a very different system he went into Essex in certain ticklish seasons in order to view the effect of hollow-draining with the assistance of narrow lands and still narrower three-feet ridges, which he found well enough adapted to loams, through which the water freely percolates; but in others so tenacious as to merit the application of clay, the deficiency was so manifest as to confirm him in his Flemish ideas. . . . The breadth [of ridge] he most approved was that of two perches, but the height did not generally exceed two feet, and in no case more than two feet and a half; in each furrow, marked by these lands, he dug and filled a well-executed hollow drain. Relative to the success of this system of draining I may observe that viewing his farm repeatedly during many years the cleanliness and magnitude of his crops formed a spectacle highly satisfactory to multitudes who viewed them. . . . The principle which governed Arbuthnot's operations is unquestionable: lay your land dry, whatever may be the method pursued, before you attempt anything else.

On the Husbandry of Three Celebrated British Farmers: Messrs Bakewell, Arbuthnot and Ducket (1811) pp. 18–20

4. EXPERIMENTAL FARMING

Young lived in a period of very considerable experimentation in farming, though the essentially empirical trials of his day were to be followed by the more strictly scientific work of such famous nineteenth-century figures as Philip Pusey, Sir John Bennet Lawes, J. H. Gilbert and J. J. Mechi. The eighteenth century was a period of progress achieved slowly and piecemeal by patient trial and error. Theoretical ideas of seventeenth-century writers were put into practical form as when, for example, Jethro Tull in about 1701 constructed the first practical seed-drill, though such a machine had been designed by Worlidge some thirty years earlier. In the later decades especially of the eighteenth century, numbers of country gentlemen and substantial farmers devoted land to 'experiment grounds', and carried out trials of new types of crops such as lucerne and chicory, attempted to assess the effects of a variety of manures and soil dressings ranging from coal ashes to seaweed, hired the rams and bulls of specialist breeders, such as those offered by Bakewell and his Leicestershire Tup Society, and spent their leisure hours in designing their own carts, ploughs, harrows and horse-rakes. They sometimes wrote papers on these subjects for Young's *Annals of Agriculture*, and they frequently joined in supporting local agricultural societies, and welcomed an invitation to visit the famous private shows held by Lord Somerville in London, the Duke of Bedford at Woburn, and the celebrated Thomas Coke, Lord Leicester, at Holkham.

The *Annals of Agriculture*, together with the papers of the Bath and West of England Society, and the later *Journal* of the Royal Agricultural Society of England, provided a forum for the views and discoveries of enthusiastic amateurs and professional farmers alike. Nevertheless, this coterie of agricultural innovators, though sufficiently numerous to sustain such publications for long periods of years, remained fairly select and circumscribed, as the circulation figures of the journals indicate. Agricultural experimentation was costly and time-consuming. It was also still in its infancy, and lacked the scientific precision and rigour, and particularly the adequate understanding of chemistry, which subsequently came to its aid. Young himself had early been bitten by the experimental bug, and many of his personal contributions to the *Annals* consist of accounts of his multifarious and often futile trials. It was this experience, stretching back over some twenty years, which informed the paper from which the first of the following excerpts is taken; in this Young compares the nature of agricultural experimentation with that of the new sciences of electricity and chemistry:

(1) ... Progress of fact depends greatly on the nature of the science. In most of the branches of philosophy there are no insurmountable difficulties in ascertaining it. When former experiments are doubted they may be repeated without any very formidable waste of time or expense. In this case the labours of one generation are appropriated by the next, and the successive age in possession of all preceding knowledge advances with an accelerated rapidity. How amusing in the history of electricity to trace the discoveries through Gilbert, Boyle, Newton, Hauksbee, Gray, &c., to Watson, Franklin, Nollet, and other electricians flourishing at present! Few of the sciences have advanced by a more regular gradation. And in the philosophy of air we may be satisfied that Boyle prepared the way for Hales and Stahl; and that without these it is not probable Black would have made the great advance

which he effected, which opened the way to Priestley and that host of disciples which in every part of Europe have lighted their flambeaux at an English torch. Not one of these great men but have made their respective discoveries that connect with the knowledge of their predecessors, and pave the way for another age to open by their means to still greater wonders. But this unbroken gradation has depended on the nature of these inquiries. In electricity, chemistry, pneumatics, the science of aeriform fluids [gaseous bodies], in medicine, anatomy, &c., experiments are under command. The able, with application and a very moderate fortune, can devise, conduct, and complete many trials in a few weeks, and repeat them with whatever variations are desired in a few months. Books have been written, and excellent ones too, on the experiments which have been made in a single year.

The rapid progress of so many sciences furnishes us, by comparison, with the true reason why that of agriculture has been so slow.

No experiment in that art is to be made in less than six months, few in less than a year, and many demand three, four, and even six years to effect. The expense also on a large scale (and many objects can be ascertained only by a large one) is very great. Nor are time and money all that are wanting. The process is in the hands of clowns, and what is oftentimes much worse, of ill-educated, conceited, ignorant, pert bailiffs, who find either pleasure or profit in a miscarriage. A man, with fortune requisite, will not, twice in an age, give the residence or the attention necessary for ascertaining facts. Rich farmers that reside and have attention give it to the common conduct of that which their fathers performed, rarely to experiment. Nor does the evil rest here: experiments are in the open fields, and consequently liable to the plundering of thieves, to accidents from birds and reptiles, to the intrusion of another sort of vermin, sportsmen, whose object of a partridge or a fox will induce them to trample on pursuits they have no relish to enjoy, nor attention to understand.

The same exposure in the fields is also to the heavens, and every experiment is in a great measure dependent on the weather: if the summer turns out very wet the result will not

be the same as if it is dry; and the dry season may come
when the wet one is wanting to the trial. When all these
circumstances are considered it will clearly appear that trials
in agriculture are quite another thing from those in any other
science. Experiments in a laboratory, which a man can lock
up when he turns his back, upon a substance that lies on a
table or is confined in a jar, with machines to be trusted in
no hands but his own – in such a situation all is within
command, and though difficulties will arise (for what pursuit
is free from them?) yet they are such as will depend very
much on his own talents, skill, and industry to remove,
perfectly free from the intrusion of storms, thieves, crows,
sparrows, rabbits, hares, sportsmen, or idlers. The contrast is
so strong that it accounts readily for the extreme backwardness of this art and its being so little removed
from its old doubt and confusion by the labours of an age
that has impelled every other science in a most rapid
course.

Besides these obvious difficulties there are others not less
effective in retarding the progress of this art. When Mr
Kirwan [the contemporary chemist] reads that Mr Boyle
put such a putrescent material into his retort, and after so
much heat obtained an empyreumatic oil [i.e. an oil tasting
or smelling of burnt organic matter], a volatile alkali, an
elastic fluid – he has very little doubt but the substance was
what it is called, and that an oil and an alkali were obtained.
And when Dr Priestley reads that Dr Hales obtained so
many cubic inches of air from such a quantity of gold in
aqua regia, he has no difficulty in knowing if the trial was
really made with gold and aqua regia; and no doubt but the
air was produced; to analyse the elastic fluid was left for
this age, but the steps that discovered its existence formed the
ground on which our philosophers stood when they took that
further flight. Turn now to agriculture, and let experimenters
at present read the works of their predecessors. With a very,
very few exceptions we do not even know the soil on which
they worked: the words clay, loam, marl, sand, &c., are used
with such a want of precision; the circumstances recorded
militate so much with the terms used that all is confusion,
and this when experiment is described; but, in general,
the writers of husbandry have given everything except

experiment – reasoning, theory, conclusion, assertion, instruction – but little observation, and less trial.

Clay sometimes means marl, and marl at others a clay with a small mixture of calcareous substance; sand is used to describe very fine sandy loams; *strong*, when applied to soils, sometimes means wetness, at others tenacity; you may suppose it a loam, a clay, or a marl. Manures are described in the same manner, rich or poor, old or new, hot or cooling; and every term used but those really descriptive of their nature. A meadow, a pasture, a wood, weeds, and a thousand other instances might be given of terms used as specific that are too loose even for generic. All this has generated error and confusion.

It is to be regretted that the writers of the present age have not often varied from the conduct of their predecessors. A book is scarcely to be opened in which endless assertions are not made, unsupported by experiment, and without any reference to particular districts where common practice might be the proof. Millions of volumes may be written on such grounds, and the sooner they are forgotten the better. Let those who wish to advance the science consider the attention that has been exerted to promote other branches of human knowledge, mark the caution that retards every step beyond experiment, that restrains conclusion; and taking nothing for granted keeps the line perpetually defined between conjecture and fact – the vigour that searches fresh truths, and the boldness that adopts them, however new and unusual. Such is the conduct that can alone advance a science, and by such only can the principles of agriculture be ascertained.

Whoever, therefore, would now attempt to give a real advance to the art, and endeavour to fix it on scientific principles, must tread back through that maze of error and opinion, and begin those experiments which ought to have been made 200 years ago, confessing that the professors of agriculture are now, on comparison with those of other sciences, much in the same state as the chemists and electricians were before Mr Boyle existed.

Annals of Agriculture, v (1786) 18–23

A number of the great landowners and gentry of the period

were sufficiently interested in farming matters to create model farms and supervise experiments. Sometimes their interest had the practical object of spreading improved practices among their tenants; or they might be in the process of enclosing common fields and waste lands, and wished to investigate the best means of bringing moors and heaths into cultivation and to ascertain the breeds best fitted for stocking newly created grasslands. In addition to the well-known pioneers, there were a number of enthusiasts among the landed aristocracy. There were, for example, Lord Ducie in Gloucestershire and Lord Halifax near Walton-on-Thames, Lord Somerville, the Duke of Portland and the Earls of Egremont. The third Earl of Egremont converted 800 acres of his park at Petworth into a model farm and held his own cattle show. Another connoisseur of livestock was the second Lord Braybrooke at Audley End. The Duke of Norfolk, Lord Shelburne, Lord Milton, Lord Clarendon and the Duke of Grafton all took a practical interest in testing new crops and introducing new methods.

In his farming *Tours* Arthur Young made a special point of visiting prominent innovators and recording the experiments currently being undertaken. Included in his *Northern Tour* was an account of the Marquis of Rockingham's model farm, which is extracted below. Young visited the Marquis at his mansion at Wentworth in 1768, and after describing the house and park he continues:

(2) But the husbandry of the Marquis of Rockingham is much more worthy of attention than that of any palace. The effects which have and must continue to result from it are of the noblest and most truly national kind. A short sketch of his Lordship's operations will convince you how much an extensive tract of country is obliged to this patriotic nobleman for introducing a cultivation unknown before.

Upon turning his attention to agriculture his Lordship found the husbandry of the West Riding of Yorkshire extremely deficient in numerous particulars. It was disgusting to him to view so vast a property cultivated in so slovenly a manner. Eager to substitute better methods in the room of such unpleasing as well as unprofitable ones, he determined to exert himself with spirit in the attempt, and he executed the noble scheme in a manner that does honour to his penetration. A very few particulars, among many of the common practice, will show how much this country wanted a Rockingham to animate its cultivation.

1. Large tracts of land, both grass and arable, yielded but a trifling profit for want of draining. In wet clays the rushes and other aquatic rubbish usurped the place of corn and grass; the seasons of tilling were retarded, and even destroyed; and those pastures which ought to have fed an ox scarcely maintained a sheep.

2. The pastures and meadows of this country were universally laid down in ridge and furrow, a practice highly destructive of profit and detestable to the eye; and the manner of laying down such lands was as miserable as their product denoted poverty, for after many years ploughing of numerous crops but insufficient fallows, when the soil was so exhausted as to disappoint the expectation of corn, a parcel of rubbish called hayseeds was scattered over the surface and the field left to time for improvement. A villainous custom, and too much practised in all parts of the kingdom.

3. The culture of turnips was become common, but in such a method that their introduction was undoubtedly a real mischief: *viz.* without hoeing, so that the year of fallow in the general management was the most capital year of slovenliness and bad husbandry.

4. The implements used in agriculture through this tract were insufficient for a vigorous culture, and consequently the husbandman sustained a constant loss.

These circumstances, among others, show how much the husbandry of this country wanted improvement. Let us in the next place examine the means taken by his Lordship to command that most beneficial purpose. He conducted himself from the beginning upon the soundest of all principles, that of *practising* himself those methods which *reason* told him were the best – well convinced that argument and persuasion would have little effect with the *John Trot* geniuses of farming, he determined to set the example of good husbandry as the only probable means of being successful.

In the pursuit of this end his Lordship's conduct was judicious and spirited. He has upwards of 2,000 acres of land in his hands, and began their improvement with draining such as were wet, rightly considering this part of husbandry as the *sine qua non* of all others. His method was the most perfect that experience has hitherto brought to light – that of covered drains.

Throughout this extensive tract of land I found very deep fosses cut or old ditches sunk so deep as to give in every field the command of a sufficient descent. These are kept open. Into them run the covered drains which are cut in number proportioned to the wetness of the land, but in general at but a small distance from each other.

Of these there are three sorts, the leading or main ones of two kinds, and the branches or secondary ones. The first sort of main drains are two feet wide at top and bottom, and four or five feet deep, walled on each side and covered at top with large broad stones. The expense 6*d.* a yard running measure. The second are a yard deep, two feet wide at top, and 10 inches at bottom; the stones used in filling them are oblong squares of 8, 9 or 10 inches length, the edges of which are rested on the sides of the bottom of the drains, and fall on each other at their tops ... then they are filled up with bits of stone within seven or eight inches of the top; and, lastly, the molds [loose earth] thrown over all.

The branches are three-quarters of a yard deep, 18 inches wide at top, and nine at bottom; they are then filled up in the same manner as the others. The expense of the operation is as follows:

	s.	d.
A cart-load of stones of 40 bushels will do 7 yards;		
the getting these, besides the leading, is		3½
the leading	1	5
digging the drains		4½
fixing in the stones and filling up		3
For 7 yards it is	2	4
or just 4*d.* a yard.		

The improvement by these drains (which you will observe last for ever) is almost immediately manifest; the summer succeeding the first winter totally eradicates in grasslands all those weeds which proceed from too much water, and leaves the surface in the depth of winter perfectly dry and sound, insomuch that the same land which before poached with the weight of a man will now bear without damage the tread of an ox. In arable lands the effect is equally striking, for the corn in winter and spring upon land that used to be stowed with rain and quite poisoned by it now lies perfectly dry throughout the year, and in the tillage of it a prodigious benefit accrues from this excellent practice for the drained fields are ready in the spring for the plough before the others can be touched; it is well-known how pernicious it is to any land to plough or harrow it while wet.

This most excellent practice his Lordship experienced, as he expected, some years before his example was followed by any of his tenants. But at last the incontestable advantages attending it opened their eyes, and some of the most unprejudiced executed in their farms what they were convinced succeeded so greatly in their landlord's; and accordingly I viewed some fields of the tenants that were drained in this way, and in a very effectual manner.

Secondly, his Lordship's management in laying down and keeping his grass lands is worthy of universal imitation, as a spirit of culture has brought forth a fertility and richness of pasture beyond anything I remember to have seen. The method of laying down is this: oats are sown (under-seeded) upon land that has been exceedingly well fallowed for a year and a half by many ploughings, harrowings, &c., by which operations the surface is laid most completely level so that not the least trace of a furrow is to be distinguished. With the corn 12 lb. of white Dutch clover and eight bushels of finely-dressed hayseeds are sown. At harvest the oats are reaped, and 6 lb. more of clover seed sown over the stubble which is then mown and raked off, and consequently the seed pretty well buried in the ground; a very rich compost is immediately spread on the field and well harrowed in, by which means the seed is completely covered; in this manner it is left the first winter. The crop is next year left until the seeds are ripe enough to shake in the mowing and making, by which means the land gains a fresh sprinkling and the whole surface ensured a total and thick covering.

The success attending this method is so very great that in several large fields I viewed the after-grass was 8 and 9 inches high soon after clearing a crop of hay of two tons per acre, and this the first year of the ley. No one would have known from walking over the field that it was not of some years growth, so thick and matted on the ground was the first year's produce. This grass in any part of the kingdom would have let for 30s. an acre, and for 40s. in most: an improvement you will think of a noble kind when you are told that the rents before this management were no more than 8s. and 9s., and let at their value. Adjoining several of these new leys some of the old pastures are to be seen yet in tenants' hands; they are over-run with every species of trumpery and weeds, the grass of a poor sort, and the quantity trifling. In leys of three or four years old the after-grass, had it been mown, would have yielded at least two tons of hay an acre.

It is observable upon this plan that no part of it is beyond the reach of a common farmer: a principal view of his Lordship in all his husbandry. Here are no two-years fallow, nor any loss by laying without a crop of corn. The seeds indeed are in large quantities, and amount in total price to near 50s. an acre; but then it is to be considered that the thickness of sowing gives it a most excellent crop the very first year, which in the common management is generally the very contrary; and it is incontestable that his Lordship's method pays its own expenses in the very first crop. Suppose the farmer's seeds cost him 20s., the excess on the side of the better manner is then, we will say, 25s.; a sum in the value of hay that does amount to little more than a fifth of the first year's produce.

But Lord Rockingham in scarce anything has acted with greater spirit than the improvement of the turnip culture by hoeing, for the disgust he felt at seeing the common slovenly management of the farmers in respect of this crop made him determine to introduce the excellent practice of hoeing, common in many of the southern parts of the kingdom. With this view he attempted to persuade his tenants to come into the method, described to them the operation, pointed out its advantages; clearly explained to them the great conse-quence of increasing the size of the root in the luxuriance of its growth and the equality of the crops; reminded them of the poor crops of spring corn gained after turnips for want of a better culture; from the difference of following a crop of weeds which will not feed cattle and consequently not improve the land, and succeeding a large produce of valuable roots, which by their thick shade and the quantity of cattle they maintained enriched the land at the same time that all weeds are destroyed in the hoeing.

Incontrovertible as this reasoning, so clearly founded on facts, must appear to the unprejudiced, yet with men of contracted ideas used to a stated road with deviations neither to the right nor left, it had very little effect: turnips continued to be sown, but were never hoed. His Lordship then finding that discourse and reasoning could not prevail over the obstinacy of their understanding, determined to convince their eyes. He sent into Hertfordshire for a husbandman used to hoeing of turnips, and gave directions for his management of a large crop. This he continued several years and by this means, by degrees, he introduced the practice which is now (though not universal) the common practice of all the good common farmers. Much does this neighbourhood owe to so patriotic a design which was truly planned with judgement and executed with spirit. Much more genuine fame ought to attend such an action than the gaining a score of battles: the senseless rabble may praise the military hero; it belongs to *the few* to venerate the spirited cultivator.

In the introduction of new implements and the improvement of old ones his Lordship was equally attentive. This will appear clearly enough from the . . . implements which are such as his Lordship has at different times either had constructed by his own directions or ordered upon the model of other counties. None of them are common in Yorkshire; you will easily perceive how much they merit attention. . . .

But these instances of spirited management, great as they certainly are, by no means are the only ones to be produced of this nobleman's attention to the improvement of husbandry. As a proof of this I shall next mention to you a new and most judicious thought which is executed with uncommon spirit. This is the establishment of two farms, managed one in the Kentish and the other in the Hertfordshire method. Those counties have the reputation of a very accurate cultivation; his Lordship therefore determined to fix a farmer from each on a distinct farm, to manage it in the best manner they had been used to: a most excellent plan as it gave rise to a beneficial emulation which could not fail of being productive of the best consequences.

Northern Tour (1770) I 307–24

Many of the gentry, in addition to the great landowners, were forward in adopting new ideas and improving their lands. The Sykeses and the Legards, for instance, put great efforts into bringing the Yorkshire wolds into cultivation, while over in Cumberland John Christian Curwen maintained large experimental farms at Schoose and Moorland Close. He fed his horses on steamed potatoes and carrots, and stall-fed his cattle on cut grass, cabbages and roots, innovations which won for him a gold medal from the Society of Arts in 1808. He experimented too with dairying, breeding and grains, and was a planter of trees on the grand scale. The Workington Agricultural Society's annual shows included a visit to his farms. Elsewhere numerous enthusiasts among the gentry and leading farmers were forming local agricultural societies, usually with the object of introducing implements and practices new to their part of the country, and they offered prizes for the farmers who made the most successful advances and for labourers who had a record of thrift, sobriety and reliability. One of the oldest of such societies was the Brecknockshire Agricultural Society, founded in 1755, and it was followed in the succeeding decades by others in various parts of the country. Young reported on the formation and activities of such societies in his *Annals*, and overleaf is part of the report given there of the 1805 Woburn 'sheep-shearing' or show, one of the most famous of the agricultural gatherings of the time:

Farm machinery, as distinct from improved designs of traditional implements such as ploughs, harrows and rollers, played little part in the agriculture of Young's time. The seed-drill and horse-hoe invented by Tull in the early years of the eighteenth century made only slow headway, partly because it was difficult and expensive to get the machines made, but also because their use was largely limited to the light-soil areas. Even the Rotherham plough, a swing-plough with a curved mouldboard based on Dutch designs, was a long time coming into favour – and this despite its advantages in lightness and size which made it possible for farmers to plough with smaller teams. The main obstacle was that

(3) TRANSACTIONS OF AGRICULTURAL SOCIETIES

WOBURN SHEEP-SHEARING, 1805

This year's attendance at His Grace the Duke of Bedford's Meeting, was equal to that of any former year, and the result highly satisfactory to all present.

Company in the Abbey

Duke of Clarence	Mr Wakefield
Colonel Dalrymple	Lord Ludlow
Lord Sheffield	Mr Francis
Mr Coke	Lord Cawdor
Mr. Anson	Sir John Wrottesley
Lord Somerville	Sir Wm. Rowley
Mr Edw. Coke	Sir Rob. Lawley
Colonel Beaumont	Mr Moseley
Lord Talbot	Mr. Motteaux
Sir Harry Featherstone	Mr. Lambert
Mr Lee Antonie	Mr Reeves
Lord Darnley	Mr Williams
Duke of Manchester	Mr Wing
Mr Northey	Rev. Bate Dudley
Lord Wm. Russell	Mr Conyers
Marquis of Huntly	Sir John Riddell
Mr Culling Smith	Mr Curwen
Mr Marshall	Lord T. Townshend
Mr M. Burgoyne	Mr Poyntz
Mr Western	Mr Isted
Mr Sandford	Mr Wiltshire
Mr Smirenove	Dr Randolph
Lord R. Spencer	

On Monday, the number that dined were 236.

On Tuesday 246.

On Wednesday 232.

On Thursday 178.

The company were from every part of the kingdom; from Ireland, from Scotland, and several foreigners.

Annals of Agriculture, XLIV (1806) 202–3

newly-designed implements had to be purchased from London or some other distinct source, or made locally from plans obtained direct from the inventor. Any parts which broke or wore out had to be replaced by hand-made substitutes specifically designed for the individual implement. It was not until the early nineteenth century that large specialist manufacturers became at all numerous, using iron instead of wood, and producing standardised parts for easy replacement. Cheaper and more efficient equipment now became more easily available, but even so many locally made implements of ancient provincial design remained in use.

The one labour-saving device of real importance which began to be adopted in Young's time was the threshing machine. Threshing was formerly performed with the hand flail, and was a slow and laborious business. Hand-operated threshing machines speeded up the process, and were eventually succeeded by improved machines powered by horses and, in due course, steam. Not until the 1820s, however, were they becoming common in the southern corn districts. The following excerpt is taken from an account of one of Young's later visits to Kent, when he spent some time in examining the practices of John Boys. He was a prominent farmer who operated on a large scale with several farms in the Sandwich area, and he wrote the county report on Kent for the Board of Agriculture. Boys had established a horse-powered thresher when it was still a novelty, and this is Young's account of it:

(4) THRESHING MILL

One of the first objects on the farm of Mr Boys is a threshing mill of his erecting. The mill itself is put up in the body of a barn from which Mr Boys added a projecting building for containing the great wheel: that wheel is 12 feet diameter, has 120 cogs which work into 12; the cogs at the end of the shaft are 87 that work into 14. The under of the two cylinders for drawing the corn through is of wood, the upper of cast iron; a wheel of 15 cogs works into 33 for turning them. The beating or flail-wheel, as it may be called, is 5 feet long and $3\frac{1}{2}$ feet diameter to outside beaters, has 4 beaters or flails fixed to it, and strikes *upwards* 1,000 strokes in a minute; whereas those I have before mentioned strike downwards, which is said not to clear away the straw equally well. In Mr Patterson's mill the sloping delivery

is a rolling canvas, but Mr Boys' is of deal and fixed, which
is found to deliver fast enough by striking upwards. The
straw is carried *over* the beating wheel and falls on a floor of
lattice work for the short broken straw and ears, &c., which
are saved as chaff, to fall through. The straw is cleared off
this floor by a man with a fork who moves it on to another
sloping floor, formed also of strips of deal, through which
chaff, &c., in like manner falls, and from the bottom of this
the straw is forked away, either into the yard or on to carts.
Four horses work the mill, a boy to drive, one man to throw
up the sheaves, a boy who supplies him, one man to spread
them on the inclined plane of delivery, and two men to fork
away the straw: the whole, four men, two boys, and four
horses. I attended several times during a day's work of eight
hours in which 36 quarters of oats were threshed. Here is a
calculation of the expense:

	£	s.	d.
Price of the machine £120: interest at 6 per cent £6, share of that say		6	0
Repairs, suppose ½d. a quarter on the corn threshed		1	6
Four horses		8	0
Four men		6	0
Two boys		1	6
	1	3	0

Such would be the expense if the machine executed well,
but being built by men who have not brought it to perfection,
there is the after-expense of dressing the corn, of $1\frac{1}{2}d.$ a
quarter; but as this belongs to the machine in its present
state, and will in this be speedily remedied, for the dressing
is the part the easiest performed in machines that are well
built, I shall take no notice of it: £1 3s. 0d. for 36 quarters
is $7\frac{3}{4}d.$ per quarter. But there is a circumstance which very
considerably lessens this expense, and that is the additional
quantity of horse-meat obtained from the machine in comparison with what the flail gives. This Mr Boys finds to be
double, and as they value this chaff, &c., called here *toff
and choff*, at 6d. per quarter of the corn threshed, this of
course deducts that amount and leaves the expense of

threshing only $1\frac{3}{4}d.$ per quarter. I have applied to some very judicious farmers for their opinion of this additional value added in chaff and they were inclined to admit it, asserting on experience that the more straw is beaten and broken in threshing the better it is and the further it will go for cattle; and that this holds good from mere common threshing to the last extreme of cutting into chaff in a box. I examined the straw attentively and found it very clean, much beyond what I ever found after a common flail. thirty-six pounds of it was threshed with a flail for trial, and a very small tea-cup of oats only gained; and on examination that was partly gained from the floor not having been swept clean. In twelve minutes we threshed twenty sheaves of wheat which yielded 17 gallons clean, or $10\frac{1}{2}$ quarters in eight hours; this is much below its work in oats.

Upon the whole this machine must be considered in its present state as very imperfect; yet it seems to prove, imperfect as it is, the profit of their use. The man who clears the straw from the machine might certainly be saved, as well as one, if not two, of the horses. The interest (here charged at 6s. for a day) will depend on the quantity of corn threshed: suppose 200 acres or 600 quarters, £6 divided would be $2\frac{1}{2}d.$ a quarter; 1,000 quarters $1\frac{1}{2}d.$ a quarter.

Annals of Agriculture, xx (1793) 248–51

CHAPTER III

Enclosure and Rural Poverty

I. ENCLOSURE AND THE OPEN FIELDS

For many years historians have debated the controversial question of the relationship between enclosure and rural poverty. Since the time of the earlier discussions by writers like J. L. and Barbara Hammond, whose well-known book, *The Village Labourer*, appeared in 1912, a great deal of detailed research has been undertaken. The general effect of the new work is to emphasise both the complexity of the subject and the great diversity of effects which flowed from enclosure. Because of local variations in the circumstances in which enclosure was carried out – the extent of the surviving open fields and commons, the nature of the soil, the size of the village community, the numbers of owners, size of the farms, access to market, cost of the enclosure, and many other conditions – generalisation is extremely hazardous. Especially doubtful are the effects which enclosure might have on the situation of the labouring class in the village. However, our brief summary of this complicated matter is postponed to a later section of this chapter, and we have first to examine Young's views on open fields and the advantages of enclosing them.

Although the great Parliamentary enclosure of the later eighteenth and early nineteenth centuries coincided precisely with Young's career as an agricultural writer, it is remarkable that he gave relatively little attention to the subject. Only a very small fraction of his large output was specifically concerned with the merits of enclosure, and with one or two exceptions (of which examples are given below) he seems to have taken it as axiomatic that enclosed farms were superior to those in open fields. Only in the later stages of his career, when in some areas rural poverty had increased to an alarming extent, did he take up the question of the effects of enclosure on the labouring poor.

Modern research has shown that open fields were far more flexible and progressive than used to be supposed. There might, for instance, be periodical reorganisation of the holdings to achieve a more compact or more equitable distribution of the strips; piecemeal enclosures were made from time to time in order to procure more land for breeding, fattening, dairying, and other purposes; the number of fields was increased (or existing ones were subdivided) in order to allow of more complex rotations; the regulations governing the communal farming might often be amended to adjust to changing conditions; and in the later seventeenth century the new fodder crops were adopted in some places. The old picture of an extremely conservative, rigid and inefficient system which persisted unchanged over the centuries has therefore to be considerably modified. Indeed, in not a few instances full-scale enclosure resulted in little technical improvement in the farming, since the farming before enclosure was already as advanced as local conditions of soil, relief, climate – and the restrictions of surviving open fields – would allow. In these circumstances the main advantage of enclosure lay not so much in improved farming as in adjustments in land use and more efficient layout and amenities of farms. These changes included the creation of more compact and consolidated farm units, the cultivation of some former commons and waste lands, the achievement of a better balance between arable and pasture, the improvement of local roads, and in some instances the abolition of tithes and the reorganisation of the old-enclosed lands in the village.

Young's references to the open fields were almost invariably brief and scathing. He made it clear that no farming improvements were to be expected from the benighted 'Goths and Vandals' who tilled them, and he deplored the loss of output that the survival of such inefficient farming entailed. Enclosure, on the other hand, was the 'first and greatest of all improvements', and alone had made the moors of northern counties 'smile with culture which before were dreary as night'. Yet, contemptuous as he was of open-field farming, he was not entirely blind to the progress that was being made. The first brief excerpt below makes clear his pleasure at seeing evidence of innovation in the open fields near Royston in Hertfordshire, while in the second excerpt he is found indulging his usual scorn of the old system, though at the same time he notes that not all enclosures, such as that at Knapwell, had good effects. The conclusion of the second passage is interesting since it shows that already in 1791 he was in favour of helping poor cottagers by giving them a larger and permanent share of the commons:

(1) I was much pleased to see about Royston many ploughs going with two horses abreast and without a driver: a very uncommon sight within the bounds of Hertfordshire. About that town the open fields let from 7s. 6d. to 10s. 6d. an acre, it is all chalk, and very good. Wheat yields from $2\frac{1}{2}$ to 4 qrs. an acre; barley up to 5 qrs. The farmers are sensible, intelligent men, for they agree among themselves to sow turnips instead of fallowing on many of their lands; and also sainfoin, by keeping off their sheep in the spring. It succeeds excellently, has been worth at one cutting £7 an acre, but they dress it well with ashes or malt-dust. They use also much oil-cake for their land, laying 1,000 cakes on 3 acres, which cost them £10 at home.

Taking the road to Stevenage I found the country continue entirely open and all chalk, with very fine crops on it; winter tares were cutting for soiling. Much trefoil was sown with clover, and as high and luxuriant as the clover, agreeing perfectly well with the soil.

Annals of Agriculture, v (1785) 145–6

(2) Taking the road from Cambridge to St Neots, view for six or seven miles the worst husbandry I hope in Great Britain. All in the fallow system, and the loss of time and the expense submitted to without the common benefit. These fallows are over-run with thistles, and the dung being spread over them forms an odd mixture of black and green that would do well enough for a meadow but is villainous in tillage. Some divisions of these fallows have not yet been broken up since reaping the last year's crops. Bid the current of national improvement roll back three centuries and we may imagine a period of ignorance adequate to the exhibition of such exertions! To what corner of the three kingdoms – to what beggarly village must we go to find in any branch of manufacture such sloth – such ignorance – such backwardness – such determined resolution to stand still while every other part of the world is at least moving? It is in the *agriculture* of the kingdom alone that such a spectacle is to be sought. There seems somewhat of a coincidence between the state of cultivation within sight of the venerable spires of Cam-

bridge and the utter neglect of agriculture in the establish-
ments of that University.

They are ploughing here with poor implements drawn by
two horses at length, and conducted by a driver. The crops of
wheat pretty good; all others bad.

At Knapwell there is a parliamentary enclosure, and such
wretched husbandry in it that I cannot well understand for
what they enclosed relative to management; rent is the only
explanation, which has risen from 5s. tithed to 10s. or 11s.
free. They sow hayseeds and clover, but little comes except
rye-grass and thistles; soil a strong loam and some clay.
Thence to St Neots, and all the way from Cambridge, must
be classed amongst the ugliest country in England. The
lands mostly open-field at 6s. an acre. The management very
bad, much strong clay, and some fallows not yet ploughed.
The course:

1. fallow, ploughed thrice; breaking up 7s. 6d., two
   stirrings, each 3s. with 4 horses and a driver;
2. wheat, produce 14 or 15 bush. per acre short of
   statute measure;
3. oats or beans.

About St Neots a vast improvement by an enclosure which
took place 16 years ago, which has made the country much
more beautiful, and has been a great benefit to the community. A gentleman of the town however complained as
I rode thither with him, that notwithstanding the produc-
tiveness of the soil was certainly greater, yet that the poor
were ill-treated by having about half a rood given them in
lieu of a *cow keep*. The enclosure of which land costing more
than they could afford, they sold the lots at £5, the money
was drunk out at the alehouse, and the men, spoiled by the
habit, came with their families to the parish; by which means
poor rates had risen from 2s. 6d. to 3s. and 3s. 6d. But pray,
sir, have not rates risen equally in other parishes where no
enclosure has taken place? Admitted. And what can be the
good of commons which would not prevent poor rates
coming to such a height? Better modes of giving the poor a
share might easily be, and have been, as in other cases,
adopted.

2. THE ADVANTAGES OF ENCLOSURE

For the individual farmer the main advantage of enclosure was that instead of having a holding made up of fragmented plots scattered through the open fields, he occupied a farm consisting of one compact block of land (or at most a few such blocks), over which the rights of other farmers to pasture their stock had been abolished. After enclosure he could freely choose (or, if a tenant, ask the permission of his landlord) to convert land to its most profitable use, break up old, weed-ridden pastures, and put worn-out arable down to grass. He was no longer tied by the restrictions of communal husbandry, and could adopt whatever practices seemed most likely to swell the output of his farm. There might also be other advantages flowing from improvements made at the enclosure to roads and drainage, possibly abolition of tithes, and sometimes much-needed reorganisation of a confused jumble of old enclosures. For the landlord these changes spelt higher rents, and even if enclosure brought about little improvement in his tenants' farming, he could still obtain a considerably advanced rent merely for the tenant's greater convenience and efficiency of managing an enclosed holding.

These, however, were the private advantages accruing to the individual farmer and landlord, and Young was generally more concerned with the public gains which enclosure brought to the community at large. He saw the post-enclosure rise in rents as an indicator of the extent of increased efficiency and enlarged output. Further, as in the first of the following excerpts, he applied his argument that higher rents made for more efficient and indus-trious farmers. He was especially enthusiastic when the cultivation of commons and waste lands – one of the enduring interests of his career – showed by the greatly increased rents produced the extent of the improvement made possible by enclosure (see excerpts (3) and (4)). He went into detail on the enclosure of Barton-upon-Humber (excerpt (4)), showing that (according to his figures) the former field land which let for between 4s. and 9s. had risen to an average of 20s., and moreover was made tithe-free. The public costs of the commissioners, etc., amounted at Barton to the very large sum of £13,000, but well over half of this expenditure had gone into the building of new roads, bridges, and jetties on the river Humber, sluices for drainage works, and the fencing of the former tithe-holder's allotment. Furthermore, the public costs, though so large, worked out at only a little over £2 per acre (to which sum must be added the costs of private fencing undertaken by each proprietor).

As the second excerpt shows, Young was well aware that enclosure usually led to an increase in employment. (The main exception to this rule was where enclosure led to a large-scale conversion of former arable to permanent grass.) The work created by the enclosure itself would employ a considerable number of men over a lengthy period in fencing, hedging and ditching, in building new farmhouses, barns and stables, in road construction and drainage, and in clearing and breaking up former commons and wastes. Subsequent upkeep of hedges and drainage works, and the abolition on the farmland of bare fallows, increased the amount of routine work available. (Abolition of bare fallows was not always possible on heavy lands, however.) The cultivation of former waste land necessarily involved a net increase in the labour demands of the village. A greater output of produce led to higher transport demands, and increased need for the services of waggoners, millers and maltsters, blacksmiths and wheelwrights. This aspect of enclosure has been appreciated by historians only in fairly recent years, though Young put forward the essence of the matter in 1774 (see excerpt (2)).

Lastly, Young strongly believed that the character of the farmers of enclosed lands was quite different from that of the occupiers of open fields. The farmers from enclosures were more progressive in their ideas, more open to the possibility of increasing output by adopting improved practices; and upon an enclosure the old open-field farmers, conservative and suspicious of change, were exposed to novel ideas and awakened to fresh opportunities. There is some exaggeration in all this, no doubt, and there were certainly progressive farmers who made advances even within the trammels of the open-field system. Young perhaps made insufficient allowance for the gradual permeation of new ideas that must have followed from the achievements of progressive farmers, the work of agricultural societies and their shows, and the influence of expanding markets and rising prices (his comments were penned in 1809, during the inflation of the Napoleonic wars); and not least, perhaps, he undervalued the effect of his own writings and those of the other experts of the day:

(1) I must take notice of one circumstance ... of particular importance, which is the amazing superiority of wool and profit in enclosed districts to open ones. It is very remarkable that every one of the places minuted in the scales of profit, from 10s. upwards, are all in enclosed districts. And one or two minutes of comparison prove the same thing. About Hagley the profit in enclosed grounds is 11s., but in open ones only 2s. 3d., which is a prodigious difference. About Bendsworth, in the Vale of Evesham, the average fleece is 9 lb. in the enclosures, but only $3\frac{1}{2}$ lb. in the open fields. Can there be a stronger argument for enclosing? The common vulgar ideas of injuring sheep and manufactures by enclosures are hence, I think, sufficiently answered. By enclosing you have 9 lb. of wool instead of three, that is, one sheep yields as much as three did; and in respect of profit, one pays as much as five. Do these wise-acres think that enclosing the moors would do mischief to manufactures? or that lessening the number of sheep that are milked instead of folded, and yield from one shilling to five or six profit per head, would lessen the quantity of British wool? Enclosures raise rents; high rents make men industrious; they put a thousand pounds in their pockets to go hire a farm, which when open would have taken only £300 or £400. Everything must be turned to good advantage when high rents are paid; the farmer knows that everything must be profitable; and that very circumstance renders them so. In such a situation will twelve-penny sheep be found? It is thus that enclosures act; and that lessening the number of sheep is increasing the quantity and value of wool.

Northern Tour (1770) IV 338–9

(2) Respecting open-field lands, the quantity of labour in them is not comparable to that of enclosures; for, not to speak of the great numbers of men that in enclosed countries are constantly employed in winter in hedging and ditching, what comparison can there be between the open-field system of one half or a third of the lands being in fallow, receiving only three ploughings, and the same portion now tilled four, five, or six times by midsummer, then sown with turnips, those hand-hoed twice, and then drawn by hand and carted to stalls for beasts, or else hurdled out in portions for

fatting sheep! What a scarcity of employment in one case, what a variety in the other! And consider the vast tracts of land in the kingdom (no less than the whole upon which turnips are cultivated) that have undergone this change since the last century. I should also remind the reader of other systems of management – beans and peas hand-hoed for a fallow – the culture of potatoes – of carrots, of coleseed, etc, – the hoeing of white corn – with the minuter improvements in every part of the culture of all crops – every article of which is an increase of labour. Then he should remember the vast tracts of country uncultivated in the last century which have been enclosed and converted into new farms, a much greater tract in eighty years than these writers dream of: all this is the effect of enclosures, and consequently they also have yielded a great increase of employment. . . .

The fact is this: in the central counties of the kingdom, particularly Northamptonshire, Leicestershire, and parts of Warwick, Huntingdon, and Buckinghamshire, there have been within thirty years large tracts of the open-field arable under that vile course: 1. fallow, 2. wheat, 3. spring corn, enclosed and laid down to grass, being much more suited to the wetness of the soil than corn; and yields in beef, mutton, hides, and wool beyond comparison a greater neat produce than when under corn. At that time the horses that tilled the land ate up the few grass enclosures near the farmhouses and a considerable part of the spring corn, whereas at present many farms of from 500 to 1,000 acres have not more than two or three nags on them for the farmers to ride and see their stock. Thus the land yields a greater neat produce in food for mankind – the landlord doubles his income, which enables him to employ so many more manufacturers and artisans – the farmer increases his income, by means of which he also does the same – the hides and wool are a creation of so much employment for other manufacturers. How anyone from such a system can deduce the melancholy prospects of depopulation, famine, and distress is to me amazing.

But further: Dr Price[1] and the other writers who assure us we should throw down our hedges and waste one-third of our farms in a barren fallow by way of making beef and

[1] See footnote on p. 33 [Ed.].

mutton cheap, will confine themselves to the enclosures
which have converted arable to grass. What say they to
those which have changed grass to arable? They choose to
be silent. I do not comprehend the amusement that is found
in constantly looking at those objects which are supposed to
be gloomy and in regularly lamenting the evils that surround
us, though they flow from causes which shower down much
superior blessings. When I look around me in this country I
think I everywhere see so great and animating a prospect
that the small specks which may be discerned in the hemi-
sphere are lost in the brilliancy that surrounds them. I cannot spread a curtain over the illumined scene and leave
nothing to view but the mere shades of so splendid a piece.

What will these gentlemen say to the enclosures in Norfolk, Suffolk, Nottinghamshire, Derbyshire, Lincolnshire,
Yorkshire, and all the northern counties? What say they to the
sands of Norfolk, Suffolk, and Nottinghamshire which yield
corn and mutton and beef from *the force of* ENCLOSURE
alone? What say they to the wolds of York and Lincoln,
which from barren heaths, at 1s. per acre, are *by* ENCLO-
SURE *alone* rendered profitable farms? Ask Sir Cecil Wray
[1734–1805: owned estates in Lincolnshire, Norfolk and
Yorkshire] if without ENCLOSURE he could advance his
heaths by sainfoin from 1s. to 20s. an acre. What say they to
the vast tracts in the peak of Derby which *by* ENCLOSURE
alone are changed from black regions of ling to fertile fields
covered with cattle? What say they to the improvement of
moors in the northern counties, where ENCLOSURES alone
have made those countries smile with culture which before
were dreary as night? What have these gentlemen to say to
these instances? Cannot they manage to assure us the prospect
is delusive? They can. Hear how they are characterised.
'Enclosures of waste lands and commons would be useful *if*
divided into *small allotments* and *given up* to be occupied at
moderate rent by the poor. But *if* besides lessening the produce of fine wool they bear hard on the poor, by depriving
them of a part of their subsistence, and *only* go towards
increasing farms already too large, the advantages attending
them may not much exceed the disadvantages.'[1] Hence

[1] This quotation was taken from Dr Price's *Observations on Rever-
sionary Payments* (1770) p. 390 [Ed.].

therefore we find all these improvements very equivocal. Before it is allowed that converting ling to corn is beneficial, it must previously be asked if the improvement is wrought by that ghostly object of dread and terror – a great farmer. Before it is acknowledged right to make that sand which would not feed rabbits produce beef and mutton, we must know whether the poor were deprived of a part of their subsistence. Before you will submit to change the heaths of Lincoln to fertile fields of sainfoin you must demand, *Were the allotments small?* I must own it is with astonishment that I thus see superior minds stooping to prejudices so unworthy of their abilities.

How, in the name of common sense, were such improvements to be wrought by little or even moderate farmers! Can such enclose wastes at a vast expense – cover them with a hundred loads an acre of marl – or six or eight hundred bushels of lime – keep sufficient flocks of sheep for folding – and conduct those (for the lower classes) mighty operations essential to new improvements? No. It is to GREAT FARMERS you owe these. Without GREAT FARMS you never would have seen these improvements – much I suppose to the satisfaction of those who declare themselves so indiscriminately their enemies.

Political Arithmetic (1774) pp. 72–3, 148–55

(3) Very few enclosures have answered better than that of Loughborough, in which the common rights, which before the enclosing sold at £10 each, rose to £50, and since even to £70; and the land that was at 7s. is now at 40s. Yet great as this is it does not equal an instance I heard the other day, in company, of Welby, near Sleaford, where heath land that let at 10d. an acre rose on the enclosure to 10s. and 12s.

Annals of Agriculture, XVI (1791) 605

(4) There are few instances of the benefit of enclosing commons greater than that of Long Sutton. The act passed in 1788, by which near 4,000 acres of common became *several* property; the rent of it, before enclosing, was £1,000 a year, or 500 rights at 40s. each; the whole now lets from 30s. to 50s. an acre, and about half of it is ploughed. Before this act the old enclosures were subservient to the common, but

now the common is subservient to those; and if all are
included in the account there is now more live stock
kept than before, and of a much better kind; though above
2,000 acres have been ploughed up to yield an enormous
produce.

About Folkingham many new as well as old parliamentary
enclosures, of arable, open, common fields, have taken place,
the improvements by which have been very great; lands
adapted to grass have been laid down; and some better for
the plough have been broken up. At Osbornby the rent of
10s. was raised to 17s. 6d.; and several others in an equal
proportion. The produce vastly more considerable: 1. fallow;
2. wheat; and 3. beans, are now changed to 1. turnips;
2. barley; 3. clover; 4. wheat. In some of these parishes the
old flocks of sheep, which were folded and sold lean, are
greatly increased in number, without folding, and sold fat.

The vast benefit of enclosing can, upon inferior soils, be
rarely seen in a more advantageous light than upon Lincolnheath. I found a large range which formerly was covered with
heath, gorse, &c., and yielding in fact little or no produce,
converted by enclosure to profitable arable farms; let on an
average at 10s. an acre; and a very extensive country, all
studded with new farm houses, barns, offices, and every
appearance of thriving industry; nor is the extent small, for
these heaths extend near seventy miles; and the progress is
so great in twenty years that very little remains to do.

The effect of these enclosures has been very great; for
while rents have risen on the heath from nothing, in most
instances, and next to nothing in the rest, to 8s. or 10s. an
acre, the farmers are in much better circumstances, a great
produce is created, cattle and sheep increased, and the poor
employed. The rectory of Navenby, one of the Cliff towns,
has become greater than the total rent of the lordship was
before.

From Lincoln to Barton all was, or very nearly all, heath,
but now enclosed by acts of parliament. And for five, six,
or seven miles every way round Hackthorne the same within
twelve or sixteen years; and of that tract the heath part was
not more than 1s. 6d. to 2s. an acre; large sheep-walks, with
pieces tilled alternately, now lets at about 10s. tithe free;
and the result otherwise has been that the tenants live much

better, and show in every circumstance signs of greater prosperity. The land is universally kept in tillage.

Around Norton-place, or rather longitudinally from it to Kirton, &c., open heath did let for 2*s*. an acre, now for 8*s*. tithe free; some, however, rising to 15*s*.; and this general, except near Lincoln, where it is much higher. In Kirton, of which Mr Harrisson has the tithes, lambs and wool paid him about £30 a year on 5,000 acres; from which may be collected how favourable open fields and heaths were to rearing sheep: for in this parish, now under the plough except the vale lands, proper for grass, the quantity of sheep is considerable; and a great culture of turnips to winterfeed them.

The expense, that is the commissioners' rate for enclosing 5,000 acres in Kirton, was about £7,000 including every public charge; roads came to near £1,000 of it.

The parish of Gainsborough is just enclosed; the old rent was 8*s*. an acre; the new 20*s*.

At Newton, the rents were 3*s*. 6*d*. twenty years ago before enclosing; now, some of it 25*s*., much 20*s*. . . .

Barton Field is one of the greatest enclosures in England; the act passed in 1793. Before the enclosures the quantities of land were supposed to be nearly as under in statute measure.

After deducting the roads and the site of the town, there may be 6,000 acres of land used in pasture and tillage.

The assessments of the commissioners under the enclosure act amounted to about £13,180 to defray the expenses of the act, fencing of tithe allotments, public and private roads, banks, jetties, cloughs [sluices], bridges, &c., &c.

The completing the public and private roads cost about £5,000. The Humber banks and jetties about £2,000, or rather more.

The parish pays yearly to the land-tax £210 8*s*. 4*d*.

The value of these lands before the enclosure were open arable let at from 4*s*. to 9*s*. per acre, of something less than three roods; little parcels for 10*s*. or 12*s*.; average about 6*s*. 6*d*. Part of the Marshes was let with the arable; thus the plough land of 72 acres arable, and eight of meadow in the ings, being four ox-gangs, were let together: all at the same

Barton upon Humber

	Acres
Open arable lands, nearly	4500
Open meadows in the *ings*, including the *growths* next the Humber, about	420
Open meadows and pastures in the Little Marshes, about	160
Open common, including the growth:	
cow-pasture	250
horse-pasture	225
Open Wold land, common, chiefly furze ground, about	270
	5825
According to the survey upon the enclosure all the open lands and grounds were found to contain	5920
From which about 110 acres were set out in roads and drains.	
The ancient enclosure within and about the town, including the sites of the homesteads, &c., in the town, contain by survey	150
The Grange and Warren farm on the Wold ancient enclosure, about	170
Therefore the whole parish contains, as nearly as may be, by survey	6240

rent. The common was stocked by the occupiers of common-right houses and lands; and also a part of the Marshes. The enclosure began directly, and they entered on the allotments in 1794. The amount of the commissioners' assessment was £13,000 for the act, tithe fencing, roads, Humber banks, jetties to secure the shore, sluices for drainage, bridges, &c. The roads alone cost £5,000. Drains £700. Now the arable fields let, on an average, at 20s. About the town, much more; at a distance, less. The Marsh land would now sell at £70 an acre, near the town; at a distance, £40. Some ploughed land, one mile from town, £40 to £50 an acre. Old enclosures near the town £100 an acre, for convenience. The common on the Wold 12s. an acre. The parish, including every thing, may now be rented at, or worth £6,000 a year; it was £2,000 and all the tenants better satisfied than before; 150 acres were given to the vicar for his small tithes; and 900 were assigned for great tithe, most conveniently for the impropriator. Many new farms, barns, &c., built, and more building.

The wheat, before enclosing, two quarters on the customary measure of three-fifth statute; the beans not more than two quarters: these crops are now changed to 1. turnips, worth 30s.; 2. barley, 4½ quarters; 3. clover, mown once, two loads per acre, worth 50s.; and a very fine after-grass of 10s. an acre; 4. wheat, four quarters. There is wheat now in the field that will be five. They formerly carted their corn and manure two miles and a half.

> *General View of the Agriculture of the County*
> *of Lincoln*, 2nd ed. (1813) 98–104

(5) In regard to the character of the Oxfordshire farmers a remark may be made at present which will not probably be just twenty years hence; and I well know was not the case twenty, thirty, and forty years ago, when I found them to be a very different race from what they are at present. They are now in the period of a great change in their ideas, knowledge, practice, and other circumstances. Enclosing to a greater proportional amount than in almost any other county in the kingdom has changed the men as much as it has improved the country; they are now in the ebullition of this change; a vast amelioration has been wrought, and is working; and a great deal of ignorance and barbarity remains. The Goths and Vandals of open fields touch the civilization of enclosures. Men have been taught to think, and till that moment arrives nothing can be done effectively. When I passed from the conversation of the farmers I was recommended to call on to that of men whom chance threw in my way, I seemed to have lost a century in time, or to have moved 1,000 miles in a day. Liberal communication, the result of enlarged ideas, was contrasted with a dark ignorance under the covert of wise suspicions; a sullen reserve lest landlords should be rendered too knowing; and false information given under the hope that it might deceive: were in such opposition, that it was easy to see *the change*, however it might work, had not done its business. The old

open-field school must die off before new ideas can become generally rooted.

General View of the Agriculture of the County of
Oxford (1809) 35–6

3. THE SOCIAL CONSEQUENCES OF ENCLOSURE

Young did not involve himself very much in the contemporary debate over the effects of enclosure on small farmers. This was partly, perhaps, because he believed the advantages of enclosure greatly outweighed any damaging effects it might have. In addition, he consistently argued that small farmers were conservative and backward, and that no improvements could be expected from them. Only the big cultivators, with their enlarged ideas and large resources of capital, could undertake the costly and time-consuming work of bringing newly enclosed commons and wastes into cultivation.

Modern research has shown that the old view of enclosure as devastating to small farmers in general, and fatal to the yeomen owner-occupiers in particular, is greatly exaggerated. Because of inflation and other factors, the costs of enclosure certainly tended to rise sharply in the later years of the eighteenth century and the period of the Napoleonic wars, and the costs were undoubtedly burdensome, perhaps fatal, in some instances. But there are a number of reasons for thinking that the financial resources of small owners were usually adequate to meet the need, and the advantages, both financial and agricultural, almost invariably outweighed the cost. Evidence produced from the land-tax records makes it clear that in heavily enclosed counties there was no marked overall decline in the numbers of small owners during the thirty years after 1780, when enclosure was at its height. It also appears that many of the small owners who decided to sell out when their land was enclosed were in fact absentees, people living at a distance, rather than occupiers. In the long run there seems little doubt but that the proportion of total farmland occupied by small owners declined – it may have fallen by as much as a half between the later seventeenth century and the end of the eighteenth century – but most of this fall appears to have occurred before 1750, i.e. before the full onset of parliamentary enclosure.

Small tenants, also, seem to have been declining fairly sharply in the half-century or so before 1750. Low prices and periods of agricultural depression in those years form the background to a marked tendency towards a consolidation of holdings, which was going on in unenclosed as much as, and perhaps more than, in enclosed villages. The changes were gradual ones, and do not appear to have been greatly accelerated by Parliamentary enclosure when it came. Tenants, as distinct from small owners, did not have to meet any part of the cost of enclosure, which was borne entirely by the property-owners in the village. Enclosure, however, did provide the large landowners with a good opportunity of consolidating their small farms, if they wished to do so, and if they could find tenants with sufficient capital and expertise to take on the larger units – which was not always possible. It seems very likely that a good deal of enclosure was accompanied, or followed, by some degree of consolidation of holdings, but on present evidence it does not appear that the effects were often very sweeping.

In his earlier years Young was critical of the choice of enclosure commissioners, usually superior landowners and farmers from outside the parish who were engaged to carry out the re-allotment of the farms. Young criticised the dilatory and costly way in which the work was sometimes executed, though it is likely that his arguments lost some of their force when, in due course, commissioners became more experienced and professional. Further, Parliament scrutinised Enclosure Bills with some care, and regulations were issued requiring due publicity to be given to the bringing of a Bill, and ensuring that the view of every proprietor on the matter was ascertained. However, Young continued to hold that the expense of enclosure was excessive, and he worked towards securing a General Enclosure Act which would simplify the procedure and reduce the costs. The eventual result, the General Enclosure Act of 1801, proved to be disappointing, however.

The commissioners were almost invariably scrupulous in respecting the rights of property-owners, whether large or small, and they often showed a greater regard for the interests of the small man. It was a fairly common practice, for instance, for the commissioners to ask the small owners to express their preference in the location of their land, and to allocate it near the homestead, or wherever requested, before proceeding to lay out the larger blocks of property. In his report on Lincolnshire Young recorded the views of a commissioner on this subject in a passage which helps to bring out the complexity of the property redistribution and the problems of achieving equity in large-scale enclosures (excerpt (1)).

As we have noted, Young was in general little concerned with the position of small owner-occupiers. His interest focused on the question of the relationship between enclosure and the growth of poverty among the labourers. That poverty was increasing, the complaints about rising poor rates and the evidence before his eyes left no doubt. It has to be remembered here, however, that in the later eighteenth century the rural population was expanding, and in some areas the numbers of labourers were growing beyond the capacity of the local economy to absorb them. This was particularly true where there was little increase in the cultivated acreage, and where old rural industries such as cloth-making and iron-working were in decline and were not being replaced by alternative sources of employment.

Inflation, too, was adding to the problem. Prices of food, which absorbed most of the spending of the poor, were rising in the later decades of the century, and rose very steeply during the bad seasons and inflationary finance of the French wars after 1793. Agricultural wages rose, but not sufficiently in many cases to keep pace with prices; and as a result the labourers relied more heavily on parish relief, particularly after the introduction of the Speenhamland bread-scale of relief in 1795, the first of the harvest crisis years of the war period. The second excerpt below is taken from Young's survey of Norfolk for the Board of Agriculture, published in 1804. By this date inflation had become severe, and Young observed with interest what rises in wages had occurred since he previously noted the wages of the area in 1770. He went on to give an estimate of the annual expenses of a labourer and his wife ('communicated by an active Magistrate'), and also their annual earnings, a calculation which showed a deficit over the year of £4 8s. 8d. This was an enormous sum in relation to the male labourer's average earings of only 1s. 11d. a day over most of the summer, and 1s. 8d. a day in the winter.

Just how widely this situation pertained is difficult to say, but it seems likely that it was fairly general in the corn-producing areas of the eastern and southern counties where labourers tended to be heavily dependent on their wages, and where an inadequacy of employment and a too restricted level of migration tended to keep labour over-abundant and depress the rates of wages. An over-supply of labour was particularly felt in the winter months when farmers required fewer men. It was in such areas that the Speenhamland system of supplementing wages spread after 1795;

and while the wages subsidy prevented labourers from starving and helped maintain employment, it may well have tended to keep farm wages from rising more than they did.

At this period there was a great deal of controversy over the problem of poverty and the burden of high poor rates. Young's main contribution was to argue the benefits of giving land to the poor. He collected evidence to show that the provision of land had the effect of instilling 'industrious and frugal habits' among the labourers, and enabled many of them to avoid seeking parish relief. He also showed that in some recently enclosed parishes, as in some still open, there remained large areas of commons or waste land which could be allotted to the poor in sufficient quantity to enable them to have a cottage and keep a cow and pigs. He estimated that to build a cottage, and provide 3 acres, a cow, a pig, seed, and some implements, would cost about £50 per family. By comparison he pointed out that it cost £60 a year to keep a family of five in a workhouse, and £20 if the same family was maintained at home on outdoor relief. In 48 parishes in Lincolnshire and Rutland, he observed, there were as many as 753 cottagers with cow-pastures, and they had nearly 1,200 cows between them: these families did not resort to the parish, and the poor rates there were under half those found elsewhere. Many Lincolnshire landowners, such as Mr Chaplin, Sir John Sheffield, Mr Goulton and Lord Carrington, had provided the poor with land for keeping cows, with very good effect (excerpt (3)). Other landlords elsewhere, such as the Duke of Bedford, the Earl of Egremont and Lord Hardwicke, had also done much to relieve poverty by providing cottage gardens and offering prizes for the best produce.

Young found that in a number of enclosures the interest of the poor had been entirely neglected. In 25 out of 37 cases of recent or active enclosure which he examined (excerpt (4)), the situation of the poor had deteriorated. It would be easy, he argued, for all Enclosure Acts to make provision for allotting land to the poor – to neglect this was contrary to 'reason, justice, and humanity'. There were many labourers, Young claimed, who, given the prospect of acquiring a cottage and a little land, would be prepared to work hard and save towards that object. But in many parishes – the old-enclosed villages where the open fields, wastes and commons had disappeared long ago – no spare land was available and the labourer had nothing to hope for. It was to this situation that Young directed his famous outburst: 'Go to an alehouse kitchen of an old enclosed country . . .' (excerpt (4)). If the landowners in such villages were unwilling to let land to the poor, then the parish itself should be authorised to act and buy land for the purpose, borrowing the necessary money on the security of the parish rates.

It seems likely that had Young's scheme been widely adopted (but only, probably, in the teeth of fierce opposition from the farmers), it might have done much to avoid the worst effects of poverty, degradation and unrest which marked parts of the eastern and southern counties in the first half of the nineteenth century. On the other hand, the rise in the numbers of the rural population would have required gradual expansion of the scheme, and indeed the enhanced security of labourers who possessed a cottage and cow-pasture might well have reduced migration from the countryside and so have exacerbated the problem of low wages and rural under-employment. A situation paralleling that of Ireland might have arisen, for, as Young noted, families settled on cow-pastures showed a marked inclination to propagate 'so that pigs and children fill every quarter'. The provision of land for labourers continued to be actively discussed after Young's death, and there were in fact two Acts, passed in 1819 and 1831, which allowed parishes to obtain land for letting to the poor, as well as an Act of 1832 which enabled allotments to be set aside at an enclosure. However, this legislation does not seem to have had much effect, though through the private efforts of parish clergy and landowners numbers of small vegetable allotments were established in the southern counties. Opposition from farmers, however, together with the levying of high rents and the unsuitability of some of the land used for allotments, limited the usefulness of these schemes. In general they had only a minor impact on a problem which has persisted down to the present century.

(1) Upon the principles on which the commissioners of enclo-
    sures should conduct themselves, Mr Elmhurst observes:
    'Where the town happens to be situated in or pretty near
    the centre of the lordship, the properties (upon the enclo-
    sures) may with great propriety be laid contiguous, or nearly
    so, to the farmhouses; and as much in squares as the nature
    and shape, &c., of the fields will admit; but when other-

wise, then the distant lands ought to be so laid out and allotted as best to suit for occupation, as a farm or farms on which houses, &c., may be built; having, as much as may be, an eye to water and different sorts of land; but to have due consideration to the *whole* of the proprietors (small as well as great) so as not to injure any one by making it *particularly* convenient to another or others. I acted as a commissioner a great many years and was at *one time* concerned in *nine* different enclosures; and from my first being in that business (which is near 28 years), I ever have attended first to what concerned the public respecting the laying out, forming and making the roads (at the expense of the proprietors) in the properest and most eligible situations for the greatest convenience of all who may travel or do business upon them; for I thought and said that the Legislature could never *intend* to place such power in any set of men as commissioners, or delegate them with such extraordinary power (as they *then* seemed to *fancy* they had) by which they should or might injure the public. And that *mode* I ever and always pursued so long as I continued to act. Another observation I at the first made, and ever after put in practice, was this, *always* to begin to line out and allot for the *smallest* proprietor *first* (whether rich or poor) in *every* parish, so as to make such allotment as proper and convenient for the occupation of such or their tenant (as that might be) to occupy; and so on, from the smallest to the greatest: for it is for the advantage of the greatest and most opulent proprietors that a Bill is presented and Act passed, and at *their* requests, and not the small ones; and as the little ones would have no weight by opposition, *they must submit*, was it ever so disadvantageous to them, as it *very often* happens; and therefore there can be no *partiality* in defending *those* who cannot help or defend themselves; and a *little* man may as well have *nothing* allotted to him as to have it so *far off* or so inconvenient for him that it is not worth his having, as it would prevent his going to his daily labour; and wherefore he *must* SELL *his* property to his rich and opulent adjoining neighbour; and *that*, in some measure, decreases population.'

*General View of the Agriculture of the County of
Lincoln*, 2nd ed. (1813) 105–7

(2) The circumstance in rural economy, which for many years distinguished Norfolk in a remarkable manner, was the cheapness wherewith the farmer carried on his business. This arose not only from a low price of labour but also from a much greater activity and spirit of exertion amongst servants and labourers than was to be found in almost any other county of the kingdom. This spirit is still highly commendable here, but by reason of the scarcities throwing the mass of the people on the parish to be supported by rates it has suffered considerably.

In 1767 I registered the price of labour in West Norfolk at 1s. a day in winter; in spring, 1s. 2d.; for the harvest £2 12s. 6d. to £3 with meat, drink, and lodging, and lasting from one month to five weeks; hoeing turnips, 3s. and 2s.; ploughing, per acre, 2s. 6d.

Holkham, 1792. In harvest, £5 5s. generally five weeks. Threshing wheat £1 1s. a last.

   "   " barley, 9s. ditto.

Thatching stacks, 1s. a yard, running measure, length of stack all widths on an average.

At Brammerton, 1770

	£	s.	d.	
For the harvest, with board	2	2	0	
„ „ Hay time	0	1	6	and beer.
„ „ Winter	0	1	0	and ditto.
Mowing grass, per acre	0	1	6	and ditto.
Hoe turnips	0	4	0	and 2s.
Clay, per 120 loads	1	5	0	
First man's wages	10	10	0	
Second, ditto	6	6	0	
Lad	3	0	0	
Dairy-maid	4	4	0	
Others	3	0	0	

In the Holkham district, winter and summer, 1s. 6d. Odd men in harvest, 2s. 6d. and 3s. Regular men, £2 2s. and board for the harvest.

Snetterton, &c., in winter   1s. 6d. ⎫
    „   „   „ Summer 1s. 9d. ⎬ no beer.
                                      ⎭

At Hingham, summer and winter 1s 8d.

The harvest 42s. to 50s. and board, generally for a month.

A custom is coming in around Waterden, &c., of allowing board-wages to farm servants instead of the old way of feeding in the house; 8s. a week are given; wages £5 5s. This is one material cause of an increased neglect of the Sabbath and looseness of morals; they are free from the master's eye, sleep where and with whom they please, and are rarely seen at church. A most pernicious practice, which will by-and-bye be felt severely in its consequences by the farmers. Mr Hill feeds his servants in the old way.

The price is raised at Waterden 6d. a day in the last two years, and the work worse done. Last winter 2s. a day, and the same in summer. But Mr Hill intends next winter to reduce it to 1s. 9d.

At Winborough in winter, 1s. 8d.; in summer 2s.; for the harvest, 50s. gloves, and 1s. hiring, with board; reaping wheat 10s. 6d. an acre, or 2s. 6d. a day, and board.

Through Loddon hundred 45s. for the harvest, and board; and allot twelve acres per man; some four load an acre, all three of spring corn, and two of wheat: dibbling wheat 10s. 6d. In winter 1s. 6d.; summer 2s., which was lately 1s. 6d.

In Fleg hundreds winter and summer 1s. 6d. a day, allowing bread-corn at 6s. a bushel; harvest, 50s. and board.

At Martham dibbling wheat 9s. an acre; peas, 8s.; bread-corn at 6s.

In parts of Happing hundred 2s. winter and summer: harvest £2 12s. 6d. and board.

At Honing harvest 50s. and board; winter 1s. 4d. and 1s. 6d. a day; summer 2s. but wheat at 5s. a bushel to the men.

At North Walsham 10s. a week, winter and summer.

Scotter 1s. 6d. and beer to harvest; then 42s. and board.

Reepham, &c., in winter 1s. 6d. to 1s. 8d.; in summer 2s.; in harvest, all included, 4s. 6d.

Thurning 2s. to harvest, for which £7 without board.

Binham 20d. to 2s. in winter and to harvest, when 52s. 6d. and board, or £6 6s. without.

Wighton harvest £6 6s. and sixteen acres a man; six wheat, and ten spring corn.

Thornham 1s. 9d. to 2s. the year round, except harvest, then £2 12s. 6d. and board; £6 6s. without: filling marl cart 28s. per 120 loads.

At Snettisham 10s. 6d. a week, winter, and to hay and turnip hoeing; in harvest £6 10s. without board. Hoeing turnips twice 6s.; mowing grass 20d. to 2s. 6d.; filling marl 25s. per 120 loads; 12s. for small low carts half loads.

At Houghton in winter 10s. 6d.; in summer 12s.; in harvest 50s. to 60s. and board.

At Wigenhall, in Marshland, the average price of reaping wheat 12s. the statute acre.

Labour at Lynn is sunk by the peace: – Sailors' wages, from £4 10s. a month, to 50s.; and that of corn-porters from 1½d. a sack to 1d.

At Walpole in Marshland, 6s. to 7s. a day general in harvest: some this year gave 9s. and 10s. a day; 2s. 6d. after Michaelmas till seed time is over: 2s. all winter; 2s. 6d. after May-day.

Near Downham in winter 20d. and beer; summer 2s.; hay-time 3s. 6d.; mowing grass 2s. to 4s.; mowing barley 5s.; reaping oats 10s. to 16s.; wheat 10s. to 12s.; in harvest, by day, 6s.

At Besthorpe 1s. 8d. in winter; 2s. at hay, and after harvest till Michaelmas; harvest 45s. and board; £6 without. No malt.

Runcton

	1770	1803
Harvest	£2 2s. and board	£2 12s. 6d. and board.
Hay	1s. 6d. and beer.	2s. and beer.
Winter	1s. 2d. and beer.	1s. 9d. and beer.
Reaping wheat	4s. to 6s.	7s. to 8s.
Reaping oats	4s.	5s.
Mowing barley	1s. 6d.	2s.
Mowing grass	2s.	3s.
Hoeing turnips	4s. and 2s.	4s. 6d. and 2s. 6d.
Threshing wheat	2s. a quarter.	3s.
Threshing barley	1s.	1s. 6d.
Threshing oats	8d.	1s.
Head man	£12	£12
Next ditto	£9	£9
Lad	£5	£6
Dairy-maid	£4 10s.	£4 10s.
Others	£3	£3

At Snettisham

1770	1803
Five weeks harvest and board, 45*s*. to 50*s*.	£2 12*s*. 6*d*.
In hay time, a day, 1*s*. 6*d*. to 2*s*.	2*s*. 6*d*.
In winter 1*s*. 2*d*.	1*s*. 9*d*.
Reaping 5*s*. per acre	12*s*.
Mowing barley 1*s*.	2*s*.
Mowing grass, artificial, 1*s*. to 2*s*.	2*s*.
natural	4*s*. 6*d*.
Hoeing turnips 4*s*. and 2*s*.	7*s*.
Filling and spreading marl 25*s*. per 120 loads	28*s*. to 30*s*.
Threshing wheat, per quarter, 1*s*. 2*d*. to 1*s*. 4*d*.	1*s*. 8*d*. to 2*s*.
Threshing barley and oats 8*d*.	8*d*. to 10*d*.
Threshing peas 1*s*. 3*d*.	8*d*. to 10*d*.
Head man's wages £10 to £12	£11 to £15
Next ditto £9	£7 to £10
Lad £4 to £7	£4 to £7
Dairy-maid £5	£5
Other ditto £3 to £4	£3 to £5
Women in harvest 1*s*. and board	1*s*.
in hay 9*d*. and beer,	1*s*. No beer
in winter 6*d*.	8*d*. No beer

Mr Henry Blythe assures me that labour in the vicinity of Burnham nearly doubled from 1795 to 1801: to satisfy me of this fact he laid his books before me, in which the fact appeared clearly; and this has taken place on his farm not at all by any extraordinary works done on it, but merely by the rise of prices: it is not, however, to be accounted for merely by the rise per week, but the men will not perform what they formerly did, and more must therefore be kept for the same work.

The labour of a sand farm of 1,000 acres near Holkham £820 last year.

Mr Marshall takes every opportunity in his work to note the great activity of the farm workmen, in the dispatch of business in this county, much exceeding any other. The observation is pointedly just; insomuch that there could hardly be a greater improvement than to introduce their system in this respect, in many other counties equally adapted to it, but managed at present at a far greater expense.

Recapitulation. General average in harvest £2 8s. 3d. the month and board; in summer 1s. 11d. a day; in winter 1s. 8d. a day. . . .

The necessary and unavoidable expenses of a labourer and his wife, without any family, for one year, calculated at the price of flour 4s. and meal 3s. per stone, and the other articles at present price, 1799*.

	£	s.	d.	£	s.	d.
Cottage rent				2	10	0
One peck of coals per day, 20 weeks, or 140 days, at 3½d. per peck	2	0	10			
Half a peck per day, 8 weeks, or 56 days	0	8	2			
A quarter of a peck per day, 24 weeks, or rather 169 days	0	12	4			
				3	1	4
Soap, 4 ounces per week, at 2½d. which is per annum	0	10	10			
Oil or candles, at 6d. per week, for 20 weeks	0	10	0			
Do. do. at 3d. per do. for 32 weeks	0	8	0			
				1	8	10
Shoemaker, one pair of shoes, one pair of highloos [boots reaching over ankles] and mending	0	16	0			
Stockings, two pair	0	5	0			
Hat	0	2	0			
Slops, jackets, &c.	0	9	0			
Breeches	0	5	0			
Two shirts	0	10	0			
				2	7	0
				£9	7	2

* Communicated by an Active Magistrate.

	£	s.	d.
Amount brought forward	9	7	2
Woman's apparel	1	15	0
Sixpence per day, for food for each person	18	5	0
Sixpence per do. additional food in the harvest month, per man	0	14	0
Expense of tools	0	8	0
	£30	9	2

In the above account no allowance is made for the wear and tear of the furniture, and sundry small articles used in the house.

Earnings

	£	s.	d.
Harvest, 4 weeks	4	14	6
48 weeks, at 8s. per week	18	4	0
Woman's gleanings	0	14	0
48 weeks, at 1s. per week	2	8	0
	£26	0	6

General View of the Agriculture of the County of Norfolk, (1804) 483–8, 493–4

(3) The management of Charles Chaplin, Esq., at Blankney and in the other lordships which he possesses cannot be too much commended: he assigns in each a large pasture sufficient to feed a cow for every cottager in the place; besides which he lets them a small croft for mowing hay to keep their cow in winter, which with the assistance of a pig and a garden are found to be of the greatest comfort to them. Upon inquiring what were poor's-rates – 8d. in the pound! In another parish 15d. nominal rent. Men are apt to complain heavily of poor's-rates in many counties yet take no steps to remedy them. Here is an instance which strongly unites with those which Lord Winchelsea has so ably explained to prove one great means of keeping rates down, by increasing benevolently the comforts of the poor. They all get cows here without difficulty: 'let them but land. and they will be sure to find stock for it', was the answer.

At Hackthorn rent of a cottage 20s.; if a cow £3 10s.; have enough for winter and summer food; not one-fourth have them; but in some towns a good many. If land could be got, all would have cows; if a cow dies, they get collections for it. The women here spin flax; a quarter of a pound of twelvepenny, or 3*d.*, is a day's work; but earn rather more by coarse work.

In the new enclosure of Glentworth, on Lincolnheath, I saw some large pieces under various crops that were in a most slovenly and wretched condition, run out, and almost waste; and on inquiry found they were allotments to cottagers who each knowing his own piece cultivated in severalty within a ring fence: it is a strong instance to prove that their shares ought always to be given in grass; they are unequal to any other tillage than that of a garden. At Kirton, in the new enclosure, there is in the vale twenty-eight acres of grass in one close, and twenty-two in another; one for the cottagers' cows in summer, and the other for hay; fifty in all: this is good, though not equal to every man having his own separate. None here find difficulty in getting cows if they can but get land. By the proportion twenty-eight acres meadow, near one acre and a half each cow, which yields two loads of hay for each gate. This fifty acres is worth £50 rent for sixteen cows for the whole year, but they pay £4 4*s.* or 28*s.* an acre; thus the land lets better by 8*s.* an acre, at the same time a great benefit to them.

It is singular that the labouring poor, with the extraordinary high price of labour at Norton, Kirton, &c., consume very little meat, except the stoutest labourers at task-work who earn 3*s.* a day: these have for dinner some meat in a pie; all consume a good many potatoes.

Upon Sir John Sheffield's estate of twenty square miles of country the rents of the cottages have never been raised, and to prevent all oppression they have been taken out of the hands of the farmers and made tenants to the landlord; they pay little or nothing, or rather less than nothing, for the cottage, as the land is worth more than they pay for both. For a comfortable habitation, a garden for potatoes of a rood or half an acre called a *garth*, with summering and wintering of two cows, which enables them to keep two or three very fine pigs (but never any poultry), they pay 40*s.* This great indulgence has no ill effect; they are very clean in every thing; remarkably well clothed; no children in rags; their beds and furniture good; are very sober, and attentive to church; but not equally so in educating their children to be industrious. Let me, however, note that in the great extent of this estate there is but one public-house; a remarkable instance that speaks strongly upon a point of infinite importance to the national manners and prosperity. In the parishes of Flixborough and Burton, the principal of the estate, poor's-rates are at the highest 1s. 10d. and this owing to militia laws and some contested settlements. Upon Mr Goulton's estate, where nearly a similar system takes place, the rates are only 1s. The cottagers are very numerous on Sir John's estate, therefore if a different system was embraced, and their habitations, gardens, and cow-grounds were raised to as much as might be, £200 a year might be added to the rents. This sum would equal 1s. in the pound on the poor's-rates of these parishes. This is a very singular fact which deserves great attention; for it may be fairly concluded that more than £200 a year is saved by this uncommon system of benevolence from which it has arisen. At this valuation of £200 a year they would still be on a par with others. They live in them from father to son, and even leave their cottages through confidence that no child or widow will ever be turned out, unless for offences that do not occur; and the effect is so great that there is a reliance on the attachment of the poor which nothing else can affect. Population increases so, that pigs and children fill every quarter. And at Burton, &c., no cottages have been pulled down but several new ones built; in the last twenty years the baptisms at Burton have exceeded the burials by 136, and though some have certainly emigrated from the parish, yet by no means in any thing like that proportion, as is visible in every circumstance that can be recurred to.

The women are very lazy; I have noted their indolence in spinning; Mr Goulton's expression was 'they do nothing but bring children, and eat cake'; nay, the men milk their cows for them; but the men very sober and industrious.

At Alkborough 9d. in the pound.

Mr Elwes's cottagers at Roxby have also each two cows, and very good houses.

In all this country the common-gate for a cottager's cow is two acres for winter, and one and a half for summer.

At Wintringham, upon Lord Carrington buying the

estate, he made all the cottagers tenants to himself, and all have cows and gardens.

Lord Yarborough's cottagers have all cows and a garden.

Mr Lloyd of Alesby has no labourers that have not cows; and it is the same with those of Mr Skipwith at Alesby. The custom seems general through all the district.

At Humberstone Lord Carrington has paid the same attention to them as at Wintringham. The whole of the parish, near Grimsby in Lincolnshire, is his property; in that parish there are thirteen cottagers, every one of whom has conveniences for the keeping of one cow, and some for the keeping of two cows. The land on which the cottages stand, with the little paddocks and gardens adjoining them, is in all about sixteen acres. Besides which, at a distance of a quarter of a mile from the town, about sixty acres of land are appropriated to the use of the cottagers. This land is divided into two plots, one of which is a pasture for the cows of the cottagers in summer, and the other is kept as meadow land to provide hay for them in the winter. Each cottager knows his own little piece of meadow land, and he lays upon it all the manure which he can obtain in order that he may have the more hay.

When one of the two plots of land has been mown for two or three years it will be converted into a summer pasture, and the other plot will become meadow land, so that no part of the land in the occupation of the cottagers will be injured by constant mowing.

The cottagers are totally independent of the larger farmers as they hold their cottages and lands directly of Lord Carrington, and not as sub-tenants. This gives them a degree of respectability which they would not otherwise enjoy; and their situation is the more desirable as the rent they pay is less than the rent paid by the farmers in general. But it is certain that in numberless places in the kingdom many a poor cottager would rejoice to give the utmost value for as much land as would keep a cow, if he could obtain it.

General View of the Agriculture of the County of Lincoln, 2nd ed. (1813) 459–64

(4) In the progress of the journey which I made in the year 1800, the more peculiar object of which was the waste lands

in the counties I should travel, I found many reasons for combining with that object two others – the state of the poor, and the amount of the rates levied for their support. Instances occurred of parishes containing great commons and waste tracts of which little or no use is made, and at the same time raising immense sums for the poor, expended in a manner which left them almost as wretched as if no such efforts had been made for their support. It did not strike me that the wastes would provide for them much better than parish rates till I met with one or two very singular instances; but when these were duly examined they opened the view to a field of such extent, and, as I thought, of such importance, as was sufficient to induce me to redouble my attention wherever any thing similar might occur. Other cases in succession did offer themselves, of which I have preserved the details.

From these I believe it will be found that of all the methods of improving waste land, none are so important or so profitable as applying them to the support of the labouring poor.

Of these particulars I have drawn out such an account as will enable the reader to judge for himself: but as the minutiae of such objects would perhaps be too unpleasant to receive the attention of those who have not time to enter into the detail of such inquiries, I have sketched a *précis* of the subject, annexing such observations as occurred; with a reply to all the objections I have in the course of my journey heard to the proposition I have built on these inquiries.

DATA

CHATTERIS, *Cambridgeshire*. About a hundred small cottages have been raised of late years on the common, so close to each other as to admit only a path around them; very few have gardens; many were built by the owners who inhabit them, and did not cost more than £10 or £12. The proprietors have no relief from the parish.

BLOFIELD, *Norfolk*. Thirty families have taken 39¾ acres of land from the common and built very good and comfortable cottages; many must have cost £40, £50, and even £60. They have 23 cows and 18 horses among them. Average of land 1⅓ acre, average of live stock 1⅔ head.

Only 16 have cows, 8 neither cows nor horses, and 11
less than an acre of land each. 150 souls thus established
have cost the parish (by a very inflamed account) £24;
while 110 others, the rest of the poor, burthened it £150
in the same half year. If 110 without land cost £150
what would 260, the total poor, have cost if none had
land?

Answer	£354
Instead of which it is	174
Saving to the parish by 40 acres	180

and 41 head of live stock, in half a year.

HETHERSETT, *Norfolk*. Enclosed by act of Parliament, and
proves how much the poor are desirous of having property
divided rather than in common. The commissioners were
enabled by the act to offer double allotments to cottagers
possessing under £5 a year if they would have them in
common under regulations and trustees, and free of all
expenses. They chose single allotments separate, though
to pay all the expenses of the enclosure equally with the
other proprietors.

WESTON COLVILLE, *Cambridgeshire*. Enclosed by act of
Parliament, when several parcels of land were laid to the
cottages; some had large gardens, others 2 or 3 acres. They
do not all keep cows, joining to plough and get bits of
corn, which they like better. In this scarcity a trifle may
have been occasionally given by the parish to one or two
of them; but, generally speaking, they are never burthensome: are very comfortable.

NAZEING, *Essex*. The common rights regulated by act of
Parliament. The poor were remarkably idle and dissolute;
but Mr Palmer offering to advance money for every poor
man who could not afford to buy live stock, many
accepted it, and every man of them repaid him in two
years, some sooner. They are converted by this property
to as sober and regular a people as they were before
licentious

ALDERSHOT, *Surrey* [*sic*]. Several cottages built on the
common, whose owners have taken from three fourths to
two acres each: some have a cow, others a pig. This not

only keeps them from the parish, but some are actually charged to and pay the rates.

WORPLESDEN, *Surrey*. An instance of an old man and his wife living in such a state of wretchedness in a miserable hovel with a small garden on the common as I have not seen any where else; but the love of property keeps them from the parish.

CHOBHAM, *Surrey*. Many poor people have built themselves cottages on the common, but very few have any live stock. Some of them receive a small matter from the parish in this scarcity, others have nothing. They assert that a cow would be a great assistance and keep them from ever being burthensome.

FARNHAM, *Surrey*. Above 100 families have built cottages on the common. I examined 47 of them, who possess about 20 acres besides some gardens. 24 of them have 103 children at home, the other families I have not noted. These (147 persons in all) are supported with no other allowance from the parish than £4 8s. 1½d. per week, or 7d. per head per week: yet there are only 4 cows among them. They would readily give up the parish for a cow, and many would agree to repay the cost by instalments. Every 5 persons in the workhouse cost £64 10s. 10d. per annum; consequently for one year's expense of a family they might establish two on the common free of expense ever after.

BUXTED, *Sussex*. A family seated on the common would rather have a cow than 6s. a week from the parish.

MAYFIELD, *Sussex*. Here is a case which proves the assertion in the preceding article: a family chargeable when there was no scarcity ceased to be chargeable in the scarcity from a cow being given by the parish.

WIMPOLE, PETWORTH, *and* WOBURN. Lord Hardwicke gives gardens to his cottagers; but observing them very badly cultivated, he offered premiums to encourage better cultivation. The effect so great that their management became exemplary. The Earl of Egremont at Petworth, and the Duke of Bedford at Woburn have each made exertions in favour of their cottagers. Mr Vernon, in Suffolk, the same.

LINCOLNSHIRE, &c. In 48 parishes, 753 labourers and their families, renting land sufficient for one or two cows, have received NOTHING from their parishes throughout the late and present scarcities.

OBSERVATIONS

It is sufficiently evident from all these cases that the great engine wherewith the poor may be governed and provided for the most easily and the most cheaply is property: but by our poor laws the effect (undesignedly) upon the poor has been that rather of impoverishment than acquisition, and of promoting idleness rather than industry, by an impolitic and expensive supply from hand to mouth. The consequences of this conduct have matured themselves into such a mass of poor rates as to be ruinous to many little housekeepers, while the poor, deprived of all spirit and ambition, have sunk into such dependence on the parish that their poverty has kept pace with the errors of the system; and has arrived at such a pitch that if some effective cure be not devised, very mischievous consequences may be expected. Rates within two or three years have doubled; and past experience tells us that although they rise by reason of the high price of corn they do not proportionably sink with a low price. If every scarcity be thus to advance them they will, in no long period, absorb the rents of the kingdom – not to give ease and comfort to the lower classes but to leave them, if possible, in a worse situation.

The evil being of such a magnitude it well deserves the consideration of the Legislature, whether a totally contrary system, proved by so many remarkable cases to be capable of producing great effects, ought not to be adopted; and the more especially as in the main point it agrees with the proposition made by Mr Pitt some years ago to the House of Commons.

Many authors have remarked with surprise the great change which has taken place in the spirit of the lower classes of the people within the last twenty years. There was formerly found an unconquerable aversion to depend on the parish, insomuch that many would struggle through life with large families never applying for relief. That spirit is annihilated: applications of late have been as numerous as the poor; and one great misfortune attending the change is that every sort of industry flags when once the parochial dependence takes place; it then becomes a struggle between the pauper and the parish, the one to do as little and to receive as much as possible, and the other to pay by no rule but the summons and order of the justice. The evils resulting are beyond all calculation, for the motives to industry and frugality are cut up by the roots when every poor man knows that if he does not feed himself the parish must do it for him; and that he has not the most distant hope of ever attaining independence, let him be as industrious and frugal as he may. To acquire land enough to build a cottage on is a hopeless aim in 99 parishes out of 100.

But the cases here detailed prove clearly that wherever there is such a hope it operates beyond all the powers of calculation. How these men were able to effect their object surpasses inquiry: that they saved money with this view is palpable, because in most of the cases the erections have been the work of regular carpenters and masons who could not have been employed without a considerable part of the expense being provided for; and this accordingly I found the case, for where mortgages had taken place it was only for a part of the expense, in many instances for only a small part, and in some, not a few, without any such assistance at all.

And here it is deserving of great attention, that during the very period in which the poor have in general become wholly dependent, and burthened their parishes to an enormous amount, these cases of saving frugality and industry have occurred in a few places with no other motive or instigation but the prospect of becoming proprietors of their own cottages. What a powerful motive has this proved, to render them such striking exceptions to a whole kingdom!

But they have done much more than at first appears in this view of the matter, for their operations have had enemies every where; they have at every place had to fight their way through a host of foes – their fences levelled – their works of all sorts viewed with the most jealous eyes – opposed – in some cases defeated – in all calumniated. That their means have been all unobjectionable I am far from asserting; but that they would have been so if their design had been viewed as it ought to have been I have not a doubt; for they received little but discouragement when they ought to have been liberally assisted, and they have in some cases been absolutely stopped from all further proceedings of the kind.

It is evident from the details that this has arisen from the parishes being without any regular system, and remaining ignorant, or without power to turn their wastes to their own immense and incalculable advantage.

Nothing can be clearer than the vast importance which all these poor people, scattered as they are through so many counties, and affected by circumstances so extremely various, attach to the object of possessing land, though no more than to set a cottage on. Of this there can be no dispute; and as an object does exist, the prospect of which will induce industry, frugality, patience, and exertion without bounds, while every where else, without this object in view, the very contrary qualities have thriven and increased to the enormous burthen of the kingdom, surely the great and unquestionable importance of using this powerful lever to work upon the people at large – to turn this deep-rooted prejudice to public account – to assist, instead of impeding its progress – and to nourish those principles of independence which are banished in every other place, is become a point essential in the management of the poor.

When we sit by our fire sides and ask how a poor labourer can afford to build a comfortable cottage, enclose some land, break up and cultivate a rough waste, acquire some live stock, and get many conveniences about him, we defy calculation; there must be some moving principle at work which figures will not count, for in such an inquiry we see nothing but impossibilities. But we forget a thousand animating principles of human feeling. Such effects could not possibly have been produced without a series of years of great industry and most economical saving – to become independent, to marry a girl and fix her in a spot they can call their own, instigates to a conduct, not a trace of which would be seen without the motive ever in view. With this powerful impulse they will exert every nerve to earn, call into life and vigour every principle of industry, and exert all the powers of frugality to save. Nothing less can account for the spectacle, and such animating prospects will account for any thing.

Go to an alehouse kitchen of an old enclosed country, and

there you will see the origin of poverty and poor rates. For whom are they to be sober? For whom are they to save? (Such are their questions.) For the parish? If I am diligent, shall I have leave to build a cottage? If I am sober, shall I have land for a cow? If I am frugal, shall I have half an acre of potatoes? You offer no motives; you have nothing but a parish officer and a workhouse! – Bring me another pot –

It is true that wastes are not every where to be found, but the principles of property are universal; and the more they are encouraged amongst the poor the less burthensome will they be found. He who cannot possess an acre may be the owner of a cow; and the man will love his country the better even for a pig.

One hundred and twenty-eight rods of potatoes are found in Ireland to be sufficient for the support of a family through much the larger part of the year; about three quarters of an acre therefore per family removes them from a dependence on wheat, placing them in that respect in such a situation that it is of little or no consequence to such families whether wheat is at 5*s*. or £5 per bushel. The prodigious importance of such a state of the poorest classes must be obvious at the first blush.

It is evident from the preceding cases that the possession of a cottage and about an acre of land, for on an average these poor people's encroachments do not exceed that portion, if they do not keep the proprietor in every case from the parish yet very materially lessen the burthen in all. If the weekly sums thus received be compared to what is paid to poor families in any part of the kingdom where wastes have not been thus applied, it will be found that the difference is much greater than could well be conceived when compared with the quantity of land, and forming a rent in this saving very much beyond the value of it in any other possible application. But the effect which is here proved to attend the possession of a cow is very extraordinary; they all agree uniformly in this point, and assert that they had rather have a cow than any parish allowance here noted, valuing it even so highly as 5*s*. or 6*s*. per week; and this by men who must know what the benefit is, having possessed and also lived without a cow. It does not follow that wastes are to be preserved in common that the poor may keep cows, but the fact clearly proved, and which applies universally where the land is good enough to keep them at all, is that the portion sufficient to feed a cow, enclosed and allotted to a cottage, is of that degree of importance.

That giving property to the poor, and that sort of property which they are most anxious to possess, would fix in their hearts a great attachment to and affection for their country is obvious; and the present state of the lower classes renders this a very essential object: I will not explain that state, it is well known. Suffice it to say that the first promulgation of such a plan as I propose would do more instantly to appease their minds and render them patient under their present sufferings than perhaps any thing that could practically be devised. Nor would the extent of the relief be inconsiderable; there are commons or wastes through much the larger part of the kingdom, and consequently the mass of the benefit would be of a magnitude well deserving the attention of the Legislature.

In periods of scarcity a considerable benefit would result to the poor from the peculiar tendency of this mode of provision to meet the exigencies of the times. Prices in such periods always rise far beyond the deficiency of the crop, then such of the poor as have land feel the advantages of it doubly. I found both the Blofield and Farnham cottagers much pleased with having reaped a tolerable and in some cases a very good crop of corn, and comfortably consoling themselves that they had potatoes of their own and were not forced to buy at the high price of the market. Whatever they have to sell produces a good return, which gives them some interest in the rise so utterly ruinous to such as are without land. Some of these cottagers had small plots of hops and told me of great advantage derived from them, even to selling as much as produced £6 or £7. Those who go much among the poor must know what a great effect this has on the mind in instigating to industry; such motives are not to be estimated; they can neither be brought to the bushel nor the scale; it is not a matter of pounds, shillings, and pence; it works in the soul; it animates the heart more than twice the value gained in any other way.

While a general enclosure of wastes is called for by one

universal voice it becomes peculiarly proper to consider what has been the effect of parliamentary ones relative to the immediate interests of the poor, as I have heard some gentlemen observe that such a measure would cure all evils. Upon right principles I believe it would, but such very general views being apt to lead to error it will be necessary to examine the question particularly.

In this journey I examined the effect of above a hundred and forty parliamentary enclosures on the production of human food – on population – on the poor rates – and on the situation and comforts of the poor. In great numbers the last article was not to be ascertained; in some, from the enclosure having taken place long ago; in others, from the want of knowledge in my informants; and for other reasons; but in the following cases I received the information I sought for.

EFFECT OF ENCLOSURES ON THE POOR

SANDY. Injured.

EATON. Injured. Their cows much lessened.

WARBOYS. Many kept cows; now few. They were certainly injured.

RAMSEY. Cottagers' cows lessened.

ALCONBURY. Highly injurious to them. Many kept cows that have not since. They could not enclose, and sold; and with those that hired the allotments thrown to the landlords, and the poor left without cows or land.

MARCH. Those of property benefited, all who hired were ruined.

WIMBLINGTON. Ditto.

BARRINGTON. One acre allotted for the right of 3 sheep and 2 cows.

LONGSTOW. Several kept cows who keep them no longer.

ABINGTON. Suffered greatly. All allotments thrown to one person, and their cows vanished. Suffered so much as to stop enclosing for many years.

MORDEN GUILDEW (the act just passed). Their cows will be dissipated. They are greatly alarmed.

STREATHAM (not enclosed, but talked of). Abhor the idea because all their cows would go.

L. WILBRAHAM. A common allotted, and never to be occupied but by cottagers.

WESTON COLVILLE. Cottagers with rights better off, others lost their cows.

CARLETON. Improved.

NORTHWOLD. Suffer. Twenty who kept stock keep it no longer. Others bettered. Allotments can neither be let nor sold from the houses.

HILLBOROUGH. Suffered.

FINCHAM. Injured in fuel, and cows gone.

SHOULDHAM. Much injured in both fuel and live stock.

GARBOISETHORPE. Poor kept 20 cows before, now none.

MARHAM. They have not suffered.

LEXHAM. Cows lessened.

HEACHAM. Much comfort from little properties of 2 to 10 acres. They keep cows, and have corn.

SEDGFORD. Injured.

BRANCASTER. Well treated.

SALTHOUSE. Ditto.

FELTHORPE. Much injured.

[?] Very well treated.

SHROPHAM. Well treated.

LANGLEY. Ditto.

ACLE. Much injured.

SHOTTISHAM. Well treated. Cows increased.

OLD BUCKENHAM. Well treated.

BARNABY. Ditto.

BARTON MILLS. Injured. Cows annihilated.

PARNDON. Their little allotments all sold.

BASINGSTOKE. Injured.

In 37 cases, not injured only in 12.

Before any observations are made on this table it is necessary to explain that by the poor being injured is not at all meant that no good results to some of them, even in these cases: in soils which are kept in tillage there is, without any question, a considerable increase of employment truly valuable to the poor. Let no one imagine that one word offered in this paper is meant generally against enclosing; all contended for is, simply, that such of the poor as kept cows in these parishes could keep them no longer after the enclosure: that instead of giving property to the poor, or preserving it, or enabling them to acquire it, the very contrary effect has taken place; and as this evil was by no means *necessarily* connected with the measure of enclosing, it was a mischief that might easily have been avoided and ought most carefully to be avoided in future.

In the minutes I took of these and many other enclosures many instances will be seen in which the small value of common rights is noted from the low rent in some cases paid for them; but this proves nothing against giving the poor land distinctly; nor is it even an argument proving the position for which it is brought, as letting to the inhabitants of other parishes is precluded, and when the home poor are unable to get the stock the price at which a right lets can be no criterion of its value.

Commissioners of enclosures are little apt to confess any thing against them, but I met with three in one county who furnished me with observations that merit notice.

Mr Forster of Norwich, after giving me an account of 20 enclosures in which he had acted as a commissioner, stated his opinion on their general effect on the poor, and lamented that he had been accessory to injuring two thousand poor people at the rate of 20 families per parish. Numbers in the practice of feeding the commons cannot prove their right; and many, indeed most who have allotments, have not more than an acre, which being insufficient for the man's cow, both cow and land are usually sold to the opulent farmers; that the right sold before the enclosure would produce much less than the allotment after it, but the money is dissipated, doing them no good when they cannot vest it in stock.

Mr Ewen, a commissioner in the same place, observed that in most of the enclosures he has known the poor man's allotment and cow are sold five times in six before the award is signed.

Mr Burton of Langley, a very able commissioner, wished for a clause in all acts on the principle of that of Northwold, which makes the allotment inalienable from the cottage, as he admits there is a considerable benefit in the poor people having land enough for a cow; from two to four acres, according to the soil.

As there is not the least necessity for the evil here complained of, and merely a call that in passing enclosure acts the rights and interests of the poor should be attended to, which it is too plainly evident they have not been, I conceive that it becomes a matter of propriety to point out such evils; and at a period in which every exertion is making to assist and relieve the poor that this necessary one should not be neglected. To pass acts beneficial to every other class in the state and hurtful to the lowest order only, when the smallest attention would prevent it, is a conduct against which reason, justice, and humanity equally plead.

The rise of poor rates in parishes that have been enclosed having kept pace with the increase in other parishes is another proof that there has been something deficient in the principles which have conducted them. Above 60,000 acres of commons have been enclosed in the places which I have registered; in the following the rise is noted particularly:

	Acres of Com.		s.		s.	d.
Lidlington	497		1	to	4	6
March	3,440	doubled to £1,300				
Chatteris	4,320		2	to	4	6
Abington	80		0	to	2	6
Wilbraham	469	more than doubled				
Hillborough	420	doubled				
Fincham	647	trebled				
Hethersett	430		5	to	10	0
Barton Mills	300		4	to	13	0
	10,603		20	to	53	0

These are selected merely because the old rates, the new, and the commons are all minuted. The rise has been equal in the rest. It should threfore seem that notwithstanding the increase of employment, yet there has been some contrary current which has been bearing heavily against the force of such employment. On the contrary, if a right use had been made of a very small portion of these commons, poor rates might have been done away altogether.

An Inquiry into the Propriety of Applying Wastes
to the better Maintenance and Support of
the Poor (1801) 1–22

CHAPTER IV

Industry and Transport

I. INDUSTRY AND POVERTY

Before the growth of rural poverty in the later eighteenth century came to puzzle farming experts like Young and Marshall, there was apparently a general consensus that the purely agricultural villages, with their regular annual routine of labour in the fields, dairies and barns, normally produced very few people who lacked a subsistence. William Marshall, for instance, held that 'agriculture occasions very few poor, on the contrary it provides them almost constant labour. It is only the blind, the extreme old, the very young children and idiots which become chargeable in a parish purely agricultural.' When he reviewed the county reports of the Board of Agriculture he was surprised to find that this was not always true.[1] In general, industrial towns, and industrialised villages invaded by the expansion of domestic crafts such as the weaving of woollen cloth, framework-knitting, and the manufacture of metal goods, had a considerably higher proportion of their inhabitants dependent on the Poor Law. This was partly because they attracted migrants who sought to enter their trades; it is clear from Young's figures that it was often possible for higher rates of pay to be earned in industry than in farming, especially by women and children. From time to time, however, the industrial centres were adversely affected by changes in fashion and the appearance of competing products, and there were periodical slumps arising from over-production, and from temporary falls in demand caused by high food prices or the closing of overseas markets in war-time.

In the following passage Young gave vent again to his view of the primacy of agriculture over industry and commerce, and argued that it was the manufacturers and merchants who complained the loudest when rates of labour rose, and who sought to keep the labouring classes poor. He seems also to be carried

[1] W. Marshall, *Review of Reports to the Board of Agriculture*, IV 203; V 118, 461.

away into asserting that the value of land was independent of the proximity of urban markets, a contention that, for all his illustrations, appears certainly to be ill-founded:

> Let the price of labour rise to its uttermost, who is it that complains? Not the 'engrossers of all vices, landed men, farmers, and jobbers', as they are politely coupled by a supercilious coxcomb,[1] but the manufacturers and traders; it is they who have turned all the melancholy ditties of ruin to the state from *loss of manufactures* by *high rates of labour*.
>
> Name me the publication in which landed men and farmers are the complainants of the rates of labour. I will in return, for every one you produce, name forty in which the other set are noisy in their exclamations on this head.
>
> If you talk of the interests of trade and manufactures, everyone but an idiot knows that the lower classes must be kept poor or they will never be industrious. I do not mean that the poor in England are to be kept like the poor of France; but the state of the country considered, they must be (like all mankind) in poverty or they will not work.
>
> Let not those, therefore, whose interest makes such policy requisite, abuse the landed interest for the miseries of the poor, which are wholly owing to manufactures and trade.
>
> Sudbury in Suffolk is named; it is a poor miserable place undoubtedly. Lavenham, its next neighbour on one side, and Colchester on the other, are in the same predicament: poor rates from 7*s.* to 17*s.* in the pound are miserable marks that they have had the curse of manufactures among them – an instance that the trading system ever stands on crazy foundations. Let the writer name a tract in which agriculture falls in ruins: even around the places above named, although husbandry is enormously burdened by the manufacturing poor, she flourishes as much, and around Colchester more, than in nine-tenths of Britain – so little truth is there in the vague assertions that the local value of land depends on the neighbourhood of manufactures. The soil around Lincoln, which possesses not one fabric [manufacture], lets higher than at Islington; nay, some of it twice as high.
>
> Go to towns where manufactures are the most flourishing,

---

[1] A reference to the author of *Considerations on the Policy, Commerce, and Circumstances of the Kingdom* (1771) [Ed.].

you will there find poor rates higher than anywhere else, except where they have nursed up great numbers of inhabitants and then fled to leave them starving.

I subscribe as readily as anyone to the importance of that general aggregate of industry, agriculture, manufactures, and commerce; but let not the possessors of one most falsely suppose the other is to be sacrificed on her altars; but if ever unfortunate questions should be started, in which a preference must be given to one, none but a fool can imagine that the landlords of this great empire of above fourscore millions of acres are to yield to the transitory sons of trade and manufacture.

Eastern Tour (1771) IV 360–2

2. THE INDUSTRIAL REVOLUTION

Young was always fascinated when in the course of his travels he saw examples of 'improvement' in industry. His belief in the overriding supremacy of agriculture, though it created an excessive prejudice, did not blind him to the significance of the remarkable industrial developments which he observed in the Black Country, Lancashire, Yorkshire, Durham, Cumberland, and elsewhere. In the following passages Young described first the rising pottery industry of Stoke-on-Trent, which he associated with the 'inventive genius' of Wedgwood, and second the great Coalbrookdale ironworks which, when he saw it, was enjoying its heyday. Young's eye for ventures which created employment, and his interest in the rates of pay that were given, are well illustrated in these descriptions.

Young's account of the Staffordshire potteries is valuable for its factual detail. He was correct in emphasising the importance of exports to the industry, and in mentioning the use of local clays for ordinary pottery, and of clays brought from Devonshire and Dorset, mixed with ground flints, for the finer qualities. (Cornish clays did not become important until a few years after his visit.) Wedgwood's cream-coloured ware became known as 'Queensware' after Queen Charlotte gave it her patronage in 1765, and, as Young notes, this type of pottery then became an important element in the success of the industry, and was widely imitated abroad. Young's figures for the employment provided by the potteries seem in line with other estimates, and his account of wages paid is accepted by R. G. Haggar in his study of the industry in the *Staffordshire Victoria County History*, vol. II (1967).

In regard to the description of Coalbrookdale, Dr Barrie Trinder of the Ironbridge Gorge Museum Trust tells me that, in general, Young's figures for wages and numbers employed seem reasonably accurate, though he was in error in saying that the local potteries made only coarse mugs and pots: they were also producing 'Jackfield ware', a very high-quality black earthenware, and by the 1770s the district's first porcelain factory, at Caughley, was in production. Young's mention of five furnaces refers to the Severn Gorge as a whole, rather than Coalbrookdale by itself; his description of the wagon ways for conveying limestone is one of the first references to railway inclined planes in Shropshire:

(1) From Newcastle-under-Lyme I had the pleasure of viewing the Staffordshire potteries at Burslem and the neighbouring villages, which have of late been carried on with such amazing success. There are 300 houses, which are calculated to employ, upon average, twenty hands each or 6,000 in the whole; but if all the variety of people that work in what may be called the preparation for the employment of the immediate manufactures [are included] the total number cannot be much short of 10,000, and it is increasing every day.

It dates its great demand from Mr *Wedgwood* (the principal manufacturer) introducing, about four years ago, the cream-coloured ware, and since that the increase has been very rapid. Large quantities are exported to Germany, Ireland, Holland, Russia, Spain, the East Indies, and much to America; some of the finest sorts to France. A considerable shopkeeper from the Pont-neuf at Paris was lately at Burslem, and bought a large quantity. It is possible, indeed, he came for more purposes than to buy; the French of that rank seldom travel for business which might be as well transacted by a single letter.

The common clay of the country is used for the ordinary sorts; the finer kinds are made of clay from Devonshire and Dorsetshire, chiefly from Bideford; but the flints from the Thames are all brought rough by sea either to Liverpool or Hull, and so by Burton. There is no conjecture formed of the original reason of fixing the manufacture in this spot, except for the convenience of plenty of coals which abound under all the country.

The flints are first ground in mills, and the clay prepared by breaking, washing, and sifting, and then they are mixed in the requisite proportions. The flints are bought first by the people about the country, and by them burnt and ground, and sold to the manufacturers by the peck.

It is then laid in large quantities on kilns to evaporate the moisture; but this is a nice work as it must not be too dry. Next it is beaten with large wooden hammers, and then is in order for throwing, and is moulded into the forms in which it is to remain. This is the most difficult work in the whole manufacture. A boy turns a perpendicular wheel which, by means of thongs, turns a small horizontal one just before the thrower with such velocity that it twirls round the lump of clay he lays on it into any form he directs it with his fingers.

The earnings of the people are various: grinders 7*s.* per week; washers and breakers 8*s.*; throwers 9*s.* to 12*s.*; engine lathe men 10*s.* to 12*s.*; handlers, who fix hands, and other kinds of finishers for adding sprigs, horns, &c., 9*s.* to 12*s.*; gilders, men 12*s.*, women 7*s.* 6*d.*; modellers, apprentices, one of £100 a year; pressers 8*s.* to 9*s.*; painters 10*s.* to 12*s.*; moulders in plaster of Paris 8*s.*

In general the men earn from 7*s.* to 12*s.*, women 5*s.* to 8*s.*, boys, chiefly apprentices, but 2*s.* a week the first year, and a rise of 3*d.* per annum afterwards; before they are apprentices 2*s.* 9*d.* per week, as they then learn nothing. But few girls.

Northern Tour (1770) III 306–9

(2) This neighbourhood [near Coalbrookdale, Shropshire] is uncommonly full of manufactures, among which the principal are the potteries, pipe-makers, colliers, and iron works. In the potteries, which are only for coarse mugs, pots, &c., the men earn 8*s.* to 10*s.* a week, boys 3*d.* to 9*d.* a day, and girls 3*d.* and 4*d.* In the pipe manufactory the men earn 10*s.* 6*d.* a week, the women 3*s.*, and children 2*s.* or 3*s.* There are three or four hundred hands employed in it. Both these fabrics are exceedingly flourishing. Great numbers of blue

tiles are also burnt here and sent by the Severn to a distance.

Walked by Benthall Hall to a steep over the river called Benthall Edge. It is a very fine woody bank which rises very steep from the Severn: you look down an immense declivity on a beautiful winding valley two miles over, cut into rich enclosures, and broken by tufts of wood. The steep on which you stand, waving from the right line, exhibits the noblest slopes of hanging wood, in one place forming a fine round hill covered with wood called Tick Wood; in front the Wrekin, three miles off, its sides cut by enclosures three parts up, and along the vale the river meanders to Shrewsbury. Further to the right at a spot called Agar's Spout, a most romantic view down a steep slope of wood with the Severn coming in a very bold reach full against it, winding away to the town in a most bending, fanciful course.

Crossing the ferry where Mr Darby has undertaken to build a bridge of one arch of 120 feet of cast iron, I passed to his works up Coalbrookdale. The waggon ways that lead down to the river are laid with cast iron instead of wood; and those made for the limestone waggons on the steep hills are so contrived that the loaded waggon winds up the empty one on a different road. Pass his new slitting mills, which are not finished, but the immense wheels, 20 feet diameter of cast iron, were there, and appear wonderful. Viewed the furnaces, forges, &c., with the vast bellows that give those roaring blasts which make the whole edifice horridly sublime. These works are supposed to be the greatest in England. The whole process is here gone through from digging the ironstone to making it into cannon, pipes, cylinders, &c., &c. All the iron used is raised in the neighbouring hills, and the coal dug likewise, which is charred, an invention which must have been of the greatest consequence after the quantity of cord wood in the kingdom declined. Mr Darby in his works employs near 1,000 people, including colliers. There are five furnaces in the Dale, and two of them are his. The next considerable proprietor is Mr Wilkinson, whose machine for boring cannon from the solid cast is at Posenail [Posenhall], and very curious.[1]

The colliers earn 20*d.* a day, those who get limestone

---

[1] Wilkinson's boring well was actually at Willey, not Posenhall [Ed.].

1s. 4d., the founderers 8s. to 10s. 6d. a week. Boys of 14 earn 1s. a day at drawing coal baskets in the pits. The coal mines are from 20 yards to 120 deep. . . . There may be about 1,000 acres of coal on the Benthall side of the river, and 2,000 on the Dale side. These ironworks are in a very flourishing situation, rising rather than the contrary.

Coalbrookdale itself is a very romantic spot. It is a winding glen between two immense hills which break into various forms and all thickly covered with wood, forming the most beautiful sheets of hanging wood. Indeed too beautiful to be much in unison with that variety of horrors art has spread at the bottom: the noise of the forges, mills, &c., with all their vast machinery, the flames bursting from the furnaces with the burning of the coal and the smoke of the limekilns are altogether sublime, and would unite well with craggy and bare rocks, like St Vincent's at Bristol.

Annals of Agriculture, IV (1785) 165–8

3. CANALS

Young made his extensive examination of the Bridgewater Canal some ten years after the beginning of this famous project. As a feat of engineering and a valuable means of exploiting the resources of the Manchester area it evidently made a great impression on him. More than thirty pages and several illustrations were devoted to the canal in the third volume of his *Northern Tour*, and it is clear that he expected his tour of inspection to become a regular excursion for visitors to the area. Indeed, the canal, with its aqueduct over the river Irwell – 250 feet of masonry carried 39 feet above the river level – its sunken roads by which land traffic was carried under it, the system of 'doors', as Young called them, which prevented loss of water should the banks be breached, and the tunnel at Worsley which took the waterway deep into the heart of the Duke's mines, became some of the most remarkable sights of the new industrial age. Though not quite the first English canal, its scale and ingenuity stirred the imagination of the time and ushered in the great period of canal-building which embraced the next seventy years.

In the following passage Young showed, as might be expected, an appreciation of the advantages which the canal offered for the drainage and manuring of farm land, the possibility it provided for reclaiming Trafford Moss, and the achievement of successfully converting the Duke's moss or bog into useful pastures by drainage works and the spreading on the surface of waste stone and spoil from the coal mines:

The original design of the Duke of Bridgewater was to cut a canal from Worsley, an estate of his Grace's abounding with coal mines, to Manchester, for the easy conveyance of his coals to so considerable a market; and in 1758–9 an Act of Parliament for that purpose was obtained. The course of the canal prescribed by this Act was afterwards varied by the same authority and the Duke further enabled greatly to extend his plan, for he now determined, and with uncommon spirit, to make his canal branch not only from Worsley to Manchester, but also form a part of the canal between both to Stockport and Liverpool. The idea was a noble one, and ranks this spirited young nobleman with the most useful geniuses of this or any age. But the execution of so great a plan teemed with difficulties that required a perpetual exertion of abilities fertile in resources.

The first point in viewing this navigation is to send from Manchester to Worsley to speak for a boat to carry your party the whole tour. (By the by, it is a strange affair that the town of Manchester does not possess a boat for the accommodation of its own inhabitants and strangers who come to see it. For want of one you may very probably wait a day or two.) And in the meantime you may employ yourself in viewing the works at Manchester. . . .

We next took possession of the pleasure boat we had before spoken for and steered for Worsley. The first objects we met with were two weirs more at Cornbrook, formed on the same principles as that in Castlefield, swallowing up rivulets in central wells, which convey the water in subterraneous passages under the canal, and permit it to rise again on the other side and flow on in its usual course.

Passing on, the canal runs chiefly along the sides of natural banks, which course was very judiciously chosen for the convenience of possessing not only one bank perfectly firm and secure, but plenty of earth ready for making the other. Just before we came to Throstlenest Bridge I observed a projecting piece of masonry in the canal which, on enquiry, I found to be the case of a canal door, for I know not what other name to

give it. It is upon the same principle as that at the mouth of
the subterranean passage in which the boats unload in Castlefield. . . .

Next we came to Leicester Bridge (under it another canal
door), and passing through it I observed on the left hand a
small waterfall which is the mouth of a main drain made by
the farmer, with smaller ones that lead into it, all covered,
the excellent effect of which is here strikingly visible, for the
land on that side was perfectly dry, but on the other side the
canal very wet, though not much rain had fallen.

At Weather-Meetings we passed another canal door. Passing
the mouth of the canal that leads to Altrincham, &c., and under
Taylor's Bridge you catch a view of Mars Bridge in a pretty
situation, the surrounding country fine: you look over it,
scattered with seats, houses, &c., in a pleasing manner. This
part of the canal runs through Trafford Moss, which is a peat-
earth, black moor. It is a great pity that the noble advantage of
a water carriage through the heart of this moor to so fine a
market as Manchester does not induce the owners to cultivate
this waste tract, which might, beyond all doubt, be applied to
numerous uses far more profitable than yielding peat in a
country so abounding with coals.

The next object that presents itself is the work at Barton
Bridge, which is one of the principal undertakings in the
whole navigation, and a wondrous one it certainly is. The canal
is here, in its usual breadth, carried (Roman aqueduct-like)
on arches over the large and navigable river Irwell. The
aqueduct is 200 yards long and 36 feet wide. It crosses the
Irwell on three large arches, the centre of which spans 63 feet;
and is carried with amazing labour through a valley filled up
to receive it. . . .

The effect of coming at once on to Barton Bridge and
looking *down* upon a large river, with barges of great burden
sailing on it, and *up* to another river, hung in the air, with
barges towing along it, form altogether a scenery somewhat
like enchantment and exhibit at once a view that must give
you an idea of prodigious labour; for the canal is here not only
carried over the Irwell but likewise across a large valley, being
banked up on each side in a surprising manner to form a mound
for the water, and the channel also filled up to the usual depth,
that the banks, at a place where they are entirely artificial and

consequently weaker than where natural, might not be endangered by the great pressure of so large a body of water as the depth here filled up would have contained. And I should remark that it is a maxim throughout this whole navigation to keep the canal of an equal depth everywhere. I believe it scarce ever varies above six inches, from four feet to four feet six inches.

The method Mr Brindley takes to fill up a channel, where too deep, is a most admirable one. He builds two very long boats, fixes them within two feet of each other and then erects upon them a triangular trough large enough to contain 17 tons of earth. The bottom of this trough is a line of trapdoors which, upon drawing a pin, fly open at once and discharge the whole burden in an instant. These boats are filled anywhere from the banks where the earth is in superfluous quantities, by wheelbarrowing it on a plank laid from the shore to the trough. The boat is then drawn over the spot which is to be filled up and the earth there dropped. It is astonishing what a vast saving is made by this invention. In common management to conduct a canal level across a valley, and without locks, would consume the revenue of a whole county; but such inventions as these ease the expense at least 5,000 per cent. . . .

I should tell you that any part of this aqueduct can be repaired without damaging the rest of the canal or losing more water than is contained within a small space on each side the decayed part; for several doors of the same nature as those already described are fixed in the channel, and also trapdoors or tubes (if I may so call them) at the bottom, &c., of the aqueduct, through which, by drawing a few plugs, the water would presently be discharged into the Irwell and the part to be repaired laid dry at once – a contrivance which is undoubtedly of vast consequence.

But there are other works at Barton which claim our attention besides the crossing the river. Two roads here came athwart the navigation, and happening in this valley where the canal is so much higher than the level of the country, to have built bridges would have cost immense sums as the rise would have required them half as long as that at Westminster. The method, therefore, taken by Mr Brindley was to sink the road gradually on both sides, and turning a large arch, to carry the canal over the roads as well as the river; and this is practised with both so that in going under it you sink gradually on one side and rise in the same manner on the other. . . .

The water in the tunnel at Worsley is upon the level of that in the canal, being the same so that the boats loaded with coals come out of the very mine itself. The first entrance, for 1,000 yards, is $6\frac{1}{2}$ feet wide and $7\frac{1}{2}$ feet high, including the water which is 3 feet 4 inches deep. It is already continued 750 yards further, 10 feet wide, and it is said (how true I know not) that it will be carried on at least a mile and a half further. I took some time to explore the horrid caverns of these mines and found on an attentive examination that the method of conducting the business of them was nearly as follows:

The seams (or in these mines, rather veins) of coal branch divers ways, some are above the tunnel, and some below it; as fast as the coal is got the space is cleared and arched for a road to move the coal on. This is done in little four-wheel waggons which contain 10 cwt. of coals, and [each] is pushed along by a man setting his head and hands against it (the road being laid on purpose for it). The roads all lead to the tunnel. When the man with the waggon comes over a well (of which there are several) that is sunk from the road through the arch of the tunnel, and under which the boats are fixed, he stops on a framework of wood, which turns on pivots, and is so contrived that upon drawing up a part of one end of the waggon some of the coals drop out, and then the waggon is tilted up and all the rest follow them, falling into the boat beneath either promiscuously, or directed through a tube to fill a box at a time at pleasure, which work is performed almost instantaneously and the waggons sent off again for a fresh cargo.

But as the arches (roads) through the mine in many places cross each other, it would there have been impracticable for a man to push so great a weight around a turning; to remove which objection the square of the floor in the cross of the roads is all of wood, and turns upon a central pivot of iron, so that a man stopping when the waggon comes exactly on to the square, and turning it till it faces the road he is to go, he then pushes on without the least interruption.

The coals that arise in the branches of the mine *below* the tunnel are drawn up through wells into those *above* it, and then conveyed like the rest in waggons to the boats. When they are loaded they are linked together in a gang; and for the convenience of drawing them out there is a rail on each side of the tunnel for the person who stands in the first boat to hold with his hands and draw himself along; which gives him so great a power that a boy of seventeen has drawn out a gang of 21 boats loaded, which at seven tons each is 147 tons. But this is only one instance, and out of the common course of business. They commonly bring out a gang at a time, which is four or six, and as soon as they are out of the tunnel they are drawn by mules to Manchester, &c.

The tunnel, where it passes through earth or coal, is surrounded with brickwork, but through the rock is only hewn out. At the distance of about a thousand yards from the mouth it divides into two, which branch different ways for the convenience of loading coals in the above compendious manner in every part of the mine, and more branches are in contemplation. It has been asserted that those who go up both passages travel therein three miles, but this is an exaggeration.

Every here and there along the tunnel are wells, bricked from it to the top of the hill for the admision of air, the exhalation of damps, and the letting down men for reparations in case of accidents. I have read of tin tubes for the conveyance of air into this mine, but there is no such thing: the shafts, passages, and tunnel supply it sufficiently.

As there generally is much superfluous water in coal mines, it was a very beneficial scheme to cut this tunnel for draining that water away, and at the same time for carrying the navigation into the heart of the colliery. Such bold and decisive strokes are the finest proof of inventive genius, of that penetration which sees into futurity, and prevents obstructions unthought of by the vulgar mind merely by foreseeing them. A man with such ideas moves in a sphere that is to the rest of the world imaginary, or at best a *terra incognita*.

The best way of viewing the extent of the mines is by going down the shaft and coming out by the tunnel, and sometimes you must either take this method (which was my own case) or not see it all, for boats are not always going in nor to be had for that purpose, but you will seldom fail of an empty boat within by which your guide (the hostler, I think, of the inn) will convey you out. . . .

The navigation is carried a mile and a half beyond Worsley

into the middle of a large bog, called here a moss, belonging to the Duke, and merely for the use of draining it and conveying manures to improve it. It is greatly to that nobleman's honour to find him attending, and at a considerable expense, to matters of husbandry in the midst of undertakings that would alone convey his name with peculiar brilliancy to the latest posterity.

The bog is of large extent, extremely wet, and so rotten that before it is improved it will not even bear a man. The Duke begins by cutting small drains, very near each other, which soon render the surface pretty firm. Then his barges bring the chippings of stone and other rubbish which arise in digging the coals, and which are brought out of the mine exactly in the same manner, only instead of going to market to be sold they are converted into money in another way by being brought hither. This rubbish is wheel-barrowed out of the barges on boards on to the land, which is greatly improved by it; the surface soon becomes sound, the aquatic spontaneous growth disappears by degrees, better herbage comes, and thus it is converted into profitable pasture without any paring, burning, or ploughing. Some of the long shivers of the stone will not crumble with the frosts; such are picked up, laid in heaps, and carried back to the stone yard where they are squared for buildings or converted to other uses.

As fast as the bog becomes improved the canal is extended for the sake of going on with the work; and almost at the end of it his Grace is building a small house for an overseer, situated upon land which once would not have borne even the men employed now in building on it.

This improvement is of a new kind, and peculiarly useful in the neighbourhood of quarries, stonemasons' yards, mines in rocks, &c., &c. In this instance it is of noble advantage for the rubbish would be troublesome at Worsley and expensive to carry out of the way; so that this improvement must be considered as another *part* of this grand WHOLE, which is so admirably connected and by itself so astonishingly supported.

Northern Tour (1770) III 251–81

On a visit to Birmingham some twenty years later, Young paused to admire the great advance in canal communications which had made Birmingham 'the first manufacturing town in the world'. The city now had connections by water with Hull, Liverpool, Bristol, Oxford and London. The recent developments to which he referred were the completion of the Oxford and Coventry Canal in 1789, which formed part of a network of canals linking the rivers Mersey, Trent, Severn and Thames, thus straddling the industrial heart of the country. Wages in Birmingham, as Young noted, were very high, which showed, he said, that cheapness of provisions was not essential for industrial growth, labour being at least 150 per cent dearer in Birmingham than in Norwich, though the prices of provisions were similar. It was not necessary, therefore, for agriculture to be ill-rewarded in order for industry to flourish. Again Young shows in the following passage his interest in economic expansion and the growth of employment:

The capital improvement wrought since I was here before is the canal to Oxford, Coventry, Wolverhampton, &c. The port, as it may be called, or double canal head in the town, crowded with coal barges, is a noble spectacle with that prodigious animation which the immense trade of this place could alone give. I looked around me with amazement at the change effected in twelve years; so great that this place may now probably be reckoned, with justice, the first manufacturing town in the world. From this port and these quays you may now go by water to Hull, Liverpool, Bristol, Oxford (130 miles), and London. The cut was opened through the coal mines to Wolverhampton in 1769, in 1783 into the new mines of Wednesbury, and to the junction with the Coventry canal at Fazeley, near Tamworth. From Birmingham to the Staffordshire canal is 22 miles, and to Fazeley 15. In the 22 miles from hence to Wolverhampton only three locks; but down to Fazeley there are 44 locks; not one rivulet to supply water, and only 30 acres of reservoirs, the water coming out of the earth. At Ocher hills they have a powerful steam engine for throwing back the waste water: and in the whole extent one that cost £4,000, another of £3,000, another of £2,500, another of £1,200, and yet another at present building that will cost £3,500. The first-mentioned works at the charge of £200 for six months. The old and new cuts were executed at the expense of about £250,000; one mile where it is open to the depth of 44 feet [cost] £30,000 for sinking only 18 feet lower than the original level. There are 13 locks between the port and Deritan, 8 feet 2 inches wide, and the boats 7 feet; to pass the 13 takes only two hours. Coals, before these canals were made, were 6d. per cwt. at Birmingham, now 4½d. The consumption is about 200,000 tons a year, which exhausts about 20 or 22 acres; it employs 40 boats, each 20 ton a day for the six summer months, besides 15 to 20 boats to Oxford, a new supply since the new cut. In the Wednesbury mines the coal is 10 yards thick, and in some even to 12 and 14 [yards], a thing elsewhere almost unheard of: a cubic yard they reckon a ton. Shares in the navigation, which were at first done at 140 per cent, are now at 1040. I was assured that shares in the Aire and Calder navigation are yet higher, even 100 per cent per annum.

These immense works, which wear so animated a face of business, correspond well with the prodigious increase of the town, which I viewed to good advantage from the top of the new church of St Paul. It is now a very great city indeed; and it was abundantly curious to have it pointed out to me the parts added since I was here. They form the greatest part of the town, and carry in their countenance undoubted marks of their modern date. In 1768 the population was under 30,000; now the common calculation is 70,000, but more accurate calculations extend it to 80,000, which I am told is the number assigned by Dr Priestley.[1] In the last ten years above 4,000 new houses have been built; and the increase is at present going on much more rapidly, for I was told that the number this year is not less than 700.

The earnings of the workmen in the manufacture are various, but in general very high: a boy of 10 or 12 years 2s. 6d. to 3s. a week; a woman from 4s. to 20s. a week, average about 6s.; men from 10s. to 25s. a week, and some much higher; colliers earn yet more. These are immense wages when it is considered that the whole family is sure of constant, steady employment; indeed they are so great that I am inclined to think labour higher at Birmingham than in any place in Europe, a most curious circumstance for the politician to reflect on, and which shows of how little effect to manufactures is cheap labour, for here is the most flourishing fabric that was

[1] The increase is exaggerated somewhat; modern figures are 35,000 in 1760 and 71,000 in 1801 [Ed.].

perhaps ever known, paying the highest rates of labour. Such an instance ought to correct those common notions that have been retailed from hand to hand a thousand times that cheap provisions are necessary for the good of manufactures because cheap provisions suppose cheap labour, which is a combination founded in ignorance and error. Provisions at Birmingham are at the same rate as everywhere else in England, for it is remarkable that the level of price at present is very general, except the division of the east and west of the kingdom for corn; but while Birmingham and Norwich eat their provisions at nearly the same price (with allowance that the former is much the more quick, ready, and active market), the price of labour is at least 150 per cent higher in one of those places than the other.

Annals of Agriculture, XVI (1791) 532–5

4. ROADS

Arthur Young's violent expostulations on the subject of English roads have entered almost into the realm of folklore. His accounts, picturesque as they are, no doubt lost something in accuracy in the telling. Nevertheless, to be fair, Young noted good roads when he came to them. His most scathing comments were reserved for the turnpiked highways which, despite the tolls, remained dangerous, toilsome and slow; and he did not hesitate to speak his mind also when the landowners and farmers had neglected to secure improvement of a heavily used but inadequate thoroughfare. With his economist's concern he was well aware that bad roads made for smaller loads and slower journeys, thus raising transport costs. When advising farmers on hiring a farm, he pointed out (excerpt (3)) that a more than average distance from market, especially in a district of bad roads, was a severe disadvantage. In his part of the country (Suffolk and Essex), where the round journey to market might be 25 miles, the carriage of wheat, according to his calculation, employed two men and five horses for two days, cost 2s. a quarter, or something approaching a twentieth of the market price, and so represented a considerable drain on a farmer's profit:

(1) Of all the cursed roads that ever disgraced this kingdom in the very ages of barbarism, none ever equalled that from Billericay to the King's Head at Tilbury. It is for near 12

miles so narrow that a mouse cannot pass by any carriage; I saw a fellow creep under his waggon to assist me to lift, if possible, my chaise over a hedge. The ruts are of an incredible depth – and a pavement of diamonds might as well be fought for as a quarter [farthing]. The trees everywhere overgrow the road so that it is totally impervious to the sun, except at a few places. And to add to all the infamous circumstances which concur to plague a traveller I must not forget the eternally meeting with chalk-waggons, themselves frequently stuck fast till a collection of them are in the same situation, and 20 or 30 horses may be tacked to each to draw them out one by one.

After this description will you – can you believe me when I tell you that a turnpike was much solicited for by some gentlemen to lead from Chelmsford to the ferry at Tilbury Fort, but was opposed by the Bruins of this country – whose horses are torn in pieces with bringing chalk through these vile roads. I do not imagine that the kingdom produces such an instance of detestable stupidity; and yet in this tract are found numbers of farmers who cultivate above £1,000 worth of land a year. Besides those already mentioned, we find a Skinner and a Towers who each rent near £1,500 a year, and a Read almost equal; but who are all perfectly well contented with their roads. . . .

[On the road to South Wales] But my dear sir, what am I to say of the roads in this country! The turnpikes! as they have the assurance to call them, and the hardiness to make one pay for. From Chepstow to the half-way house between Newport and Cardiff they continue mere rocky lanes, full of hugeous stones as big as one's horse and abominable holes. The first six miles from Newport they were so detestable, and without either direction-posts or milestones, that I could not well persuade myself I was on the turnpike but had mistook the road, and therefore asked everyone I met, who answered me to my astonishment, Ya-as. Whatever business carries you into this country avoid it, at least till they have good roads. If they were good, travelling would be very pleasant, for cultivated hills are of all other tracts of country the most picturesque, and most of these hills (which in more level countries would be called mountains) are cultivated to the very tops, and cut into very beautiful enclosures by quick

hedges. I must, however, allow that the last 16 miles to
Cowbridge they are exceeding good, the stones bound
firmly together, no loose ones, nor any ruts.

Southern Tour (1768) pp. 72–3, 120–1

(2) [An account of some roads in northern England.] From
Newton to Stokesley in Cleveland. Cross [i.e. connecting road
between turnpikes], and execrably bad. You are obliged to
cross the moors they call Black Hambledon over which the
road runs in narrow hollows that admit a south-country
chaise with such difficulty that I reckon this part of the
journey made at the hazard of my neck. The going down
into Cleveland is beyond all description terrible, for
you go through such steep, rough, narrow, rocky precipices
that I would sincerely advise any friend to go a hundred
miles about to escape it. The name of this pass is very
judicious, Scarthneck, that is scare nick, or frighten the
devil.

To Kirkleatham. Cross. This road is a rare instance of the
public spirit of the gentlemen of Cleveland who determined not only to convert the worst roads in England
into good ones, but to effect it without the least tax upon
the traveller. They are doing it by subscription. It was
set on foot and greatly promoted by Charles Turner,
esquire. . . .

To Preston. Turnpike. Very bad.

To Wigan. Ditto. I know not in the whole range of
language terms sufficiently expressive to describe this infernal
road. To look over a map and perceive that it is a principal
one, not only to some towns, but even whole counties, one
would naturally conclude it to be at least decent; but let me
most seriously caution all travellers who may accidentally
purpose to travel this terrible country to avoid it as they
would the devil, for a thousand to one but they break their
necks or limbs by overthrows or breakings down. They will
here meet with ruts, which I actually measured, four feet
deep, and floating with mud only from a wet summer; what
therefore must it be after a winter? The only mending it in
places receives is the tumbling in some loose stones which
serve no other purpose but jolting a carriage in the most
intolerable manner. These are not merely opinions but facts,

for I actually passed three carts broken down in these 18 miles of execrable memory.

Northern Tour (1770) IV 576–81

(3) [One must consider] the loss of carrying a *small* load of every commodity on account of bad roads when a *large* one would be carried were the roads good. This raises the expenses of every journey prodigiously; but very slight calculations will show this point in its true colours.

The distance from the market to which the corn is carried is also a point of great consequence. Perhaps the average distance over the whole kingdom does not exceed a day's journey in going and returning. I believe the average distance is not so great, as in many counties the nearest market-town is the place to carry to, as well as to sell at. A day's work may be reckoned 10 miles, which is done with ease. Now if a farm in this respect is above the average of farms the person who hires it should consider the evil in the rent he offers.

In Suffolk and Essex 25 miles are a common distance, and the roads none of the best. It is there two complete and hard days' work to carry 20 quarters of wheat, or even barley, to market. The expense is enormous, as will appear from a slight calculation:

	£	s.	d.
The use of 5 horses on such an occasion is undoubtedly to be reckoned at 2s. 6d. a horse per day	1	5	0
The two men are allowed for their expenses		5	0
They carry with them a meal of bread and cheese, and 2 or 3 quarts of ale; call it		2	0
Their time		4	0
Wear and tear of the wagon and harness: this cannot be reckoned at less than		3	0
Sundry small expenses		1	0
	2	0	0

It is true they sometimes gain back-carriage of coals, for which 18s. is paid, but then the wear and tear and use of the horses are greater, and consequently the profit by it the less. But back-carriage is, however, a mere uncertainty, and therefore not to be taken into any account.

Here we find the expense of carrying out the corn amounts alone to 2s. a quarter, which is prodigious. Suppose a farmer raises 500 quarters in a year, the expense of the carriage runs up so high as £50, full £30 of which ought to be reckoned as extraordinary and charged to the land with rent.

Some savings may be made, it is true, by using broad-wheeled waggons, for which reason they should ever be used on farms large enough for 9 or 10 horses; but then others not so large will raise greater quantities of corn than I have calculated, and consequently cannot have those machines for want of the proper number of horses.

These hints, I apprehend, are sufficient to prove that goodness of roads, and a moderate distance from market, are circumstances highly necessary to be attended to in the hiring a farm; and that, if they are wanting, the rent ought to be estimated accordingly.

The Farmer's Guide in Hiring and Stocking Farms
(1770) pp. 62–4

CHAPTER V

Arthur Young Abroad

I. THE TOUR IN IRELAND

Young made a number of visits to Ireland between 1776 and 1779 when he was employed as the agent of Lord Kingsborough, and his account of the country has long been regarded as one of the most valuable sources for the period. In his *A Tour in Ireland* Young followed his usual procedure of first recounting the course of his journeys round the countryside, filled out with 'minutes' or notes on the standards of farming, systems of tenure, and the conditions of the peasants, followed by extended summaries of his material together with the conclusions which he drew from them. The first selection below consists of passages taken from the travel minutes, illustrating the variety of conditions to be found in the country, and showing also that, despite their extreme poverty, the Irish peasants exhibited a love of sports and amusements. The second and third selections deal with the practice of letting land to cottagers through the medium of middlemen, and conclude with Young's views on the state of the labouring poor. Both of these are taken from Part II of the work, that in which he brought together and summarised his impressions of the country.

Many of his pages are of considerable interest, not merely for their vivid descriptions of labouring life in Ireland at this time but also because of the incidental light thrown on English conditions, for Young was naturally inclined to draw comparisons and contrasts between the two countries. His findings on Irish poverty were not perhaps so adverse as might be expected, although it should be remembered that he visited the country much before the worst effects of over-population and under-employment became felt. It is clear, however, that already many of the peasants were subsisting on a diet consisting mainly of milk and potatoes, and were living under miserable conditions. Very noticeable, too, was the contrast between the degree of independence and equality before the law enjoyed by the English labourer and the state of subjection in which many Irish peasants existed. Emigration from the Protestant manufacturing districts was apparently well under way in Young's time, and he has some interesting remarks on the causes of this movement which was to become so marked a feature of Ireland in the next hundred years and more:

(1) [Carton, Co. Kildare, to Summerhill, Co. Meath] The country is cheerful and rich; and if the Irish cabins continue like what I have hitherto seen, I shall not hesitate to pronounce their inhabitants as well off as most English cottagers. They are built of mud walls 18 inches or 2 feet thick, and well thatched, which are far warmer than the thin clay walls in England. Here are few cottars without a cow, and some of them two. A bellyful invariably of potatoes, and generally turf for fuel from a bog. It is true they have not always chimneys to their cabins, the door serving for that and window too. If their eyes are not affected with the smoke it may be an advantage in warmth. Every cottage swarms with poultry, and most of them have pigs. . . .

In general the complete family of cows, calves, hogs, poultry, and children pig together in the cabin; fuel they have in the utmost plenty. Great numbers of families are also supported by the neighbouring lakes, which abound prodigiously with fish. A child with a packthread and a crooked pin will catch perch enough in an hour for the family to live on the whole day. Besides perch, there is pike upwards of five feet long, bream, tench, trout of ten pounds, and as red as salmon, and fine eels. All these are favourable circumstances, and are very conspicuous in the numerous and healthy families among them.

Reverse the medal: they are ill-clothed and make a wretched appearance, and what is worse, are much oppressed by many who make them pay too dear for keeping a cow, horse, &c. They have a practice also of keeping accounts with the labourers, contriving by that means to let the poor wretches have very little cash for their year's work. This is a great oppression, farmers and gentlemen keeping accounts with the poor is a cruel abuse: so many days' work for a cabin, so many for a potato garden, so many for keeping a horse, and so many for a cow, are clear accounts which a poor man can understand well, but farther it ought never to go; and when he has worked out what he has of this sort, the rest of his work ought punctually to be paid him every

Saturday night. Another circumstance mentioned was the excessive practice they have in general of pilfering. They steal everything they can lay their hands on, and I should remark that this is an account which has been very generally given me: all sorts of iron hinges, chains, locks, keys, &c.; gates will be cut in pieces, and conveyed away in many places as fast as built; trees as big as a man's body and that would require ten men to move, gone in a night. Lord Longford has had the new wheels of a car stolen as soon as made. Good stones out of a wall will be taken for a fire-hearth, &c., though a breach is made to get at them. In short, everything, and even such as are apparently no use to them; nor is it easy to catch them for they never carry their stolen goods home but to some bog-hole. Turnips are stolen by car-loads, and two acres of wheat plucked off in a night. In short, their pilfering and stealing is a perfect nuisance. How far it is owing to the oppression of laws aimed solely at the religion of these people, how far to the conduct of the gentlemen and farmers, and how far to the mischievous disposition of the people themselves, it is impossible for a passing traveller to ascertain. I am apt to believe that a better system of law and management would have good effects. . . .

The state of the poor in the whole county of Kerry is represented as exceedingly miserable, owing to the conduct of men of property, who are apt to lay the blame on what they call land pirates or men who offer the highest rent, and who, in order to pay this rent, must and do re-let all the cabin lands at an extravagant rise, which is assigning over all the cabins to be devoured by one farmer. The cottars on a farm cannot go from one to another in order to find a good master, as in England; for all the country is in the same system, and no redress to be found. Such being the case, the farmers are enabled to charge the price of labour as *low* as they please, and rate the land as *high* as they like. This is an evil which oppresses them cruelly, and certainly has its origin in its landlords when they set their farms, setting all the cabins with them, instead of keeping them tenants to themselves. The oppression is the farmer valuing the labour of the poor at fourpence or fivepence a day, and paying that in land rated much above its value. Owing to this the poor are depressed; they live upon potatoes and sour milk, and the poorest of them only salt and water to them, with now and then a herring. Their milk is bought; for very few keep cows, scarce any pigs, but a few poultry. Their circumstances are incomparably worse than they were twenty years ago; for they had all cows, but then they wore no linen: all now have a little flax. To these evils have been owing emigrations, which have been considerable. . . .

Dancing is very general among the poor people, almost universal in every cabin. Dancing-masters of their own rank travel through the country from cabin to cabin, with a piper or blind fiddler, and the pay is sixpence a quarter. It is an absolute system of education. Weddings are always celebrated with much dancing, and a Sunday rarely passes without a dance. There are very few among them who will not, after a hard day's work, gladly walk seven miles to have a dance. John is not so lively, but then a hard day's work with him is certainly a different affair from what it is with Paddy. Other branches of education are likewise much attended to, every child of the poorest family learning to read, write, and cast accounts.

There is a very ancient custom here for a number of country neighbours among the poor people to fix upon some young woman that ought, as they think, to be married. They also agree upon a young fellow as a proper husband for her. This determined, they send to the fair one's cabin to inform her that on the Sunday following 'she is to be horsed', that is, carried on men's backs. She must then provide whisky and cider for a treat, as all will pay her a visit after mass for a hurling match. As soon as she is horsed the hurling begins, in which the young fellow appointed for her husband has the eyes of all the company fixed on him. If he comes off the conqueror, he is certainly married to the girl; but if another is victorious he as certainly loses her, for she is the prize of the victor. . . . Hurling is a sort of cricket, but instead of throwing the ball in order to knock down a wicket the aim is to pass it through a bent stick, the end stuck in the ground. In these matches they perform such feats of activity as ought to evidence the food they live on to be far from deficient in nourishment.

A Tour in Ireland, Dublin ed. (1780) I 28, 67–9;
II 249–51

OF THE TENANTRY OF IRELAND

It has been probably owing to the small value of land in Ireland before, and even through a considerable part of the present century, that landlords became so careless of the interests of posterity as readily to grant their tenants leases for ever. It might also be partly owing to the unfortunate civil wars and other intestine divisions, which for so long a space of time kept that unhappy country in a state rather of devastation than improvement. When a castle, or a fortified house, and a family strong enough for a garrison were essentially necessary to the security of life and property among protestants, no man could occupy land unless he had substance for defence as well as cultivation; short, or even determinable tenures were not encouragement enough for settling in such a situation of warfare. To increase the force of an estate leases for ever were given of lands, which from their waste state were deemed of little value. The practice once become common, continued long after the motives which originally gave rise to it, and has not yet ceased entirely in any part of the kingdom. Hence, therefore, tenants holding large tracts of land under a lease for ever, and which have been relet to a variety of under-tenants, must in this enquiry be considered as landlords.

The obvious distinction to be applied is that of the occupying and unoccupying tenantry: in other words, the real farmer, and the middle man. The very idea, as well as the practice, of permitting a tenant to relet at a profit rent, seems confined to the distant and unimproved parts of every empire. In the highly cultivated counties of England the practice has no existence, but there are traces of it in the extremities; in Scotland it has been very common; and I am informed that the same observation is partly applicable to France. In proportion as any country becomes improved the practice necessarily wears out.

It is in Ireland a question greatly agitated, whether the system has or has not advantages which may yet induce a landlord to continue in it. The friends to this mode of letting lands contend that the extreme poverty of the lower classes renders them such an insecure tenantry that no gentleman of fortune can depend on the least punctuality in the payment of rent from such people; and therefore to let a large farm to some intermediate person of substance at a lower rent, in order that the profit may be his inducement and reward for becoming a collector from the immediate occupiers and answerable for their punctuality, becomes necessary to any person who will not submit to the drudgery of such a minute attention. Also, that such a man will at least improve a spot around his own residence, whereas the mere cottar can do nothing. If the intermediate tenant is, or from the accumulation of several farms becomes, a man of property, the same argument is applicable to his reletting to another intermediate man, giving up a part of his profit to escape that trouble which induced the landlord to begin this system, and at the same time accounts for the number of tenants, one under another, who have all a profit out of the rent of the occupying farmer. In the variety of conversations on this point of which I have partook in Ireland I never heard any other arguments that had the least foundation in the actual state of the country; for as to ingenious theories which relate more to what might be than to what is, little regard should be paid to them.

That a man of substance whose rent is not only secure, but regularly paid, is in many respects a more eligible tenant than a poor cottar or little farmer, cannot be disputed; if the landlord looks no farther than those circumstances the question is at an end, for the argument must be allowed to have its full weight even to victory. But there are many other considerations: I was particularly attentive to every class of tenants throughout the kingdom, and shall therefore describe these middle men from whence their merit may be the more easily decided. Sometimes they are resident on a part of the land, but very often they are not. Dublin, Bath, London, and the country towns of Ireland contain great numbers of them; the merit of this class is surely ascertained in a moment; there cannot be a shadow of a pretence for the intervention of a man whose single concern with an estate is to deduct a portion from the rent of it. They are however sometimes resident on a part of the land they hire, where it is natural to suppose they would work some improvements; it is however very rarely the case. I have in different parts of the kingdom seen farms just fallen in after leases of three lives, of the duration of fifty, sixty, and even seventy years, in which the residence of the principal tenant was not to be distinguished from the cottared fields surrounding it. I was at first much surprised at this, but after repeated observation I found these men very generally were the masters of packs of wretched hounds, with which they wasted their time and money, and it is a notorious fact that they are the hardest drinkers in Ireland. Indeed the class of the small country gentlemen, chiefly consisting of these profit renters, seem at present to monopolize that drinking spirit which was, not many years ago, the disgrace of the kingdom at large: this I conjecture to be the reason why those who might improve are so very far from doing it; but there are still greater objections to them.

Living upon the spot, surrounded by their little under-tenants, they prove the most oppressive species of tyrant that ever lent assistance to the destruction of a country. They relet the land at short tenures to the occupiers of small farms, and often give no leases at all. Not satisfied with screwing up the rent to the uttermost farthing, they are rapacious and relentless in the collection of it. Many of them have defended themselves in conversation with me upon the plea of taking their rents partly in kind, when their undertenants are much distressed: 'What', say they, 'would the head landlord, suppose him a great nobleman, do with a miserable cottar, who, disappointed in the sale of a heifer, a few barrels of corn, or firkins of butter, brings his five instead of his ten guineas? But we can favour him by taking his commodities at a fair price, and wait for reimbursement until the market rises. Can my lord do that?' A very common plea, but the most unfortunate that could be used to anyone whoever remarked that portion of human nature which takes the garb of an Irish land jobber! For upon what issue does this remark place the question? Does it not acknowledge that calling for their rents when they cannot be paid in cash, they take the substance of the debtor at the very moment when he cannot sell it to another? Can it be necessary to ask what the price is? It is at the option of the creditor; and the miserable culprit meets his oppression, perhaps his ruin, in the very action that is trumpeted as a favour to him. It may seem harsh to attribute a want of feeling to any class of men, but let not the reader misapprehend me; it is the *situation*, not the *man*, that I condemn. An injudicious system places a great number of persons, not of any liberal rank in life, in a state abounding with a variety of opportunities of oppression, every act of which is profitable to themselves. I am afraid it is human nature for men to fail in such posts; and I appeal to the experience of mankind in other lines of life whether it is ever found advantageous to a poor debtor to sell his products or wares to his richer creditor at the moment of demand.

But farther: the dependence of the occupier on the resident middle man goes to other circumstances, personal service of themselves, their cars and horses, is exacted for leading turf, hay, corn, gravel, &c., insomuch that the poor undertenants often lose their own crops and turf from being obliged to obey these calls of their superiors. Nay, I have even heard these jobbers gravely assert that without undertenants to furnish cars and teams at half or two-thirds the common price of the country they could carry on no improvements at all; yet taking a merit to themselves for works wrought out of the sweat and ruin of a pack of wretches, assigned to their plunder by the inhumanity of the landholders.

In a word, the case is reducible to a short compass; intermediate tenants work no improvements; if non-resident they *cannot*, and if resident they *do not*; but they oppress the occupiers, and render them as incapable as they are themselves unwilling. The kingdom is an aggregate proof of these facts; for if long leases at low rents and profit incomes given would have improved it, Ireland had long ago been a garden. . . .

Let me next mention the circumstances of the occupiers. The variety of these is very great in Ireland. In the North, where the linen manufacture has spread, the farms are so small that ten acres in the occupation of one person is a large one, five or six will be found a good farm, and all the agriculture of the country so entirely subservient to the manufacture that they no more deserve the name of farmers than the occupier of a mere cabbage garden. In Limerick, Tipperary, Clare, Meath and Waterford there are to be found the greatest graziers and cow-keepers perhaps in the world, some who rent and occupy from £3,000 to £10,000 a year: these of course are men of property, and are the only

occupiers in the kingdom who have any considerable substance. The effects are not so beneficial as might be expected.
Rich graziers in England who have a little tillage usually
manage it well, and are in other respects attentive to various
improvements, though it must be confessed not in the same
proportion with great arable farmers; but in Ireland these
men are as errant slovens as the most beggarly cottars. The
rich lands of Limerick are in respect of fences, drains,
buildings, weeds, &c., in as waste a state as the mountains of
Kerry; the fertility of nature is so little seconded that few
tracts yield less pleasure to the spectator. From what I
observed I attributed this to the idleness and dissipation so
general in Ireland. These graziers are too apt to attend to
their claret as much as their bullocks, live expensively, and
being enabled from the nature of their business to pass nine-
tenths of the year without any exertion to industry, contract
such a habit of ease that works of improvement would be
mortifying to their sloth.

In the arable counties of Louth, part of Meath, Kildare,
Kilkenny, Carlow, Queen's, and part of King's, and Tipperary, they are much more industrious. It is the nature
of tillage to raise a more regular and animated attention to
business; but the farms are too small and the tenants too
poor to exhibit any appearances that can strike an English
traveller. They have a great deal of corn, and many fine
wheat crops; but being gained at the expense and loss of a
fallow, as in the open fields of England, they do not suggest
the ideas of profit to the individual or advantage to the state
which worse crops in a well-appointed rotation would do.
Their manuring is trivial, their tackle and implements
wretched, their teams weak, their profit small, and their
living little better than that of the cottars they employ. These
circumstances are the necessary result of the smallness of
their capitals, which even in these tillage counties do not
usually amount to a third of what an English farmer would
have to manage the same extent of land. The leases of these
men are usually three lives to protestants, and thirty-one years
to catholics.

The tenantry in the more unimproved parts, such as Cork,
Wicklow, Longford, and all the mountainous counties where
it is part tillage and part pasturage, are generally in a very

backward state. Their capitals are smaller than the class I just mentioned, and among them is chiefly found the practice of many poor cottars hiring large farms in partnership. They make their rents by a little butter, a little wool, a little corn, and a few young cattle and lambs. Their lands at extreme low rents are the most unimproved (mountain and bog excepted) in the kingdom. They have, however, more industry than capital; and with a very little management might be brought greatly to improve their husbandry. I think they hold more generally from intermediate tenants than any other set; one reason why the land they occupy is in so waste a state. In the mountainous tracts I saw instances of greater industry than in any other part of Ireland. Little occupiers who can get leases of a mountain side make exertions in improvement which, though far enough from being complete or accurate, yet prove clearly what great effects encouragement would have among them.

In the King's county and also in some other parts I saw many tracts of land, not large enough to be relet, which were occupied under leases for ever, very well planted and improved by men of substance and industry.

The poverty among the small occupying tenantry may be pretty well ascertained from their general conduct in hiring a farm. They will manage to take one with a sum surprisingly small; they provide labour, which in England is so considerable an article, by assigning portions of land to cottars for their potato gardens, and keeping one or two cows for each of them. To lessen the live stock necessary they will, whenever the neighbourhood enables them, take in the cattle at so much per month or season of any person that is deficient in pasturage at home, or of any labourers that have no land. Next, they will let out some old ley for grass potatoes to such labourers; and if they are in a county where corn acres are known they will do the same with some corn land. If there is any meadow on their farm they will sell a part of it as the hay grows. By all these means the necessity of a full stock is very much lessened, and by means of living themselves in the very poorest manner and converting every pig, fowl, and even egg into cash, they will make up their rent, and get by very slow degrees into somewhat better circumstances. Where it is the custom to take in partnership, the difficulties are easier got over, for one man brings a few sheep, another a cow, a third a horse, a fourth a car and some seed potatoes, a fifth a few barrels of corn, and so on, until the farm among them is tolerably stocked and hands upon it in plenty for the labour.

Ibid., Part II, II 17–23

(3)   FOOD

The food of the common Irish, potatoes and milk, have been produced more than once as an instance of the extreme poverty of the country, but this I believe is an opinion embraced with more alacrity than reflection. I have heard it stigmatized as being unhealthy and not sufficiently nourishing for the support of hard labour, but this opinion is very amazing in a country many of whose poor people are as athletic in their form, as robust, and as capable of enduring labour as any upon earth. The idleness seen among many when working for those who oppress them is a very contrast to the vigour and activity with which the same people work when themselves alone reap the benefit of their labour. To what country must we have recourse for a stronger instance than lime carried by little miserable mountaineers thirty miles on horses' backs to the foot of their hills, and up the steeps on their own. When I see the people of a country in spite of political oppression with well-formed vigorous bodies, and their cottages swarming with children; when I see their men athletic, and their women beautiful, I know not how to believe them subsisting on an unwholesome food.

At the same time, however, that both reason and observation convince me of the justice of these remarks, I will candidly allow that I have seen such an excess in the laziness of great numbers, even when working for themselves, and such an apparent weakness in their exertions when encouraged to work, that I have had my doubts of the heartiness of their food. But here arise fresh difficulties: were their food ever so nourishing I can easily conceive an habitual inactivity of exertion would give them an air of debility compared with a more industrious people. Though my residence in Ireland was not long enough to become a perfect master of the question, yet I have employed from twenty to fifty men for several months and found their habitual laziness or weakness so great, whether working by measure or by day, that I am absolutely convinced 1s. 6d. and even 2s. a day in Suffolk or Hertfordshire much cheaper than sixpence halfpenny at Mitchelstown. It would not be fair to consider this as a representation of the kingdom, that place being remarkably backward in every species of industry and improvement; but I am afraid this observation would hold true in a less degree for the whole. But is this owing to habit or food? Granting their food to be the cause, it decides very little against potatoes, unless they were tried with good nourishing beer instead of their vile potations of whisky. When they are encouraged or animate themselves to work hard, it is all by whisky, which though it has a notable effect in giving a perpetual motion to their tongues, can have but little of that invigorating substance which is found in strong beer or porter; probably it has an effect as pernicious as the other is beneficial. One circumstance I should mention which seems to confirm this: I have known the Irish reapers in Hertfordshire work as laboriously as any of our own men, and living upon potatoes which they procured from London but drinking nothing but ale. If their bodies are weak I attribute it to whisky, not potatoes; but it is still a question with me whether their miserable working arises from any such weakness or from an habitual laziness. A friend of mine always refused Irishmen work in Surrey, saying his bailiff could do nothing but settle their quarrels.

But of this food there is one circumstance which must ever recommend it, they have a bellyful, and that let me add is more than the superfluities of an Englishman leaves to his family: let any person examine minutely into the receipt and expenditure of an English cottage, and he will find that tea, sugar and strong liquors can come only from pinched bellies. I will not assert that potatoes are a better food than bread and cheese; but I have no doubt of a bellyful of the one being much better than half a bellyful of the other; still less have I that the milk of the Irishman is incomparably better than the small beer, gin, or tea of the Englishman; and this even for the father, how much better must it be for the poor infants; milk to them is nourishment, is health, is life.

If anyone doubts the comparative plenty which attends the board of a poor native of England and Ireland, let him attend to their meals: the sparingness with which our labourer eats his bread and cheese is well known; mark the Irishman's potatoe bowl placed on the floor, the whole family upon their hams around it, devouring a quantity almost incredible, the beggar seating himself to it with a hearty welcome, the pig taking his share as readily as the wife, the cocks, hens, turkeys, geese, the cur, the cat, and perhaps the cow – and all partaking of the same dish. No man can often have been witness of it without being convinced of the plenty, and I will add the cheerfulness, that attends it.

CLOTHING

The common Irish are in general clothed so very indifferently that it impresses every stranger with a strong idea of universal poverty. Shoes and stockings are scarcely ever found on the feet of children of either sex; and great numbers of men and women are without them: a change however, in this respect as in most others is coming in, for there are many more of them with those articles of clothing now than ten years ago.

An Irishman and his wife are much more solicitous to feed than to clothe their children: whereas in England it is surprising to see the expense they put themselves to to deck out children whose principal subsistence is tea. Very many of them in Ireland are so ragged that their nakedness is scarcely covered, yet are they in health and active. As to the want of shoes and stockings I consider it as no evil, but a much more cleanly custom than the beastiality of stockings and feet that are washed no oftener than those of our own poor. Women are oftener without shoes than men; and by washing their clothes nowhere but in rivers and streams, the cold, especially as they roast their legs in their cabins till they are *fire* spotted, must swell them to a wonderful size and horrid black and blue colour always met with both in young and old. They stand in rivers and beat the linen against the great stones found there with a beetle [club].

I remarked generally that they were not ill dressed of Sundays and holidays, and that black or dark blue was almost the universal hue.

HABITATIONS

The cottages of the Irish, which are all called cabins, are the most miserable looking hovels that can well be conceived: they generally consist of only one room; mud kneaded with straw is the common material of the walls; these are rarely above seven feet high, and not always above five or six; they are about two feet thick, and have only a door which lets in light instead of a window, and should let the smoke out instead of a chimney but they had rather keep it in: these two conveniences they hold so cheap that I have seen them both stopped up in stone cottages built by improving landlords; the smoke warms them, but certainly is as injurious to their eyes as it is to the complexions of the women, which in general in the cabins of Ireland has a near resemblance to that of a smoked ham. The number of the blind poor I think greater there than in England, which is probably owing to this cause.

The roofs of the cabins are rafters raised from the tops of the mud walls, and the covering varies; some are thatched with straw, potato stalks, or with heath, others only covered with sods of turf cut from a grass field; and I have seen several that were partly composed of all three. The bad repair these roofs are kept in, a hole in the thatch being often mended with turf, and weeds sprouting from every part, gives them the appearance of a weedy dunghill, especially when the cabin is not built with regular walls, but supported on one or perhaps on both sides by the banks of a broad dry ditch, the roof then seems a hillock, upon which perhaps the pig grazes. Some of these cabins are much less and more miserable habitations than I had ever seen in England. I was told they were the worst in Connaught, but I found it an error; I saw many in Leinster to the full as bad, and in Wicklow some worse than any in Connaught. When they are well roofed, and built not of stones, ill put together, but of mud, they are much warmer, independently of smoke, than the clay or lath and mortar cottages of England, the walls of which are so thin that a rat hole lets in the wind to the annoyance of the whole family. The furniture of the cabins is as bad as the architecture; in very many, consisting only of a pot for boiling their potatoes, a bit of a table, and one or two broken stools. Beds are not found universally, the family lying on straw, equally partook of by cows, calves and pigs, though the luxury of sties is coming in in Ireland, which excludes the poor pigs from the warmth of the bodies of their master and mistress. I remarked little hovels of earth thrown up near the cabins, and in some places they build their turf stacks hollow in order to afford shelter to the hogs. This is a general description, but the exceptions are very numerous. I have been in a multitude of cabins that had much useful furniture, and some even superfluous; chairs, tables, boxes, chest of drawers, earthenware, and in short most of the articles found in a middling English cottage; but upon enquiry, I very generally found that these acquisitions were all made within the last ten years, a sure sign of a rising national prosperity. I think the bad cabins and furniture the greatest instances of Irish poverty, and this must flow from the mode of payment for labour, which makes cattle so valuable to the peasant that every farthing they can spare is saved for their purchase: from hence also results another observation, which is that the apparent poverty of it is greater than the real; for the house of a man that is master of four or five cows will have scarce anything but deficiencies; nay, I was in the cabins of dairymen and farmers, not small ones, whose cabins were not at all better or better furnished than those of the poorest labourer; before, therefore, we can attribute it to absolute poverty we must take into the account the customs and inclinations of the people. In England a man's cottage will be filled with superfluities before he possesses a cow. I think the comparison much in favour of the Irishman; a hog is a much more valuable piece of goods than a set of tea things; and though his snout in a *crock* of potatoes is an idea not so poetical as

> ... *Broken tea cups, wisely kept for shew,*
> *Rang'd o'er the chimney, glisten'd in a row*

yet will the cottar and his family, at Christmas, find the solidity of it an ample recompence for the ornament of the other.

OPPRESSION

Before I conclude this article of the common labouring poor

in Ireland, I must observe that their happiness depends not
merely upon the payment of their labour, their clothes, or
their food; the subordination of the lower classes, degener-
ating into oppression, is not to be overlooked. The poor in
all countries, and under all governments, are both paid and
fed, yet is there an infinite difference between them in
different ones. This enquiry will by no means turn out so
favourable as the preceding articles. It must be very
apparent to every traveller through that country that
the labouring poor are treated with harshness, and are in all
respects so little considered that their want of importance
seems a perfect contrast to their situation in England,
of which country, comparatively speaking, they reign the
sovereigns. The age has improved so much in humanity
that even the poor Irish have experienced its influence, and
are everyday treated better and better; but still the remnant
of the old manners, the abominable distinction of religion,
united with the oppressive conduct of the little country
gentlemen, or rather vermin of the kingdom, who never were
out of it, altogether bear still very heavy on the poor people,
and subject them to situations more mortifying than we ever
behold in England. The landlord of an Irish estate inhabited
by Roman catholics is a sort of despot who yields obedience
in whatever concerns the poor, to no law but that of his
will. To discover what the liberty of a people is we must
live among them and not look for it in the statutes of the
realm: the language of written law may be that of liberty,
but the situation of the poor may speak no language but
that of slavery; there is too much of this contradiction
in Ireland; a long series of oppressions, aided by many very
ill-judged laws, have brought landlords into a habit of
exerting a very lofty superiority and their vassals into that
of an almost unlimited submission: speaking a language that
is despised, professing a religion that is abhorred, and being
disarmed, the poor find themselves in many cases slaves even
in the bosom of *written* liberty. Landlords that have resided
much abroad are usually humane in their ideas, but the habit
of tyranny naturally contracts the mind, so that even in this
polished age there are instances of a severe carriage towards
the poor which is quite unknown in England.

A landlord in Ireland can scarcely invent an order which

a servant, labourer, or cottar dares to refuse to execute. Nothing satisfies him but an unlimited submission. Disrespect or anything tending towards sauciness he may punish with his cane or his horsewhip with the most perfect security; a poor man would have his bones broke if he offered to lift his hand in his own defence. Knocking down is spoken of in the country in a manner that makes an Englishman stare. Landlords of consequence have assured me that many of their cottars would think themselves honoured by having their wives and daughters sent for to the bed of their master; a mark of slavery that proves the oppression under which such people must live. Nay, I have heard anecdotes of the lives of people being made free with without any apprehension of the justice of a jury. But let it not be imagined that this is common; formerly it happened every day, but law gains ground. It must strike the most careless traveller to see whole strings of cars whipped into a ditch by a gentleman's footman to make way for his carriage; if they are overturned or broken in pieces no matter, it is taken in patience; were they to complain they would perhaps be horsewhipped. The execution of the laws lies very much in the hands of justices of the peace, many of whom are drawn from the most illiberal class in the kingdom. If a poor man lodges a complaint against a gentleman, or any animal that chooses to call itself a gentleman, and the justice issues out a summons for his appearance, it is a fixed affront and he will infallibly be *called out*. Where MANNERS are in conspiracy against LAW, to whom are the oppressed people to have recourse? It is a fact that a poor man having a contest with a gentleman must – but I am talking nonsense, they know their situation too well to think of it; they can have no defence but by means of protection from one gentleman against another, who probably protects his vassal as he would the sheep he intends to eat. . . .

EMIGRATION

Before the American war broke, the Irish and Scotch emigrations were a constant subject of conversation in England and occasioned much discourse even in parliament. The common observation was that if they were not stopped those countries would be ruined, and they were generally attributed to a great rise of rents. Upon going over to Ireland I determined to omit no opportunities of discovering the cause and extent of this emigration, and my information, as may be seen in the minutes of the journey, was very regular. I have only a few general remarks to make on it here.

The spirit of emigrating in Ireland appeared to be confined to two circumstances, the presbyterian religion, and the linen manufacture. I heard of very few emigrants except among manufacturers of that persuasion. The catholics never went, they seem not only tied to the country but almost to the parish in which their ancestors lived. As to the emigration in the north, it was an error in England to suppose it a novelty which arose with the increase in rents. The contrary was the fact: it has subsisted perhaps forty years, insomuch that at the ports of Belfast, Derry, &c., the *passenger trade*, as they called it, had long been a regular branch of commerce which employed several ships and consisted in carrying people to America. The increasing population of the country made it an increasing trade, but when the linen trade was low the *passenger trade* was always high. At the time of Lord Donegal's letting his estate in the North the linen business suffered a temporary decline, which sent great numbers to America, and gave rise to the error that it was occasioned by the increase of his rents: the fact, however, was otherwise, for great numbers of those who went from his lands actually sold those leases for considerable sums, the hardship of which was supposed to have driven them to America. Some emigration, therefore, always existed, and its increase depended on the fluctuations of linen; but as to the *effect*, there was as much error in the conclusions drawn in England as before in the *cause*.

It is the misfortune of all manufactures worked for a foreign market to be upon an insecure footing; periods of declension will come, and when in consequence of them great numbers of people are out of employment the best circumstance is their enlisting in the army or navy; and it is the common result; but unfortunately the manufacture in Ireland (of which I shall have occasion to speak more hereafter) is not confined as it ought to be to towns, but spreads into all the cabins of the country. Being half farmers, half manufacturers, they have too much property in cattle, &c., to enlist when idle; if they convert it into cash it will enable them to pay their passage to America, an alternative always chosen in preference to the military life. The consequence is that they must live without work till their substance is quite consumed before they will enlist. Men who are in such a situation that from various causes they cannot work, and won't enlist, should emigrate; if they stay at home they must remain a burthen upon the community: emigration should not, therefore, be condemned in states so ill governed as to possess many people willing to work but without employment.

Ibid., Part II, II 32–7, 40–3

2. TRAVELS IN FRANCE

Young's *Travels in France*, first published in 1792, is his best-known and most easily accessible work, though unfortunately most modern editions omit the journeys in Catalonia and Italy which formed part of the original. The interest of the *Travels* is enhanced by their being in countries quite strange to Young himself and unknown to many of his readers. His commentaries, therefore, were broader in scope and more detailed, and he described aspects of the country – scenery, inns, manners, the extent of poverty – which in England he would have taken for granted or passed over very briefly. His visits to France took place in a period which saw the beginnings of the Revolution – he was in Paris during the deliberations of the States-General and witnessed the captivity of the royal family – and this gives to his first-hand accounts an additional interest which is almost as vital today as it was to contemporaries who lived through those years. Indeed, historians on both sides of the Channel have drawn heavily on Young for their picture of France at this critical juncture.

Young undertook three journeys in France in the years 1787–90. The route of his first journey, which lasted from 15 May to 11 November 1787, was from Calais to Paris, and then southwards via Orléans, Châteauroux, Limoges and Toulouse to Bagnères-de-Luchon, a spa in the Pyrenees. While his French travelling companions stayed in Bagnères-de-Luchon enjoying the company and diversions, Young, always eager to see as much as possible and fretful when idle, crossed into Spain. With a single companion he threaded his way through the wild and

Map 1 *Young's Travels in France*, 1787–90
(Contemporary international boundaries shown)

rugged Pyrenees, and proceeded as far south as Barcelona before returning to France. His return journey from Spain included an excursion through Languedoc along the Gulf of Lions as far as the Roman aqueduct at Pont-du-Gard, beyond Nîmes, before turning west again by a more inland route to Bagnères-de-Luchon. His homeward journey was via Bayonne, Auch, Bordeaux, Poitiers, Tours, Orléans, Fontainebleau, Paris, Lille, Dunkirk and Calais – a total of 2,200 miles travelled within the borders of France.

Young's experience of this journey determined him to make a second visit on his own so that he could be free to travel as he pleased and see what most interested him. His fame as an agriculturist had already gained him friends among the French aristocracy and, armed with letters of introduction Young was able to call on a number of leading French landowners and see many things that would not have been available to the ordinary traveller. The second journey, taken between 4 August and 15 October 1788, was his shortest, but still involved a route of some 1,200 miles through the provinces of Normandy and Brittany. Young's course took him from Calais via Amiens, Rouen, Le Havre, Caen, Cherbourg, Rennes, Brest, Nantes, Angers, and so back to Rouen, and thence to Dieppe, where he found a boat ready to sail for Brighton. He was not unduly put out by his mare's going blind at an early stage of the journey, but completed his route, and by the end of October he and his blind mare were safely back in Bradfield.

Young's third and longest journey followed between 6 June 1789 and 29 January 1790, and encompassed about 2,100 miles in France alone, besides an extensive excursion into Italy. On this last occasion he left Paris in greater style in a one-horse cabriolet or gig, which allowed him to carry more in the way of luggage as well as the samples of curious soils and products which he collected along the way. He spent three weeks in Paris between 8 and 27 June, visiting the French Royal Society of Agriculture, the Bibliothèque Royale, and the meetings of the States-General at Versailles. His route from Paris lay through north-eastern France via Nangis, Meaux, Épernay, Rheims and Châlons to Metz. From Metz he struck south-east towards Nancy and Strasbourg before turning south-west on a line through Colmar, Belfort, Dôle and Dijon to Moulins, some 160 miles south of Paris. Having completed this circuit of the north-east, Young next turned towards the south-east, leaving Moulins for Riom, Le Puy, Avignon, Aix and Marseilles. From Marseilles he proceeded eastwards along the Côte d'Azur to Toulon, reaching Nice, the gateway to Italy, on 16 September. At Toulon he sold his horse and chaise (having been wrongly advised not to take them into Italy) by the simple expedient of advertising them in the main street and waiting with them until a satisfactory buyer appeared. His return to France was made on 25 December via Chambéry and Lyons, and he moved rapidly northwards through Moulins, Briare and Nemours to reach Paris on 3 January, finally arriving home at Bradfield on 30 January 1790.

(a) Agriculture

Though much of the interest attaching to Young's continental journeys lies in the detail of a wide range of observations, his primary concern remained with agriculture. It is fitting, therefore,

that our first excerpt should deal, in part, with the striking
contrast which Young noted between the English aristocracy and
the French nobility in regard to their interest in promoting better
farming. This passage, incidentally, also brings out Young's
interest in the theatre: he seems to have gone to performances at
every opportunity and evidently had sufficient command of the
language to follow the plays; there is, too, a rather touching
tribute to his blind mare on quitting France at the end of his
second visit in 1788.

The other excerpts in this section record, first, Young's visit
to the Royal Society of Agriculture in Paris on 12 June 1789
and his doubts concerning the value of such societies, whether in
France or in England; and second, his summary of the findings of
his three years' examination of French farming. Among the interesting points which he makes are his conclusion that the value
of land in the two countries was roughly equal, but with England
having a decided advantage in yields of corn. French farmers
were under-equipped, and under-stocked in livestock, by English
standards, but the greatest weakness of French agriculture in his
view was the small size of the farms over much of the country,
a situation which gave rise to low standards of cultivation, poverty
among the farmers, and over-population of the countryside. It
is clear from Young's account that the rural backwardness still
evident in parts of France today had deep-seated origins, and
was plainly evident even before the Revolution, which in itself
merely relieved the peasants of their feudal obligations and did
little to solve the long-standing causes of rural poverty:

(1) La Roche-Guyon, OCT 10TH 1788

The Duc de la Rochefoucauld had the kindness to order the
steward to give me all the information I wanted relative to
the agriculture of the country, and to speak to such persons
as were necessary on points that he was in doubt about. At
an English nobleman's there would have been three or four
farmers asked to meet me, who would have dined with the
family amongst the ladies of the first rank. I do not exaggerate when I say that I have had this at least an hundred
times in the first houses of our islands. It is however a thing
that in the present state of manners in France would not be
met with from Calais to Bayonne, except by chance in the
house of some great lord that had been much in England,

and then not unless it was asked for. The nobility in France have no more idea of practising agriculture, and making it an object of conversation, except on the mere theory, as they would speak of a loom or a bowsprit, than of any other object the most remote from their habits and pursuits. I do not so much blame them for this neglect as I do that herd of visionary and absurd writers on agriculture who, from their chambers in cities, have, with an impertinence almost incredible, deluged France with nonsense and theory, enough to disgust and ruin the whole nobility of the kingdom.

OCT. 12TH. Part with regret from a society I had every reason to be pleased with.

OCT. 13TH. The 20 miles to Rouen, the same features. First view of Rouen sudden and striking; but the road doubling, in order to turn more gently down the hill, presents from an elbow the finest view of a town I have ever seen; the whole city with all its churches and convents, and its cathedral proudly rising in the midst, fills the vale. The river presents one reach, crossed by the bridge, and then dividing into two fine channels, forms a large island covered with wood; the rest of the vale of verdure and cultivation, of gardens and habitations, finish the scene in perfect unison with the great city that forms the capital feature. Wait on Mons. Dambourney, secretary of the Society of Agriculture, who was absent when I was here before. We had an interesting conversation on agriculture and on the means of encouraging it. I found, from this very ingenious gentleman that his plan of using madder green, which many years ago made so much noise in the agricultural world, is not practised at present anywhere; but he continues to think it perfectly practicable.

In the evening to the play, where Madame Crétal from Paris acted *Nina*, and it proved the richest treat I have received from the French theatre. She performed it with an inimitable expression, with a tenderness, a *naïveté*, and an elegance withal, that mastered every feeling of the heart against which the piece was written. Her expression is as delicious as her countenance is beautiful; in her acting, nothing overcharged, but all kept within the simplicity of nature. The house was crowded, garlands of flowers and laurel were thrown on the stage, and she was crowned by the other actors, but modestly removed them from her head as often as they were placed there. – 20 miles.

OCT. 14TH. Take the road to Dieppe. Meadows in the vale well-watered, and hay now making. Sleep at Tôtes.

OCT. 15TH. To Dieppe. I was lucky enough to find the passage-boat ready to sail; go on board with my faithful sure-footed blind friend. I shall probably never ride her again, but all my feelings prevent my selling her in France. Without eyes she has carried me in safety above 1,500 miles; and for the rest of her life she shall have no other master than myself; could I afford it this should be her last labour; some ploughing, however, on my farm she will perform for me, I dare say cheerfully.

Landing at the neat, new-built town of Brighthelmston [Brighton], offers a much greater contrast to Dieppe, which is old and dirty, than Dover does to Calais; and in the Castle inn I seemed for a while to be in fairyland; but I paid for the enchantment.

Travels in France, ed. C. Maxwell (Cambridge, 1950)
128–9 (10–15 Oct 1788)

(2) JUNE 12TH

To the Royal Society of Agriculture, which meets at the Hôtel de Ville, and of which being an *associé*, I voted and received a *jeton*, which is a small medal given to the members every time they attend in order to induce them to mind the business of their institution. It is the same at all royal academies, etc., and amounts in a year to a considerable and ill-judged expense; for what good is to be expected from men who would go only to receive their *jeton*? Whatever the motive may be, it seems well attended; near thirty were present; among them Parmentier, Vice-President, Cadet-de-Vaux, Fourcroy, Tillet, Desmarest, Broussonnet, secretary, and Cretté-Palluel, at whose farm I was two years ago, and who is the only practical farmer in the society. The secretary reads the titles of the papers presented, and gives some little account of them; but they are not read unless particularly interesting; then memoirs are read by the members, or reports of references; and when they discuss or debate there is no order, but all speak together as in a warm private conversation. The Abbé Raynal has given

them 1200 *livres* [£52 10s.] for a premium on some important subject; and my opinion was asked what it should be
given for. Give it, I replied, in some way for the introduction
of turnips. But that they conceive to be an object of impossible attainment; they have done so much, and the Government so much more, and all in vain, that they consider it as
a hopeless object. I did not tell them that all hitherto done
has been absolute folly; and that the right way to begin was
to undo everything done. I am never present at any societies
of agriculture, either in France or England, but I am much
in doubt with myself whether, when best conducted, they
do most good or mischief; that is, whether the benefits a
national agriculture may by great chance owe to them are
not more than counterbalanced by the harm they effect; by
turning the public attention to frivolous objects, instead of
important ones, or dressing important ones in such a garb
as to make them trifles?

　　　　　　　　　　　　Ibid., 137 (12 June 1789)

(3) RENT, PRICE OF LAND, AND PRODUCE OF CORN

The average price of all the cultivated land in the kingdom
is, per English acre, £20. The rent of such part as is let is
15s. 7d. The average produce of wheat and rye is 18 bushels.

　　In order to judge the better of these particulars it will be
necessary to contrast them with the similar circumstances
of England, by which method their merit or deficiency may
be more clearly discriminated. In respect to England, may
be remarked, in the first place, a very singular circumstance,
which is the near approximation of the two kingdoms in the
two articles of *price* and *rent*. The rent of cultivated land in
England, if it could be known accurately, would be probably
found not much to exceed 15s. 7d. per acre. Now 15s. 7d.
at 26 years purchase, which I take to be the present average
price of land in this kingdom (1790 and 1791), is £20 5s. 2d.
The two kingdoms are, therefore, on a foot of equality in
this respect. If it be thought extraordinary that land should
sell for as high a price in France as in England, there are
not wanted circumstances to explain the reason. In the first
place, the net profit received from estates is greater, There
are no poor rates in that kingdom, and tithes were much
more moderately exacted. Repairs, which form a consider-

able deduction with us are a very trifling one with them. But what operates as much or perhaps more than these circumstances, is the number of small properties. All the savings which are made by the lower classes in France are invested in land, but this practice is scarcely known in England where such savings are usually lent on bond or mortgage, or invested in the public funds. This causes a competition for land in France which, very fortunately for the prosperity of agriculture, does not obtain here.

As to the acreable produce of corn land, the difference will be found very great indeed, for in England the average produce of wheat and rye is 24 bushels, which form a vast superiority to 18, the produce of France. But the superiority is greater than is apparent in the proportion of those two numbers; for the corn of England as far as respects *dressing*, that is cleaning from dirt, chaff, seeds of weeds, etc., is as much better than that of France as would make the difference at least 25 (instead of 24) to 18; and I am inclined to think even more. There is not a plank threshing floor in France, and no miller can grind corn as he receives it from the farmer without further cleaning. Another point yet more important is that English wheat, in much the greater part of our kingdom, succeeds other preparatory crops, whereas the wheat of France follows almost universally a dead fallow on which is spread all the dung of the farm.

The importance of a country producing 25 bushels per acre instead of 18 is prodigious, but it is an idle deception to speak of 25, for the superiority of English spring corn (barley and oats) is doubly greater than that of wheat and rye, and would justify me in proportioning the corn products of England in general, compared with those of France as 28 to 18, and I am well persuaded that such a ratio would be no exaggeration. The difference between the corn products of France and England is so great that it would justify some degree of surprise how any political writer could ever express any degree of amazement that a territory, naturally so inconsiderable as the British Isles on comparison with France, should ever become equally powerful, yet this sentiment, founded in mere ignorance, has been very common. With such an immense superiority in the produce of corn the more obvious surprise should have been that the resources of England, compared with those of France, were not yet more decisive. But it is to be observed that there are other articles of culture to which recourse must be had for an explanation; vines are an immense object in the cultivation of the latter kingdom, and yield all the advantages, and even superior ones to those afforded by the assiduous culture of corn in England. Maize is also an article of great consequence in the French husbandry; olives, silk and lucerne are not to be forgotten, nor should we omit mentioning the fine pastures of Normandy, and every article in the rich acquisitions of Flanders, Alsace and part of Artois, as well as on the banks of the Garonne. In all this extent, and it is not small, France possesses a husbandry equal to our own, and it is from well seconding the fertility of nature in these districts, and from a proper attention to the plants adapted to the soil, that there has arisen any equality in the resources of the two kingdoms; for, without this, France, with all the ample advantages she otherwise derives from nature, would be but a petty power on comparison with Great Britain.

CAPITAL EMPLOYED IN HUSBANDRY

There is no light in which the agriculture of France can appear to less advantage than upon this head. It is scarcely credible how the *métayers* are able to support themselves with a stock so much inferior to what would be necessary to a good cultivation. In all the provinces which are backward in point of agriculture, as Bretagne, Anjou, Maine, Touraine, Sologne, Berry, La Marche, Limousin, Angoumois, Poitou, part of Guienne and Languedoc; in Champagne, Lorraine, Franche Comté, Bourbonnais, Nivernais, Lyonnais and part of Auvergne, Dauphiné and Provence, the stock of every sort upon the farms, whether belonging to the landlord or the tenant, would not rise to 20s. per English acre, and in many districts not to 15s. The pastures of Normandy, and the arable lands of Flanders and part of Artois, are well stocked, but there is a great deficiency in every other part of the kingdom even in the best provinces. The quantity of sheep and cattle everywhere trifling in comparison of what it ought to be. The implements of husbandry are contrived for cheapness, not for duration and effect; and such stacks of hay in store as are found all over England are rarely seen in France. Improvements invested in the land, by marling, draining, etc., which on farms in England amount to large sums of money, are inconsiderable even in the best parts of France. And besides the stock, transferable from tenant to tenant, the investments which in England fall upon the landlord, such as all sorts of conveniences in building, fencing, gates, stiles, posts, rails, etc., which he must provide or repair for a new tenant, are done in England at an expense unknown in the greatest part of France – not but that in some provinces, especially in the northern ones, the buildings are substantial and erected on a large scale. I shall however have no doubt in calculating the inferiority of France in its present state to that of England in the circumstances of building, enclosing, marling, claying, draining, laying to meadow, and other *permanent* improvements, at 30s. an acre over the whole territory. It is 40s. or 50s. inferior to all our well-improved counties, but as we have some backward in agriculture, as well as France, I calculate the whole at 30s.

I have calculated the capital of the farmers in all the provinces of the kingdom, and the medium of my notes is 40s. an acre. A similar calculation of the capital employed in the husbandry of England gives £4 an acre*; in other words 40s. more than is found in France; add 30s. for the less quantity of permanent improvements, and we have the total of £3 10s. per acre for the inferiority of French to English capital employed in agriculture, which upon 131,000,000 of acres forms a deficiency of £458,500,000 sterling, or 10,480,000,000 of *livres* – above 10 milliards.

* It will be proper here to explain what I mean by *capital*. A farmer in England, who stocks a farm, finds it necessary on entering to have a given sum of money for engaging in and carrying on the business through the first year, in which is reckoned a year's labour, rent, tithe, seed, etc., and this sum varies generally from £3 to £5 an acre; if the accounts of the same farmer be examined some years after, he will be found to have stock to a greater value, having increased it in cattle, sheep, manuring, and other improvements, for which he would be paid if he suddenly left his farm. Now take the average of all farms, of all stocks and of all periods of leases, and I value the capital employed at £4 an acre, which I have reason to believe to be a very moderate estimate.

Hence it is that it would demand this vast sum to be expended and invested in the agriculture of France, to bring the whole of that kingdom to an acreable equality with England; and I am confident that I have not been guilty of the least exaggeration.

THE TENANTRY

I. The small properties of the peasants are found everywhere, to a degree we have no idea of in England; they are found in every part of the kingdom, even in those provinces where other tenures prevail; but in Quercy, Languedoc, the whole district of the Pyrenees, Béarn, Gascony, part of Guienne, Alsace, Flanders and Lorraine, they abound to a greater degree than common. In Flanders, Alsace, on the Garonne, and Béarn, I found many in comfortable circumstances, such as might rather be called small farmers than cottagers, and in Bas Bretagne, many are reputed rich; but in general they are poor and miserable, much arising from the minute division of their little farms among all the children. In Lorraine, and the part of Champagne that joins it, they are quite wretched. I have more than once seen division carried to such an excess that a single fruit tree, standing in about 10 perch of ground, has constituted a farm, and the local situation of a family decided by the possession.

II. Hiring at money rent is the general practice in Picardy, Artois, part of Flanders, Normandy (except the Pays de Caux), Isle of France, and Pays de Beauce; and I found some in Béarn and about Navarreux. Such tenures are found also in most parts of France, scattered among those which are different and predominant; but, upon a moderate estimate they have not yet made their way through more than a sixth or seventh of the kingdom.

III. Feudal tenures are fiefs granted by the seigneurs of parishes under a reservation of fines, quit-rents, forfeitures, services, etc. I found them abounding most in Bretagne, Limousin, Berry, La Marche, etc., where they spread through whole provinces; but they are scattered very much in every part of the kingdom. About Vierzon, Vatan, etc., in Berry, they complained so heavily of these burdens that the mode of levying and enforcing them must constitute much of the evil; they are everywhere much more burden-some than apparent from the amount which I attribute to that circumstance. Legal adjudications, they assert, are very severe against the tenant in favour of the seigneur.

IV. Monopoly is commonly practised in various of the provinces where *métayage* is known. Men of some substance hire great tracts of land at a money rent and re-let it in small divisions to *métayers*, who pay half the produce. I heard many complaints of it in La Marche, Berry, Poitou and Angoumois, and it is met with in other provinces. It appears to flow from the difficulties inherent in the *métayage* system, but is itself a mischievous practice, well-known in Ireland where these middlemen are almost banished.

V. *Métayers* [*Métayage*] is the tenure under which perhaps seven-eighths of the lands of France are held. It pervades almost every part of Sologne, Berry, La Marche, Limousin, Anjou, Burgundy, Bourbonnais, Nivernais, Auvergne, etc., and is found in Bretagne, Maine, Provence, and all the southern counties. In Champagne there are many at *tiers franc*, which is the third of the produce, but in general it is half. The landlord commonly finds half the cattle and half the seed, and the *métayer* labour, implements, and taxes; but in some districts the landlord bears a share of these. In Berry some are at half, some one-third, some one-fourth produce. In Roussillon the landlord pays half the taxes, and in Guienne many landlords pay all. Near Aiguillon on the Garonne, the *métayers* furnish half the cattle. At Nangis in the Isle of France I met with an agree-ment for the landlord to furnish live stock, implements, harness and taxes; the *métayer* found labour and his own capitation tax. The landlord repaired the house and gates; the *métayer* the windows; the landlord provided seed the first year; the *métayer* the last; in the intervening years they supply half and half. Produce sold for money divided. In the Bourbonnais the landlord finds all sorts of live stock, yet the *métayer* sells, changes, and buys at his will, the steward keeping an account of these mutations, for the landlord has half the product of sales, and pays half the purchases. The tenant carts the landlord's half of the corn to the barn of the château, and comes again to take the straw. The consequences of this absurd system are striking;

land which in England would let at 10s. pays about 2s. 6d.
for both land and live stock.

At the first blush, the great disadvantage of the *métayage*
system is to landlords; but on a nearer examination the
tenants are found in the lowest state of poverty, and some of
them in misery. At Vatan, in Berry, I was assured that the
métayers almost every year borrowed their bread of the
landlord before the harvest came round, yet hardly worth
borrowing, for it was made of rye and barley mixed. I tasted
enough of it to pity sincerely the poor people. In Limousin
the *métayers* are considered as little better than menial
servants, removable at pleasure, and obliged to conform in
all things to the will of the landlords. It is commonly com-
puted that half the tenantry are deeply in debt to the proprietor, so that he is often obliged to turn them off with the
loss of these debts in order to save his land from running
waste.

In all the modes of occupying land the great evil is the
smallness of farms. There are large ones in Picardy, the Isle
of France, the Pays de Beauce, Artois and Normandy; but in
the rest of the kingdom such are not general. The division of
the farms and population is so great that the misery flowing
from it is in many places extreme; the idleness of the people
is seen the moment you enter a town on market day; the
swarms of people are incredible. At Landivisiau in Bretagne,
I saw a man who walked 7 miles to bring 2 chickens, which
would not sell for 24 *sous* the couple, as he told me himself.
At Avranches, men attending each a horse, with a pannier
load of sea ooze, not more than 4 bushels. Near Ensisheim
in Alsace, a rich country, women, in the midst of harvest,
where their labour is nearly as valuable as that of men,
reaping grass by the road side to carry home to their cows.

The hard plea of necessity can alone be urged in favour
of [*métayage*]; the poverty of the farmers being so great
that the landlord must stock the farm or it could not be
stocked at all. This is a most cruel burden to a proprietor
who is thus obliged to run much of the hazard of farming
in the most dangerous of all methods, that of trusting his
property absolutely in the hands of people who are generally
ignorant, many careless, and some undoubtedly wicked.
Among some gentlemen I personally knew, I was acquainted

with one at Bagnères-de-Luchon who was obliged to sell his
estate because he was unable to re-stock it, the sheep having
all died of epidemical distempers, proceeding doubtless from
the execrable methods of the *métayers* cramming them into
stables as hot as stoves, on reeking dung hills, and then, in
the common custom of the kingdom, shutting every hole and
crack that could let in air. In this most miserable of all the
modes of letting land, after running the hazard of such
losses, fatal in many instances, the defrauded landlord
receives a contemptible rent; the farmer is in the lowest
state of poverty; the land is miserably cultivated; and the
nation suffers as severely as the parties themselves.

SMALL PROPERTIES

Before I travelled I conceived that small farms, in property,
were very susceptible of good cultivation, and that the
occupier of such, having no rent to pay, might be sufficiently
at his ease to work improvements and carry on a vigorous
husbandry; but what I have seen in France has greatly
lessened my good opinion of them. In Flanders I saw
excellent husbandry on properties of 30 to 100 acres; but
we seldom find here such small patches of property as are
common in other provinces. In Alsace, and on the Garonne,
that is, on soils of such exuberant fertility as to demand no
exertions, some small properties also are well cultivated.
In Béarn I passed through a region of little farmers whose
appearance, neatness, ease, and happiness, charmed me; it
was what property alone could, on a small scale, effect; but
these were by no means contemptibly small; they are, as I
judged by the distance from house to house, from 40 to 80
acres. Except these, and a very few other instances, I saw
nothing respectable on small properties except a most unre-
mitting industry. Indeed, it is necessary to impress on the
reader's mind, that though the husbandry I met with in a
great variety of instances on little properties was as bad as
can well be conceived, yet the industry of the possessors was
so conspicuous, and so meritorious, that no commendations
would be too great for it. It was sufficient to prove that
property in land is, of all others, the most active instigator
to severe and incessant labour. And this truth is of such force
and extent that I know no way so sure of carrying tillage to

a mountain top, as by permitting the adjoining villagers to acquire it in property; in fact, we see that in the mountains of Languedoc, etc., they have conveyed earth in baskets on their backs to form a soil where nature had denied it.

Having in this manner admitted the merit of such small farms in property, I shall, in the next place, state the inconveniences I have observed to result from them in France. The first and greatest is the division which universally takes place after the death of the proprietor, commonly amongst all the children, but in some districts amongst the sons only. Forty or fifty acres in property are not incapable of good husbandry; but when divided, twenty acres *must* be ill-cultivated; again divided, they become farms of ten acres, of five, of two, and even one; and I have seen some of half, and even a quarter of a rood, with a family as much attached to it as if it were a hundred acres. The population flowing from this division is in some cases great, but it is the multiplication of wretchedness. Couples marry and procreate on the *idea*, not the *reality*, of a maintenance; they increase beyond the demands of towns and manufactures, and the consequence is distress, and numbers dying of diseases arising from insufficient nourishment. Hence, therefore, small properties much divided prove the greatest source of misery that can be conceived; and this has operated to such an extent and degree in France that a law undoubtedly ought to be passed to render all division, below a certain number of arpents, illegal.

Ibid., 284–7, 295–9 (1792)

(b) *Canals and Roads*

The next excerpts, taken from the first journey of 1787, reflect Young's interest in new undertakings of economic significance. Here he lauds Louis XIV for the magnificent enterprise of the Canal of Languedoc (Canal du Midi), and ponders on the enormous sums expended in creating the magnificent roads of the region. The roads, however, seemed much in excess of requirements; traffic was negligible, and far below the roads' capacity, though here Young was neglecting the military aspect of rapid land communications, a consideration which hardly arose in England. He also attacked the system of levying *tailles*, under which the lands owned by nobles were assessed, according to his information, at well under a quarter of the figure set on lands owned by commoners:

(1) The Canal of Languedoc [Canal du Midi] is the capital feature of all this country. The mountain through which it pierces is insulated in the midst of an extended valley and only half-a-mile from the road. It is a noble and stupendous work, goes through the hill about the breadth of three *toises* [fathoms], and was dug without shafts.

Leave the road, and crossing the canal, follow it to Béziers; nine sluice-gates let the water down the hill to join the river at the town. A noble work! The port is broad enough for four large vessels to lie abreast; the greatest of them carries from 90 to 100 tons. Many of them were at the quay, some in motion, and every sign of an animated business. This is the best sight I have seen in France. Here Louis XIV thou art truly great! Here with a generous and benignant hand thous dispensest ease and wealth to thy people! *Si sic omnia,* thy name would indeed have been revered. To effect this noble work of uniting the two seas less money was expended than to besiege Turin or to seize Strasbourg like a robber. Such an employment of the revenues of a great kingdom is the only laudable way of a monarch's acquiring immortality; all other means make their names survive with those only of the incendiaries, robbers, and violators of mankind.

Ibid., 40–1 (24 July 1787)

(2) The roads here are stupendous works. I passed a hill cut through to ease a descent that was all in the solid rock, and cost 90,000 *livres* (£3,937), yet it extends but a few hundred yards. Three leagues and an half from St Jean to Narbonne cost 1,800,000 *livres* (£78,750). These ways are superb even to a folly. Enormous sums have been spent to level even gentle slopes. The causeways are raised and walled on each side, forming one solid mass of artificial road carried across the valleys to the height of six, seven, or eight feet, and never less than 50 wide. There is a bridge of a single arch, and a causeway to it, truly magnificent; we have not an idea of what such a road is in England. The traffic of the way, however, demands no such exertions; one-third of the breadth is beaten, one-third rough, and one-third covered

with weeds. In 36 miles I have met one cabriolet, half-a-dozen carts, and some old women with asses. For what all this waste of treasure? In Languedoc, it is true, these works are not done by *corvées*; but there is an injustice in levying the amount not far short of them. The money is raised by *tailles*, and in making the assessment lands held by a noble tenure are so much eased, and others by a base one so burdened, that 120 arpents in this neighbourhood held by the former pay 90 *livres* [£3 19*s*.], and 400 possessed by a plebeian right, which ought proportionally to pay 300 livres [£13 2*s*. 6*d*.], is, instead of that, assessed at 1,400 *livres* [£61 5*s*.]. At Narbonne the canal [Canal de la Robine] which joins that of Languedoc deserves attention; it is a very fine work, and will, they say, be finished next month.

Ibid., 39–40 (23 July 1787)

(c) *The Inns of France*

When approaching Bagnères-de-Luchon towards the end of his first extended period of travel in France, Young was tempted to compare the inns with those of his native England. French inns, he found, were cheaper, and they offered a wide variety of fare; the wine was better, and so were the beds; the rooms, on the other hand, were far from weather-proof, were badly furnished and uncomfortable, and the kitchens dirty and the service surly. Subsequent experience, however, modified this early impression: cheapness, he discovered, might mean going hungry, as he found at his hotel in Rouen. Further, the table d'hôte was lacking in conversation and the guests deficient in curiosity, a feature of the company at French inns which he noted over and over again:

(1) Having now crossed the kingdom and been in many French inns, I shall in general observe that they are on an average better in two respects, and worse in all the rest, than those in England. We have lived better in point of eating and drinking beyond a question than we should have done in going from London to the Highlands of Scotland, at double the expense. But if in England the best of everything is ordered, without any attention to the expense, we should for double the money have lived better than we have done in France. The common cookery of the French gives great advantage; it is true they roast everything to a chip if they

are not cautioned, but they give such a number and variety
of dishes that if you do not like some there are others to
please your palate. The dessert at a French inn has no rival
at an English one; nor are the liqueurs to be despised. We
sometimes have met with bad wine, but upon the whole far
better than such port as English inns give. Beds are better
in France; in England they are good only at good inns; and
we have none of that torment, which is so perplexing in
England, to have the sheets aired; for we never trouble our
heads about them, doubtless on account of the climate. After
these two points, all is a blank. You have no parlour to eat
in, only a room with two, three, or four beds. Apartments
badly fitted up; the walls white-washed; or paper of different
sorts in the same room; or tapestry so old, as to be a fit nidus
for moths and spiders; and the furniture such that an English
innkeeper would light his fire with it. For a table you have
everywhere a board laid on cross bars, which are so conveniently contrived as to leave room for your legs only at the
end. Oak chairs with rush bottoms, and the back universally
a direct perpendicular that defies all idea of rest after fatigue.
Doors give music as well as entrance; the wind whistles
through their chinks; and hinges grate discord. Windows
admit rain as well as light; when shut they are not easy to
open; and when open not easy to shut. Mops, brooms, and
scrubbing-brushes are not in the catalogue of the necessaries
of a French inn. Bells there are none; the *fille* must always
be bawled for; and when she appears, is neither neat, well-
dressed, nor handsome. The kitchen is black with smoke;
the master commonly the cook, and the less you see of the
cooking the more likely you are to have a stomach to your
dinner; but this is not peculiar to France. Copper utensils
always in great plenty, but not always well-tinned. The
mistress rarely classes civility or attention to her guests among
the requisites of her trade.

Ibid., 30–1 (27 June 1787)

(2) Rouen is dearer than Paris, and therefore it is necessary for
the pockets of the people that their bellies should be whole-
somely pinched. At the *table d'hôte* at the hotel *Pomme de
Pin* we sat down, sixteen, to the following dinner: a soup,
about 3 lb. of *bouilli*, one fowl, one duck, a small fricassee

of chicken, *rôti* of veal, of about 2 lb. and two other small
plates with a salad; the price 45 *sous* [1s. 11d.] and 20 *sous*
[10½d.] more for a pint of wine. At an ordinary of 20d. a
head in England, there would be a piece of meat which
would, literally speaking, outweigh this whole dinner! The
ducks were swept clean so quickly that I moved from table
without half a dinner. Such *table d'hôtes* are among the
cheap things of France! Of all *sombre* and *triste* meetings a
French *table d'hôte* is foremost; for eight minutes a dead
silence, and as to the politeness of addressing a conversation
to a foreigner, he will look for it in vain. Not a single word
has anywhere been said to me unless to answer some question; Rouen not singular in this.

Ibid., 98 (13 Aug 1788)

(d) *Poverty and the Peasantry*

Historians have seen significance in Young's remarks on the extent
of poverty in rural France. Many of the peasantry, he found,
were in a distressed condition, ill-housed, harder-worked, and
worse clothed in comparison with the English labourer. The
miserable state of the overburdened peasantry was one of the
predisposing factors in the Revolution, and the high grain prices
of 1789, commented on several times by Young, undoubtedly
hit the poor very hard. Even a thriving little market-town like
Souillac, by the Dordogne, had as waiting-girls at the inn 'some
things that called themselves by the courtesy of Souillac women,
but in reality walking dung-hills'.

The first of three passages included here comes from the 1787
journey, and remarks on conditions in the district just across the
Dordogne. (The river was crossed, Young noted in passing, by
means of an excellent and cheap ferry, the boat 'well-contrived
for driving in at one end, and out at the other, without the
abominable operation, common in England, of beating horses
till they leap into them', the cost was also very low – 2s. 1d. for
two carriages, one saddle-horse and six persons, when in England
2s. 6d. was charged per wheel 'for execrable ferries, passed over
at the hazard of the horses' limbs'.) The second excerpt, taken from
the 1788 journey, remarks on part of Brittany, a province Young
found to be generally backward and poverty-stricken; and the
third records his comments on conditions between Les Islettes and
Mars-la-Tour, on his way from Châlons to Metz in July 1789:

(1) Pass Payrac, and meet many beggars, which we had not done before. All the country girls and women are without shoes or stockings; and the ploughmen at their work have neither sabots nor stockings to their feet. This is a poverty that strikes at the root of national prosperity; a large consumption among the poor being of more consequence than among the rich. The wealth of a nation lies in its circulation and consumption; and the case of poor people abstaining from the use of manufactures of leather and wool ought to be considered as an evil of the first magnitude. It reminded me of the misery of Ireland.

Pass Pont-de-Rhodes, and come to high land, whence we enjoyed an immense and singular prospect of ridges, hills, vales, and gentle slopes, rising one beyond another in every direction, with few masses of wood but many scattered trees. At least forty miles are tolerably distinct to the eye, and without a level acre; the sun, on the point of being set illumined part of it, and displayed a vast number of villages and scattered farms. The mountains of Auvergne, at the distance of 100 miles, added to the view. Pass by several cottages, exceedingly well-built of stone and slate or tiles, yet without any glass to the windows; can a country be likely to thrive where the great object is to spare manufactures? Women picking weeds into their aprons for their cows, another sign of poverty I observed, during the whole way from Calais.

Ibid., 23–4 (10 June 1787)

(2) To Combourg. The country has a savage aspect; husbandry not much further advanced, at least in skill, than among the Hurons, which appears incredible amidst enclosures; the people almost as wild as their country, and their town of Combourg one of the most brutal filthy places that can be seen: mud houses, no windows, and a pavement so broken as to impede all passengers but ease none; yet here is a château, and inhabited. Who is this Mons. de Chateaubriand, the owner, that has nerves strung for a residence amidst such filth and poverty? Below this hideous heap of wretchedness is a fine lake surrounded by well-wooded enclosures. Coming out of Hédé there is a beautiful lake belonging to Mons. de Blossac, Intendant of Poitiers, with a fine

accompaniment of wood. A very little cleaning would make
here a delicious scenery. There is a château [Château de
Blossac], with four rows of trees, and nothing else to be seen
from the windows in the true French style. Forbid it, taste,
that this should be the house of the owner of that beautiful
water; and yet this Mons. de Blossac has made at Poitiers
the finest promenade in France! But that taste which draws
a straight line, and that which traces a waving one, are
founded on feelings and ideas as separate and distinct as
painting and music – as poetry or sculpture. The lake
abounds with fish, pike to 36 lb., carp to 24 lb., perch 4 lb.
and tench 5 lb. To Rennes the same strange wild mixture
of desert and cultivation, half savage, half human. . . .

To Montauban. The poor people seem poor indeed; the
children terribly ragged, if possible worse clad than if with
no clothes at all; as to shoes and stockings they are luxuries.
A beautiful girl of six or seven years playing with a stick,
and smiling under such a bundle of rags as made my heart
ache to see her. They did not beg, and when I gave them
anything seemed more surprised than obliged. One-third of
what I have seen of this province seems uncultivated, and
nearly all of it in misery. What have kings, and ministers,
and parliaments, and States, to answer for their prejudices,
seeing millions of hands that would be industrious, idle and
starving, through the execrable maxims of despotism or the
equally detestable prejudices of a feudal nobility. Sleep at
the *Lion d'Or* at Montauban, an abominable hole.

Ibid., 107–9 (1 and 5 Sep 1788)

(3) Walking up a long hill, to ease my mare, I was joined by a
poor woman, who complained of the times, and that it was
a sad country. Demanding her reasons, she said her husband
had but a morsel of land, one cow, and a poor little horse,
yet they had a *franchar* (42 lb.) of wheat and three chickens
to pay as a quit-rent to one seigneur; and four *franchar* of
oats, one chicken and 1 *sou* to pay to another, besides very
heavy tailles and other taxes. She had seven children, and
the cow's milk helped to make the soup. But why, instead of
a horse, do not you keep another cow? Oh, her husband
could not carry his produce so well without a horse; and
asses are little used in the country. It was said, at present,

that *something was to be done by some great folks for such poor ones, but she did not know who nor how,* but God send us better, *car les tailles et les droits nous écrasent.* This woman at no great distance might have been taken for sixty or seventy, her figure was so bent, and her face so furrowed and hardened by labour; but she said she was only twenty-eight. An Englishman who has not travelled cannot imagine the figure made by infinitely the greater part of the country-women in France; it speaks, at the first sight, hard and severe labour. I am inclined to think that they work harder than the men, and this, united with the more miserable labour of bringing a new race of slaves into the world, destroys absolutely all symmetry of person and every feminine appearance. To what are we to attribute this difference in the manners of the lower people in the two kingdoms? To GOVERNMENT.

                                        Ibid., 173 (12 July 1879)

(e) Paris in 1787

In one of his best descriptive passages Young gives us a vivid account of the French capital as it appeared to him on his first visit. The reference to reckless driving in the city's narrow streets and the mention of the run-over child bring to mind the similar incident in *A Tale of Two Cities*, and makes one think that perhaps Dickens was familiar with Young's *Travels*.

Young refers also to the active intellectual life of Paris and the attention paid to science and literature. He was himself an active member of the cultured circles while in the capital, and in the second of the two passages which follow he recounts his visit to Lavoisier, the famous chemist, who was subsequently a victim of the Revolution. Young had personally carried out experiments in an attempt to ascertain the food of plants, and it was with some practical knowledge and interest that he inspected the equipment of Lavoisier's laboratory. The day of his visit to Lavoisier was completed by a meeting with Lhomond, another scientist and inventor, whose discovery of a kind of electric telegraph greatly intrigued Young:

(1) This great city appears to be in many respects the most ineligible and inconvenient for the residence of a person of small fortune of any that I have seen, and vastly inferior

to London. The streets are very narrow, and many of them crowded, nine-tenths dirty, and all without foot pavements. Walking, which in London is so pleasant and so clean that ladies do it every day, is here a toil and a fatigue to a man, and an impossibility to a well-dressed woman. The coaches are numerous and what are much worse, there are an infinity of one-horse cabriolets which are driven by young men of fashion and their imitators, alike fools, with such rapidity as to be real nuisances, and render the streets exceedingly dangerous without an incessant caution. I saw a poor child run over and probably killed, and have been myself many times blackened with the mud of the kennels. This beggarly practice of driving a one-horse booby hutch about the streets of a great capital flows either from poverty or a wretched and despicable economy; nor is it possible to speak of it with too much severity. If young noblemen at London were to drive their chaises in streets without footways, as their brethren do at Paris, they would speedily and justly get very well thrashed or rolled in the kennel. This circumstance renders Paris an ineligible residence for persons, particularly families that cannot afford to keep a coach; a convenience which is as dear as at London. The *fiacres* (hackney coaches) are much worse than at that city; and chairs there are none, for they would be driven down in the streets. To this circumstance also it is owing that all persons of small or moderate fortune are forced to dress in black with black stockings; the dusky hue of this in company is not so disagreeable a circumstance as being too great a distinction; too clear a line drawn in company between a man that has a good fortune and another that has not. With the pride, arrogance, and ill temper of English wealth this could not be borne; but the prevailing good humour of the French eases all such untoward circumstances. Lodgings are not half so good as at London, yet considerably dearer. If you do not hire a whole suite of rooms at an hotel you must probably mount three, four, or five pair of stairs, and in general have nothing but a bedchamber. After the horird fatigue of the streets such an elevation is a delectable circumstance. You must search with trouble before you will be lodged in a private family, as gentlemen usually are at London, and pay a higher price. Servants' wages are about the same as at that city. It is to be regretted that Paris should have these disadvantages, for in other respects I take it to be a most eligible residence for such as prefer a great city. The society for a man of letters, or [for one] who has any scientific pursuit, cannot be exceeded. The intercourse between such men and the great, which if it is not upon an equal footing ought never to exist at all, is respectable. Persons of the highest rank pay an attention to science and literature, and emulate the character they confer. I should pity the man who expected, without other advantages of a very different nature, to be well received in a brilliant circle at London because he was a fellow of the Royal Society. But this would not be the case with a member of the Academy of Sciences at Paris; he is sure of a good reception everywhere. Perhaps this contrast depends in a great measure on the difference of the governments of the two countries. Politics are too much attended to in England to allow a due respect to be paid to anything else; and should the French establish a freer government, academicians will not be held in such estimation when rivalled in the public esteem by the orators who hold forth liberty and property in a free parliament.

Ibid., 90–1 (25 Oct. 1787)

(2) To Mons. Lavoisier, by appointment. Madame Lavoisier, a lively, sensible, scientific lady, had prepared a *déjeuné Anglois* of tea and coffee, but her conversation on Mr Kirwan's Essay on Phlogiston, which she is translating from the English, and on other subjects, which a woman of understanding that works with her husband in his laboratory knows how to adorn, was the best repast. That apartment, the operations of which have been rendered so interesting to the philosophical world, I had pleasure in viewing. In the apparatus for aerial experiments nothing makes so great a figure as the machine for burning inflammable and vital air to make or deposit water; it is a splendid machine. Three vessels are held in suspension with indexes for marking the immediate variations of their weights; two that are as large as half hogsheads contain the one inflammable, the other the vital air, and a tube of communication passes to the third, where the two airs unite

and burn; by contrivances, too complex to describe without
plates, the loss of weight of the two airs, as indicated by their
respective balances, equal at every moment to the gain in
the third vessel from the formation or deposition of the water,
it not being yet ascertained whether the water be actually
made or deposited. If accurate (of which I must confess
I have little conception), it is a noble machine. Mons.
Lavoisier, when the structure of it was commended, said,
Mais oui monsieur, et même par un artiste François! with
an accent of voice that admitted their general inferiority to
ours. It is well known that we have a considerable exportation of mathematical and other curious instruments to every
part of Europe, and to France amongst the rest. Nor is this
new, for the apparatus with which the French academicians
measured a degree in the polar circle was made by Mr
George Graham. Another engine Mons. Lavoisier showed us
was an electrical apparatus enclosed in a balloon for trying
electrical experiments in any sort of air. His pond of quick-
silver is considerable, containing 250 lb., and his water
apparatus very great, but his furnaces did not seem so well
calculated for the higher degrees of heat as some others I
have seen. I was glad to find this gentleman splendidly
lodged, and with every appearance of a man of considerable
fortune. This ever gives one pleasure; the employments of a
State can never be in better hands than of men who thus
apply the superfluity of their wealth. From the use that is
generally made of money, one would think it the assistance
of all others of the least consequence in affecting any business
truly useful to mankind; many of the great discoveries that
have enlarged the horizon of science having been in this
respect the result of means seemingly inadequate to the end,
the energic exertions of ardent minds, bursting from obscu-
rity, and breaking the bands inflicted by poverty, perhaps by
distress. . . .

In the evening to Mons. Lhomond, a very ingenious and
inventive mechanic, who has made an improvement of the
jenny for spinning cotton. Common machines are said to
make too hard a thread for certain fabrics, but this forms it
loose and spongy. In electricity he has made a remarkable
discovery: you write two or three words on a paper; he takes
it with him into a room and turns a machine enclosed in a

cylindrical case, at the top of which is an electrometer, a
small fine pith ball; a wire connects with a similar cylinder
and electrometer in a distant apartment; and his wife, by
remarking the corresponding motions of the ball, writes
down the words they indicate; from which it appears that
he has formed an alphabet of motions. As the length of the
wire makes no difference in the effect, a correspondence
might be carried on at any distance; within and without a
besieged town, for instance; or for a purpose much more
worthy, and a thousand times more harmless, between two
lovers prohibited or prevented from any better connection.
Whatever the use may be, the invention is beautiful. Mons.
Lhomond has many other curious machines, all the entire
work of his own hands; mechanical invention seems to be
in him a natural propensity.

Ibid., 82–4 (16 Oct 1787)

(f) The Revolution

In 1789 Young was in Paris from 8 June to 27 June, and subsequently, after his tour of the eastern provinces and Italy, he
returned there on 3 January 1790. He left Paris for the last time
on 20 January 1790 after parting from his old friend M.
Lazowski, with whom Young spent his last evening – 'he en-
deavouring to persuade me to reside upon a farm in France, and I
enticing him to quit French bustle for English tranquility'.

'Bustle' was an understatement for the conditions of the Paris
which Young left behind him. In the summer of 1789 he found
both in Paris and in the eastern provinces a great ferment of
political agitation, though the provincial centres were starved of
reliable news of events in Paris and so were prey to all kinds
of wild rumours. Young was evidently in favour of a moderate
reform which would create in France the kind of constitutional
monarchy which existed in England. Impressed, however by the
short-sighted stubbornness of the aristocracy and the ineptitude of
the government, he perceived that matters were in danger of going
very much further. The following excerpts, taken from his
journals for the period between 9 and 27 June 1789, vividly
convey the atmosphere of feverish activity, the day-to-day flux of
events, and the excitement and uncertainty which filled Paris at
the time of the critical meetings of the States-General:

(1) JUNE 9TH. The business going forward at present in the

pamphlet shops of Paris is incredible. I went to the Palais-
Royal to see what new things were published, and to procure
a catalogue of all. Every hour produces something new.
Thirteen came out today, sixteen yesterday, and ninety-two
last week. We think sometimes that Debrett's or Stockdale's
shops at London are crowded, but they are mere deserts
compared to Desenne's and some others here, in which one
can scarcely squeeze from the door to the counter. The price
of printing two years ago was from 27 *livres* [23s. 6d.] to 30
livres [26s. 3d.] per sheet, but now it is from 60 *livres*
[£2 12s. 6d.] to 80 *livres* [£3 10s.]. This spirit of reading
political tracts, they say, spreads into the provinces, so that
all the presses of France are equally employed. Nineteen-
twentieths of these productions are in favour of liberty, and
commonly violent against the clergy and nobility. I have
today bespoken many of this description that have reputation; but inquiring for such as had appeared on the other
side of the question, to my astonishment I find there are but
two or three that have merit enough to be known. Is it not
wonderful, that while the press teems with the most levelling
and even seditious principles that if put in execution would
overturn the monarchy, nothing in reply appears, and not
the least step is taken by the Court to restrain this extreme
licentiousness of publication? It is easy to conceive the spirit
that must thus be raised among the people. But the coffee-
houses in the Palais-Royal present yet more singular and
astonishing spectacles; they are not only crowded within,
but other expectant crowds are at the doors and windows,
listening *à gorge déployée* to certain orators, who from chairs
or tables harangue each his little audience. The eagerness
with which they are heard, and the thunder of applause
they receive for every sentiment of more than common
hardiness or violence against the present government, cannot
easily be imagined. I am all amazement at the ministry permitting such nests and hotbeds of sedition and revolt which
disseminate amongst the people every hour principles that by
and by must be opposed with vigour, and therefore it seems
little short of madness to allow the propagation at present.

JUNE 10TH. Everything conspires to render the present
period in France critical; the want of bread is terrible;
accounts arrive every moment from the provinces of riots

and disturbances, and calling in the military to preserve the peace of the markets. The prices reported are the same as I found at Abbeville and Amiens; 5 *sous* (2½*d*.) a pound for white bread, and 3½ *sous* to 4 *sous* for the common sort eaten by the poor; these rates are beyond their faculties, and occasion great misery. At Meudon the police, that is to say the Intendant, ordered that no wheat should be sold on the market without the person taking at the same time an equal quantity of barley. What a stupid and ridiculous regulation, to lay obstacles on the supply in order to be better supplied; and to show the people the fears and apprehensions of Government, creating thereby an alarm, and raising the price at the very moment they wish to sink it. I have had some conversation on this topic with well-informed persons who have assured me that the price is, as usual, much higher than the proportion of the crop demanded, and there would have been no real scarcity if Mr Necker would have let the corn trade alone; but his edicts of restriction, which have been mere comments on his book on the legislation of corn, have operated more to raise the price than all other causes together. It appears plain to me that the violent friends of the Commons are not displeased at the high price of corn, which seconds their views greatly, and makes any appeal to the common feeling of the people more easy and much more to their purpose than if the price was low.

JUNE 26TH. Every hour that passes seems to give the people fresh spirit: the meetings at the Palais-Royal are more numerous, more violent, and more assured; and in the assembly of electors at Paris for sending a deputation to the National Assembly, the language that was talked, by all ranks of people, was nothing less than a revolution in the government, and the establishment of a free constitution. What they mean by a free constitution is easily understood – *a republic*; for the doctrine of the times runs every day more and more to that point; yet they profess that the kingdom ought to be a monarchy too; or, at least, that there ought to be a king. In the streets one is stunned by the hawkers of seditious pamphlets, and descriptions of pretended events that all tend to keep the people equally ignorant and alarmed. The supineness and even stupidity of the Court is without example; the moment demands the greatest decision, and yesterday, while it was actually a question whether he should be a doge of Venice or a king of France, the King went a hunting! The spectacle the Palais-Royal presented this night till eleven o'clock, and as we afterwards heard almost till morning, is curious. The crowd was prodigious, and fireworks of all sorts were played off, and all the building was illuminated. These were said to be rejoicings on account of the Duc d'Orléans and the nobility joining the Commons; but united with the excessive freedom and even licentiousness of the orators, who harangue the people. With the general movement which before was threatening, all this bustle and noise, which will not leave them a moment tranquil, has a prodigious effect in preparing them for whatever purposes the leaders of the Commons shall have in view; consequently they are grossly and diametrically opposite to the interests of the Court; but all these are blind and infatuated. . . .

JUNE 27TH. The whole business now seems over, and the revolution complete. The King has been frightened by the mobs into overturning his own act of the *séance royale* by writing to the presidents of the orders of the nobility and clergy requiring them to join the Commons, full in the teeth of what he had ordained before. It was represented to him that the want of bread was so great in every part of the kingdom that there was no extremity to which the people might not be driven; that they were nearly starving, and consequently ready to listen to any suggestions, and on the *qui vive* for all sorts of mischief; that Paris and Versailles would inevitably be burnt; and in a word, that all sorts of misery and confusion would follow his adherence to the system announced in the *séance royale*. His apprehensions got the better of the party who had for some days guided him; and he was thus induced to take this step, which is of such importance that he will never more know where to stop or what to refuse; or rather he will find that in the future arrangement of the kingdom his situation will be very nearly that of Charles I; a spectator, without power, of the effective resolutions of a long parliament. The joy this step occasioned was infinite; the Assembly, uniting with the people, all hurried to the château. *Vive le Roi* might have been heard at Marly; the King and Queen appeared in the balcony, and were received with the loudest shouts of applause; the leaders, who governed these motions, knew the value of the concession much better than those who made it. I have today had conversation with many persons on this business, and to my amazement there is an idea, and even among many of the nobility, that this union of the orders is only for the verification of their powers, and for *making the constitution*, which is a new term they have adopted, and which they use as if a constitution was a pudding to be made by a receipt [recipe]. In vain I have asked, where is the power that can separate them hereafter if the Commons insist on remaining together, which may be supposed, as such an arrangement will leave all the power in their own hands?

Ibid., 134–5 (9 June 1789); 158–9
(26 June 1789); 159–60 (27 June 1789)

On leaving Paris for the eastern provinces in late June 1789, Young found further evidence of the unrest arising from the current scarcity and high prices of grain. He comments on this state of affairs at Nangis, not many miles east of Paris, and again when he reached Strasbourg in the extreme north-east of the country (see excerpts (2) and (3)). At Strasbourg he was an eye-witness of an attack made upon the city's *hôtel de ville*, in which the mob was assisted, rather than deterred, by a body of troops. At Dijon (excerpt (4)) he was very struck by the scarcity of newspapers and the consequent prevalence of rumours, and he dined at his inn with two noblemen driven from their estates by the mob; one of these entered into conversation with Young and gloomily forecast ruin arising from an expected civil war and the collapse of the government. At Moulins (excerpt (5)), some 180 miles south of Paris, there was again no newspaper, and two weeks later, at Thueyts, Young himself ran into difficulties with the local militia. A mob along the road had already forced him to wear the white cockade of the *tiers état*, and at L'Isle-sur-le-Doubs it was only with some trouble that he was able to convince a menacing crowd that he was an innocent English traveller and not a seigneur. At Thueyts (excerpt (6)), on the road to Avignon, his detailed measurement of a parcel of mulberry trees brought him under suspicion as a tax agent of the unpopular Queen, Marie-Antoinette, but again he was able to extricate himself. Only the next day, however, on reaching Villeneuve-de-Berg (excerpt (7)), he was once more under necessity of explaining himself to a suspicious detachment of *milice bourgeoise*. After these experiences a less determined or more prudent man might will have abandoned his mission and taken the shortest way home, but Young pressed on to reach Toulon and the road to Italy on 11 September:

(2) Nangis, JULY 1ST 1789

Nangis is near enough to Paris for *the people* to be politicians; the perruquier that dressed me this morning tells me that everybody is determined to pay no taxes, should the National Assembly so ordain. But the soldiers will have something to say. No Sir, never: – be assured, as we are, that the French soldiers will never fire on the people; but, if they should, it is better to be shot than starved. He gave me a frightful account of the misery of the people; whole families in the utmost distress; those that work have a pay insufficient to feed them, and many that find it difficult to get work at all. I inquired of Mons. de Guerchy concerning this, and found it true. By order of the magistrates no person is allowed to buy more than two bushels of wheat at a market to prevent monopolizing. It is clear to common sense that all such regulations have a direct tendency to increase the evil, but it is in vain to reason with people whose ideas are immovably fixed. Being here on a market-day I attended and saw the wheat sold out under this regulation, with a party of dragoons drawn up before the market-cross to prevent violence. The people quarrel with the bakers, asserting the prices they demand for bread are beyond the proportion of wheat, and proceeding from words to scuffling, raise a riot, and then run away with bread and wheat for nothing. This has happened at Nangis, and many other markets; the consequence was that neither farmers nor bakers would supply them till they were in danger of starving, and when they did come prices under such circumstances must necessarily rise enormously, which aggravated the mischief, till troops became really necessary to give security to those who supplied the markets.

(3) Strasbourg, JULY 21ST 1789

I have spent some time this morning at the *cabinet littéraire*, reading the gazettes and journals that give an account of the transactions at Paris; and I have had some conversation with several sensible and intelligent men on the present revolution. The spirit of revolt is gone forth into various parts of the kingdom; the price of bread has prepared the populace everywhere for all sorts of violence. At Lyons there have been commotions as furious as at Paris, and the same at a great many other places. Dauphiné is in arms; and Bretagne in absolute rebellion. The idea is that the people will, from hunger, be driven to revolt; and when once they find any other means of subsistence than that of honest labour everything will be to be feared. Of such consequence it is to a country, and indeed to every country, to have a good police of corn; a police that shall by securing a high price to the farmer encourage his culture enough to secure the people at the same time from famine. . . .

Night – I have been witness to a scene curious to a foreigner, but dreadful to Frenchmen that are considerate. Passing through the square of the Hôtel de Ville, the mob were breaking the windows with stones, notwithstanding an officer and a detachment of horse was in the square. Perceiving that their numbers not only increased but that they grew bolder and bolder every moment, I thought it worth staying to see what it would end in, and clambered on to the roof of a row of low stalls opposite the building against which their malice was directed. Here I beheld the whole commodiously. Perceiving that the troops would not attack them, except in words and menaces, they grew more violent and furiously attempted to beat the doors in pieces with iron crows, placing ladders to the windows. In about a quarter of an hour, which gave time for the assembled magistrates to escape by a back door, they burst all open and entered like a torrent with a universal shout of the spectators. From that minute a shower of casements, sashes, shutters, chairs, tables, sofas, books, papers, pictures, etc., rained incessantly from all the windows of the house, which is 70 or 80 feet long, and which was then succeeded by tiles, skirting boards, bannisters, framework, and every part of the building that force could detach. The troops, both horse and foot, were quiet spectators. They were at first too few to interpose, and when they became more numerous, the mischief was too far advanced to admit of any other conduct than guarding every avenue around, permitting none to go to the scene of action, but letting everyone that pleased retire with his plunder; guards being at the same time placed at the doors of the churches and all public buildings. I was for two hours a spectator at different places of the scene, secure myself from the falling furniture, but near enough to see a fine lad of about fourteen crushed to death by something as he was handing plunder to a woman, I suppose his mother, from the horror that was pictured in her countenance. I remarked several common soldiers, with their white cockades, among the plunderers, and instigating the mob even in sight of the officers of the detachment. There were amongst them people so decently dressed that I regarded them with no small surprise. They destroyed all the public archives; the streets for some way around strewed with papers. This has been a wanton mischief, for it will be the ruin of many families unconnected with the magistrates.

(4) Dijon, JULY 31ST 1789

I went to search coffee-houses; but will it be credited that I could find but one in this capital of Burgundy where I could read the newspapers? At a poor little one in the square I read a paper, after waiting an hour to get it. The people I have found everywhere desirous of reading newspapers; but it is rare that they can gratify themselves; and the general ignorance of what is passing may be collected from this, that I found nobody at Dijon had heard of the riot at the town-house of Strasbourg. I described it to a gentleman, and a party collected around me to hear it; not one of them had heard a syllable of it, yet it is nine days since it happened; had it been nineteen, I question whether they would more than have received the intelligence; but, though they are slow in knowing what has really happened, they are very quick in hearing what is impossible to happen. The current report at present, to which all possible credit is given, is, that the Queen has been convicted of a plot to poison the King and Monsieur, and give the regency to the Count d'Artois; to set fire to Paris, and blow up the Palais-Royal by a mine! Why do not the several parties in the States cause papers to be printed that shall transmit only their own sentiments and opinions in order that no man in the nation, arranged under the same standard of reasoning, may want the facts that are necessary to govern his arguments and the conclusions that great talents have drawn from those facts? The King has been advised to take several steps of authority against the States, but none of his ministers have advised the establishment of journals and their speedy circulation that should undeceive the people in those points his enemies have misrepresented. When numerous papers are published in opposition to each other the people take pains to sift into and examine the truth; and that inquisitiveness alone, the very act of searching, enlightens them; they become informed, and it is no longer easy to deceive them.

At the *table d'hôte* only three, myself, and two noblemen, driven from their estates, as I conjecture by their conversation, but they did not hint at anything like their houses being burnt. Their description of the state of that part of the province they come from, in the road from Langres to Gray, is terrible; the number of châteaux burnt not considerable, but three in five plundered, and the possessors driven out of the country and glad to save their lives. One of these gentlemen is a very sensible well-informed man; he considers all rank, and all the rights annexed to rank, as destroyed in fact in France; and that the leaders of the National Assembly having no property, or very little themselves, are determined to attack that also, and attempt an equal division. The expectation is got among many of the people; but whether it takes place or not he considers France as *absolutely ruined*. That, I replied, was going too far, for the destruction of rank did not imply *ruin*. 'I call nothing ruin,' he replied, 'but a general and confirmed civil war, or dismemberment of the kingdom; in my opinion, both are inevitable; not perhaps this year, or the next, or the year after that, but whatever government is built on the foundation now laying in France cannot stand any rude shocks; an unsuccessful or a successful war will equally destroy it.' He spoke with great knowledge of historical events, and drew his political conclusions with much acumen. I have met very few such men at *table d'hôtes*.

(5) Moulins Aug. 7TH 1789
Moulins appears to be but a poor ill-built town. I went to

the *Belle Image*, but found it so bad that I left it and went
to the *Lion d'Or*, which is worse. This capital of the
Bourbonnais, and on the great post road to Italy, has not
an inn equl to the little village of Chevagnes. To read the
papers I went to the coffee-house of Madame Bourgeau, the
best in town, where I found near twenty tables set for company, but as to a newspaper I might as well have demanded
an elephant. Here is a feature of national backwardness,
ignorance, stupidity, and poverty! In the capital of a great
province, the seat of an Intendant, at a moment like the
present, with a National Assembly voting a revolution, and
not a newspaper to inform the people whether La Fayette,
Mirabeau, or Louis XVI is on the throne. Companies at a
coffee-house, numerous enough to fill twenty tables, and
curiosity not active enough to command one paper. What
impudence and folly! Folly in the customers of such a house
not to insist on half-a-dozen papers, and all the journals of the
Assembly; and impudence of the woman not to provide
them! Could such a people as this ever have made a revolution, or become free? Never in a thousand centuries. The
enlightened mob of Paris, amidst hundreds of papers and
publications, have done the whole. I demanded why they had
no papers? *They are too dear*; but she made me pay 24 *sous*
[1s.] for one dish of coffee, with milk, and a piece of butter
about the size of a walnut. It is a great pity there is not a
camp of *brigands* in your coffee-room, Madame Bourgeau.

(6) Thueyts, Aug. 19th 1789
In conversation with him [the Marquis Deblou] and another
gentleman, on agriculture, particularly the produce of mulberries, they mentioned a small piece of land that produced,
by silk only, 120 *livres* [£5 5s.] a year, and being contiguous
to the road we walked to it. Appearing very small for such
a produce, I stepped it to ascertain the contents and minuted
them in my pocket-book. Soon after, growing dark, I took
my leave of the gentlemen and retired to my inn.

What I had done had more witnesses than I dreamt of;
for at eleven o'clock at night, a full hour after I had been
asleep, the commander of a file of twenty *milice bourgeoise*,
with their muskets, or swords, or sabres, or pikes, entered my
chamber, surrounded my bed, and demanded my passport.

A dialogue ensued, too long to minute; I was forced first to give them my passport, and that not satisfying them, my papers. They told me that I was undoubtedly a conspirator with the Queen, the Count d'Artois, and the Count d'Entraigues (who has property here), who had employed me as an *arpenteur*, to measure their fields in order to double their taxes. My papers being in English saved me. They had taken it into their heads that I was not an Englishman, only a pretended one; for they speak such a jargon themselves that their ears were not good enough to discover by my language that I was an undoubted foreigner. Their finding no maps or plans, nor anything that they could convert by supposition to a *cadastre* of their parish, had its effect, as I could see by their manner, for they conversed entirely in patois. Perceiving, however, that they were not satisfied, and talked much of the Count d'Entraigues, I opened a bundle of letters that were sealed; these, gentlemen, are my letters of recommendation to various cities of France and Italy, open which you please, and you will find, for they are written in French, that I am an honest Englishman, and not the rogue you take me for. On this they held a fresh consultation and debate, which ended in my favour; they refused to open the letters, prepared to leave me, saying, that my numerous questions about lands and measuring a field, while I pretended to come after volcanoes, had raised great suspicions, which they observed were natural at a time when it was known to a certainty that the Queen, the Count d'Artois, and the Count d'Entraigues were in a conspiracy against the Vivarais; and thus, to my entire satisfaction, they wished me good night and left me to the bugs, which swarmed in the bed like flies in a honey-pot. I had a narrow escape; it would have been a delicate situation to have been kept prisoner probably in some common gaol, or, if not, guarded at my own expense while they sent a courier to Paris for orders and me to pay the piper.

(7) Villeneuve-de-Berg, AUG. 20TH 1789

Reach Villeneuve-de-Berg. I was immediately hunted out by the *milice bourgeoise*. *Where is your certificate?* Here again the old objection that my features and person were not described. *Your papers?* The importance of the case, they said, was great, and looked as big as if a marshal's baton was in hand. They tormented me with an hundred questions; and then pronounced that I was a suspicious-looking person. They could not conceive why a Suffolk farmer should travel into the Vivarais? Never had they heard of any person travelling for agriculture! They would take my passport to the Hôtel de Ville; have the permanent council assembled; and place a sentinel at my door. I told them they might do what they pleased, provided they did not prohibit my dinner as I was hungry; they then departed. In about half-an-hour a gentleman-like man, a *Croix de St Louis*, came, asked me some questions very politely, and seemed not to conclude that Maria Antoinetta and Arthur Young were at this moment in any very dangerous conspiracy. He retired, saying he hoped I should not meet with any difficulties. In another half hour a soldier came to conduct me to the Hôtel de Ville, where I found the council assembled. I had a good many questions asked; and some expressions of surprise that an English farmer should travel so far for agriculture; they had never heard of such a thing; but all was in a polite liberal manner; and though travelling for agriculture was as new to them as if it had been like the ancient philosopher's tour of the world on a cow's back, and living on the milk, yet they did not deem anything in my recital improbable, signed my passport very readily, assured me of every assistance and civility I might want, and dismissed me with the politeness of gentlemen.

Ibid., 166, 182–3, 194–5, 202, 215–16,
217–18 (7 July–20 Aug 1789)

On the day immediately following his return to Paris, 4 January 1790, Young hurried to 'the most extraordinary sight that either French or English eyes could ever behold at Paris' – Louis XVI and his Queen walking in the Tuileries gardens as virtual prisoners in their own capital (excerpt (8)). Young was gratified to find that some small signs of respect were still accorded the royal family, though he rightly conjectured that the treatment of the King was likely to put the whole revolution in danger. Our last glimpse of Paris in this period shows Young, on his last night but one before quitting the city for good, visiting the Jacobin Club and accepting election to that body as the distinguished author of *Political Arithmetic*, an honour which he found intriguing if not entirely flattering (excerpt (9)):

(8) After breakfast, walk in the gardens of the Tuileries, where there is the most extraordinary sight that either French or English eyes could ever behold at Paris. The King, walking with six grenadiers of the *milice bourgeoise*, with an officer or two of his household, and a page. The doors of the gardens are kept shut in respect to him, in order to exclude everybody but deputies or those who have admission-tickets. When he entered the palace the doors of the gardens were thrown open for all without distinction, though the Queen was still walking with a lady of her court. She also was attended so closely by the *gardes bourgeoises* that she could not speak, but in a low voice without being heard by them. A mob followed her, talking very loud, and paying no other apparent respect than that of taking off their hats wherever she passed, which was indeed more than I expected. Her Majesty does not appear to be in health; she seems to be much affected, and shows it in her face; but the King is as plump as ease can render him. By his orders there is a little garden railed off for the Dauphin to amuse himself in, and a small room is built in it to retire to in case of rain; here he was at work with his little hoe and rake, but not without a guard of two grenadiers. He is a very pretty good-natured-looking boy, of five or six years old, with an agreeable countenance; wherever he goes, all hats are taken off to him, which I was glad to observe. All the family being kept thus close prisoners (for such they are in effect) affords, at first view, a shocking spectacle; and is really so, if the act were not absolutely necessary to effect the revolution; this I conceive to be impossible; but if it were necessary, no one can blame the people for taking every measure possible to secure that liberty they had seized in the violence of a revolution. At such a moment, nothing is to be condemned but what endangers the national freedom. I must, however, freely own that I have my doubts whether this treatment of the royal family can be justly esteemed any security to liberty; or, on the contrary, whether it were not a very dangerous step that exposes to hazard whatever had been gained.

Ibid., 246–7 (4 Jan 1790)

(9) At night, Mons. Décretot and Mons. Blin carried me to the Revolution Club at the *Jacobins*; the room where they assemble is that in which the famous league was signed, as it has been observed above. There were above one hundred deputies present, with a president in the chair; I was handed to him, and announced as the author of the *Arithmétique Politique*; the president standing up, repeated my name to the company, and demanded if there were any objections. None; and this is all the ceremony, not merely of an introduction, but an election; for I was told that now I was free to be present when I pleased, being a foreigner. Ten or a dozen other elections were made. In this club, the business that is to be brought into the National Assembly is regularly debated; the motions are read that are intended to be made there, and rejected or corrected and approved. When these have been fully agreed to, the whole party are engaged to support them. Plans of conduct are there determined; proper persons nominated for being of committees, and presidents of the Assembly named. And I may add that such is the majority of numbers that whatever passes in this club is almost sure to pass in the Assembly.

Ibid., 261–2 (18 Jan 1790)

(g) *Manners and Customs in France*

Our first passage, taken from the first journey of 1787, describes the life of high society at the Pyrenean spa of Bagnères-de-Luchon. It is perhaps as interesting for the light it throws on Young himself, his restless, enquiring nature, as for what it tells us of the French aristocracy and their amusements – which seem very similar, indeed, to the daily round one might find at Bath or Cheltenham in the same period:

The life led here has very little variety. Those who bathe or drink the waters do it at half after five or six in the morning; but my friend and myself are early in the mountains, which are here stupendous; we wander among them to admire the wild and beautiful scenes which are to be met with in almost every direction. The whole region of the Pyrenees is of a nature and aspect so totally different from everything that I had been accustomed to that these excursions were productive of much amusement. Cultivation is here carried to a considerable perfection in several articles, especially in the irrigation of meadows. We seek-out the most intelligent peasants, and have many and long conversations with those who understand French, which however is not the case with all for the language of the country is a mixture of Catalan, Provençal, and French. This, with examining the minerals (an article for which the Duke de la Rochefoucauld likes to accompany us, as he possesses a considerable knowledge in that branch of natural history), and with noting the plants with which we are acquainted, serves well to keep our time employed sufficiently to our taste. The ramble of the morning finished, we return in time to dress for dinner at half after twelve or one; then adjourn to the drawing-room of Madame de la Rouchefoucauld, or the Countess of Grandval alternately, the only ladies who have apartments large enough to contain the whole company. None are excluded; as the first thing done by every person who arrives is to pay a morning visit to each party already in the place; the visit is returned, and then everybody is of course acquainted at these assemblies, which last till the evening is cool enough for walking. There is nothing in them but cards, trick-track [a form of backgammon], chess, and sometimes music; but the great feature is cards. I need not add that I absented myself often from these parties, which are ever mortally insipid to me in England, and not less so in France. In the evening the company splits into different parties for their promenade, which lasts till half-an-hour after eight; supper is served at nine; there is after it an hour's conversation in the chamber of one of our ladies, and this is the best part of the day; for the chat is free, lively, unaffected and uninterrupted, unless on a post day, when the Duke has such packets of papers and pamphlets that they turn us all into politicians. All the world are in bed by eleven. In this arrangement of the day, no circumstance is so objectionable as that of dining at noon, the consequence of eating no breakfast; for as the ceremony of dressing is kept up, you must be at home from any morning's excursion by twelve o'clock. This single circumstance, if adhered to, would be sufficient to destroy any pursuits except the most frivolous. Dividing the day exactly in halves destroys it for any expedition, inquiry, or business that demands seven or eight hours' attention, uninterrupted by any calls to the table or the toilette: calls which, after fatigue or exertion, are obeyed with refreshment and with pleasure. We dress for dinner in England with propriety, as the rest of the day is dedicated to ease, to converse, and relaxation; but by doing it at noon too much time is lost. What is a man good for after his silk breeches and stockings are on, his hat under his arm, and his head *bien poudré*? Can he botanize in a watered meadow? Can he clamber the rocks to mineralize? Can he farm with the peasant and the ploughman? He is in order for the conversation of the ladies, which to be sure is in every country, but particularly in France where the women are highly cultivated, an excellent employment; but it is an employment that never relishes better than after a day spent in active toil or animated pursuit; in something that has enlarged the sphere of our conceptions, or added to the stores of our knowledge. I am induced to make this observation because the noon dinners are customary all over France, except by persons of considerable fashion at Paris. They cannot be treated with too much ridicule or severity for they are absolutely hostile to every view of science, to every spirited exertion, and to every useful pursuit in life.

Ibid., 32–4 (28 June 1787)

Young's last reminiscences before taking his final leave of France concerned the differences between that country's manners and customs and those of his native England. At this time French manners, as Young observed, were held up as the model to be admired and imitated all over Europe. Young took particular note of the practice of using separate glasses at the dinner table, with each person keeping to his own glass, and also the regular use of clean table linen and napkins, all of which were neglected in England. The French were also cleaner in the person, and made regular use of the bidet. On the other hand, privies were much dirtier than in England, as was the habit of spitting indoors, a practice found in all ranks of French society. French cooking, Young confirmed, was much superior in its quality and variety, and he voiced the familiar complaint of the lack of flavour of English vegetables boiled in water. Even the roast beef was better in Paris than in London, and the French served a dessert as a matter of course rather than as a luxury. The English, however, dressed better and at greater expense, especially the ladies, but were more subject to rapidly changing whims of fashion. The

French, he noted in conclusion, so far from living up to their reputation for high spirits, volubility and politeness, revealed a more cautious, phlegmatic and reserved nature than the English, though he believed them to be better-tempered. In sum, his remarks make an interesting study in comparison and contrast, written by a gentleman of mature years who had spent the better part of three years in France, had long training in the art of observation, and was used to moving in all levels of society from the highest nobility to the poorest peasantry on both sides of the Channel:

One of the most amusing circumstances of travelling into other countries is the opportunity of remarking the difference of customs amongst different nations in the common occurrences of life. In the art of living, the French have generally been esteemed by the rest of Europe to have made the greatest proficiency, and their manners have been accordingly more imitated and their customs more adopted than those of any other nation. Of their cookery there is but one opinion; for every man in Europe that can afford a great table either keeps a French cook, or one instructed in the same manner. That it is far beyond our own, I have no doubt in asserting. We have about half-a-dozen real English dishes that exceed anything, in my opinion, to be met with in France; by English dishes I mean a turbot and lobster sauce; ham and chicken; turtle; a haunch of venison; a turkey and oysters; and after these there is an end of an English table. It is an idle prejudice to class roast beef among them; for there is not better beef in the world than at Paris. Large handsome pieces were almost constantly on the considerable tables I have dined at. The variety given by their cooks to the same thing is astonishing; they dress an hundred dishes in an hundred different ways, and most of them excellent; and all sorts of vegetables have a savouriness and flavour from rich sauces, that are absolutely wanted to our greens boiled in water. This variety is not striking in the comparison of a great table in France with another in England; but it is manifest in an instant between the tables of a French and English family of small fortune. The English dinner of a joint of meat and a pudding, as it is called, or *pot luck* with a neighbour, is bad luck in England; the same fortune in France gives, by means of cookery only, at least four dishes to one among us, and spreads a small table incomparably better. A regular dessert with us is expected at a considerable table only, or at a moderate one when a formal entertainment is given; in France it is as essential to the smallest dinner as to the largest; if it consists only of a bunch of dried grapes or an apple, it will be as regularly served as the soup. I have met with persons in England who imagine the sobriety of a French table carried to such a length that one or two glasses of wine are all that a man can get at dinner; this is an error; your servant mixes the wine and water in what proportion you please; and large bowls of clean glasses are set before the master of the house and some friends of the family at different parts of the table for serving the richer and rarer sorts of wines, which are drunk in this manner freely enough. The whole nation are scrupulously neat in refusing to drink out of glasses used by other people. At the house of a carpenter or blacksmith a tumbler is set to every cover. This results from the common beverage being wine and water; but if at a large table, as in England, there were porter, beer, cider, and perry, it would be impossible for three or four tumblers or goblets to stand by every plate; and equally so for the servants to keep such a number separate and distinct. In table-linen they are I think, cleaner and wiser than the English; that the change may be incessant, it is everywhere coarse. The idea of dining without a napkin seems ridiculous to a Frenchman, but in England we dine at the tables of people of tolerable fortune without them. A journeyman carpenter in France has his napkin as regularly as his fork; and at an inn the *fille* always lays a clean one to every cover that is spread in the kitchen for the lowest order of pedestrian travellers. The expense of linen in England is enormous from its fineness; surely a great change of that which is coarse would be much more rational.

In point of cleanliness, I think the merit of the two nations is divided; the French are cleaner in their persons, and the English in their houses; I speak of the mass of the people, and not of individuals of considerable fortune. A *bidet* in France is as universally in every apartment as a basin to wash your hands, which is a trait of personal cleanliness I wish more common in England; on the other hand, their necessary houses are temples of abomination; and the practice of spitting about a room, which is amongst the highest as well as the lowest ranks, is detestable. I have seen a gentleman spit so near the clothes of a duchess that I have stared at his unconcern.

In everything that concerns the stables, the English far exceed the French; horses, grooms, harness, and change of equipage; in the provinces you see cabriolets undoubtedly of the last century; an Englishman, however small his fortune may be, will not be seen in a carriage of the fashion of forty years past; if he cannot have another, he will walk on foot. It is not true that there are no complete equipages at Paris, I have seen many; the carriage, horses, harness, and attendance without fault or blemish; but the number is certainly very much inferior to what are seen at London. English horses, grooms, and carriages have been of late years largely imported.

In all the articles of the fitting up and furnishing houses, including those of all ranks in the estimate, the English have made advances far beyond their neighbours. Mahogany is scarce in France, but the use of it is profuse in England. Some of the hotels in Paris are immense in size from a circumstance which would give me a good opinion of the people, if nothing else did, which is the great mixture of families. When the eldest son marries he brings his wife home to the house of his father, where there is an apartment provided for them; and if a daughter does not wed an eldest son, her husband is also received into the family, in the same way, which makes a joyous number at every table. This cannot altogether be attributed to economical motives, though they certainly influence in many cases, because it is found in families possessing the first properties in the kingdom. It does with French manners and customs, but in England it is sure to fail, and equally so amongst all ranks of people; may we not conjecture, with a great probability of truth, that the nation in which it succeeds is therefore better tempered? Nothing but good humour can render such a jumble of families agreeable, or even tolerable. In dress they have given the *ton* to all Europe for more than a century; but this is not among any but the highest rank an object of such expense as in England, where the mass of mankind wear much better things (to use the language of common conversation) than in France; this struck me more amongst ladies who, on an average of all ranks, do not dress at one half of the expense of English women. Volatility and changeableness are attributed to the French as national characteristics, but in the case of dress with the grossest exaggeration. Fashions change with ten times more rapidity in England, in form, colour, and assemblage; the vicissitudes of every part of dress are fantastic with us; I see little of this in France; and to instance the mode of dressing the gentlemen's hair, while it has been varied five times at London, it has remained the same at Paris. Nothing contributes more to make them a happy people than the cheerful and facile pliancy of disposition with which they adapt themselves to the circumstances of life; this they possess much more than the high and volatile spirits which have been attributed to them; one excellent consequence is a greater exemption from the extravagance of living beyond their fortunes than is met with in England. In the highest ranks of life there are instances in all countries; but where one gentleman of small property in the provinces of France runs out his fortune, there are ten such in England that do it. In the blended idea I had formed of the French character from reading, I am disappointed from three circumstances which I expected to find predominant. On comparison with the English, I looked for great talkativeness, volatile spirits, and universal politeness. I think, on the contrary, that they are not so talkative as the English; have not equally good spirits, and are not a jot more polite; nor do I speak of certain classes of people, but of the general mass. I think them, however, incomparably better tempered; and I propose it as a question, whether good temper be not more reasonably expected under an arbitrary, than under a free government?

Ibid., 262–5 (18 Jan 1790)

3. A JOURNEY IN CATALONIA

Young's brief journey in Catalonia was made as an extension of his first visit to France in 1787, and he undertook it in order to pass the time while his French friends, with whom he had travelled from Paris, enjoyed the placid round of social life at the Pyrenean watering-place of Bagnères-de-Luchon. His Catalonian expedition was a rapid one, covering 347 miles of mostly rugged, mountainous country in the space of only a little over three weeks, and involving some twelve or fourteen hours a day in the saddle in the hottest season of the year. Young's route lay across the central Pyrenees through Viella, Escalo, Pobla de Segur, and Montserrat to Barcelona, his destination; the return journey ran further east along the coastal plain through Calella, Gerona,

Figueras and Bellegarde on the boundary between Spain and France.

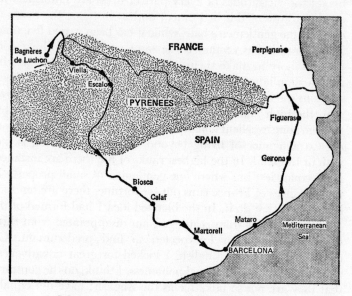

Map 2 *Young's Tour in Catalonia*, 1787

(a) Poverty and its Causes

Young's first impressions of Spain were of spectacular scenery, hazardous roads, farming which was surprisingly productive where the land could be irrigated, and poverty of a most wretched and extreme kind in the towns of the Pyrenees. At Escalo (excerpt (1)) the inn was so bad that Young took refuge in the residence of the *curé*, though he said the *curé*'s wine was putrid and the bed as hard as the pavement. The town could not boast a single window that was glazed, and with the exception of the *curé*'s house had no chimney but only smokeholes in the roofs. Further acquaintance with the country led Young to speculate on the causes of the general poverty which he found (excerpt (2)). He noticed a lack of livestock, though there was plenty of un-cultivated land capable of carrying sheep and goats. Even the poor and arid land could be cultivated with vines and olives. Ordinary commodities of life, Young observed, were dearer than in France, from which country came the mules and many of the cattle and sheep. The basic cause of this scarcity and waste of land, Young believed, lay in the absence of resident proprietors who, if they chose to bring their energy and intelligence into this backward region, could have given an impetus to improved farming and would have set about making the rivers navigable and the roads capable of bearing wheeled carriages:

(1) Reach Escalo; the inn so bad that our guide would not permit us to enter it, so he went to the house of the Curé. A scene followed so new to English eyes that we could not refrain from laughing very heartily. Not a pane of glass in the whole town, but our reverend host had a chimney in his kitchen; he ran to the river to catch trout; a man brought us some chickens which were put to death on the spot. For light they kindled splinters of pitch-pine, and two merry wenches, with three or four men, who collected to stare at us, as well as we at them, were presently busy in satisfying our hunger. They gave us red wine so dreadfully putrid from the borachio that I could not touch it. Brandy, but poisoned with aniseed, what then to do? A bottle of excellent rich white wine came forth, resembling good mountain, all was well; but when we came to examine our beds there was only one; my friend would again do the honours and insisted on my taking it, he made his on a table; and what with bugs, fleas, rats, and mice, slept not. I was not attacked, and though the bed and a pavement might be ranked in the same class of softness, fatigue converted it to down. This town and its inhabitants are to the eye equally wretched, the smoke holes instead of chimneys, the total want of glass windows – the cheerfulness of which to the eye is known only by the want – the dress of the women all in black, with cloth of the same colour about their heads, and hanging half down their backs – no shoes – no stockings – the effect upon the whole dismal – savage as the rocks and mountains.

(2) The poverty of the people in the interior country is striking; their towns old, ill-built, dirty, and wretched; the people ill-dressed and generally deficient in the wealth best adapted to such a country, cattle; in the higher Pyrenees this is not so much the case; they have cattle, and are in every respect in a better condition owing to the plenty which great commons give in a country of good pasturage, and where wood is in profusion. The number of sheep we saw in general was

not the twentieth part of what the wastes, bad as they are, for that animal would maintain; and that of goats so small as to indicate the same thing strongly. This poverty, not being the effect of a want of industry, must result from a government inattentive to their interests, and probably oppressive, and from a total want of the higher classes residing amongst them. Till we came to the rich country near Barcelona, that is to say in about 200 miles, we saw nothing that had the least resemblance to a gentleman's country seat; those who have estates let in it are absent, those we heard of live at Barcelona, and the whole country is thus abandoned to the very lowest classes, and the wealth and intelligence which might contribute to its improvement diverted into distant and very different channels; this is a great misfortune to the people and which will long contribute to keep things in their present state. To the same cause it is owing that the roads, so essential in the improvement of a country, are left in a state which precludes the use of wheel carriages, which with the unnavigable state of all the rivers, except for rafters of timber grossly put together, cuts off that system of reciprocal purchase and sale, that interior commerce which is the best a country can possess. These are also evils which the residence of men of fortune is the most likely to correct; and much above the power of peasants and mountaineers. With all these disadvantages there are still circumstances which make it surprising that more land is not cultivated. Vines and olives succeed very well on the poorest and the most arid soils. Their growth and luxuriance in spots surrounded on every side with wastes, and in soils not better, yield a conviction which leaves nothing to doubt that the adjoining lands would, if planted, give a similar produce. The profit of doing it will not be suspected if the revenue and value of cultivated lands, on comparison with wastes, be considered. Two points here force themselves on our notice; first, the want of capitals for undertaking the work, and secondly, the wastes being in all probability in the possession of absent landlords who will not give sufficient encouragement to others to do what they neglect doing themselves.

Where cultivation climbs up the mountain sides, it is by small proprietors, who purchase of the communities of the parishes the property of the land; wherever the soil is in hands that will sell just the portion which is in the power of a man to buy, great exertions are sure to be the consequence. There is no spur to industry so great as the possession of a piece of land, which in a country where the means of subsistence are contracted for want of more diffusive and more various employments, is the only comfortable dependence of a man who wishes to be the father of a family. The parish that will sell a waste at a moderate price will be almost sure to see it cultivated; but the great lord, who rarely or never sells any of his property, unless ruin forces him to sell the whole, is equally sure of perpetuating the deserts which are the disgrace of his country. He would let them, and perhaps upon advantageous terms; but it demands considerable capitals, and a very enlightened state of agriculture for speculations of that sort to take place; the only capitals which can be found in Catalonia for such a purpose are the hands of men willing to work; aided, perhaps, by some little savings, which have originated from the view of wastes that are to be purchased. All that has been done, and it is much in some districts, is to be traced clearly to this origin.

That these observations are just will be confirmed by the prices of all the necessaries of life in that province; they have nothing very cheap; every article of consumption is somewhat dearer than in France; and it is more than once noted that all the meat they eat comes from that kingdom. Their mules are bred in France, and great imports of cattle and sheep are common. This is a direct premium upon every species of rural industry, and its not having operated greater improvements must be owing to the causes on which I have touched.

'A Tour in Catalonia', *Annals of Agriculture*, VIII (1787) 209–10, 262–6 (July 1787)

(b) Agriculture in Catalonia

Farming in the Pyrenees ran all the way from crops of a 'contemptible' variety to the luxuriant vines and tall maize to be found on irrigated land (excerpt (3)). Near Villafranca (excerpt (4)), on the way to Barcelona, there were many vines, good mulberries, thick maize and fine hemp. It was the practice to follow hemp with wheat, and then sow French beans in the wheat stubbles, giving three crops in the space of two years:

(3) More deserts for several miles. Some alternate fallow husbandry between vines, and the crops so contemptible that they produce not more than the seed. Pass some vineyards surrounded on every side by deserts; no water, and yet the vines and grapes are of the most beautiful luxuriance; from which I conclude that immense tracts of these waste lands might be applied with equal profit if there were men and capitals enough in the country. Pass Rivellias, a village whose white church and houses on the pinnacle of a rocky hill has a singular effect in the midst of an uncultivated dreary tract. Dine at Sanaouzier, the day excessively hot, and the flies so innumerable as to be a perfect plague. They have a clever contrivance for keeping them off the table you eat at, a moveable and very light frame of canvas is suspended from the ceiling by two pivots, and a girl keeps pulling it backwards and forwards while you are at table, the motion it gives the air drives off the flies; where this invention is not adopted they use a hand-flapper for the same purpose. Watered maize here seven to nine feet high. Every time we see any irrigation we are struck more and more with the importance of water, even on soils which are apparently mere rock, and on the most arid deserts it gives at once the utmost luxuriance of vegetation. Vines and olives, however, stand in no need of it, but thrive admirably on the driest soils without it. Not one acre, however, in 20 is planted with them that might be. Meet a farmer who pointed out to us a piece of land, containing exactly a Catalonian Journal, from which it appeared to be pretty nearly the same measure as an English acre. They stack their corn by the threshing floor, drive mules, &c., around upon it, and draw the straw, when cleared, with ropes by a mule to the stack, in which it is deposited for winter use. Come to more watered grounds; gardening and husbandry mixed; peaches; apples; ripe pears; pomegranates in the hedges, as large now as walnuts in the shell; onions and lettuces, in great plenty. Some watered lands have been sold at 1,300 *livres* the Journal.

(4) Come to a noble road, making by the King of Spain. It is 50 or 60 feet wide, and walled on each side to support the

earth of which it is formed: the men are paid 18 to 25 *sous* a day, besides a pint of wine given if they work well.

The country now is far more populous and better built: many vines and great cultivation, but with fallows. The soil all a strong red loam; a way cut through a vineyard of this soil, which showed it to be 7 feet deep; at the bottom was a crop of fine hemp; indeed the soil to the eye was as good at bottom as on the surface. Pass a large paper-mill. Continuing on this road, it joins another of the same size, which leads to Villafranca. Turn to the left over a very fine bridge, built all of red granite. It is a solid, durable, and noble work, 440 paces long, but the style of architecture bad, built 8 years ago. They have rolled their lands here, which is the first time we have seen it in Spain. Exceeding fine hemp, watered – maize thick and in ear; – many fine and tall poplars by the river.

Meet great numbers of carts and carriages with very fine mules, and every sign of approaching a great city. They are now ploughing their stubbles for French beans, their course is 1. hemp, 2. wheat, and after wheat French beans. Three crops are therefore gained in two years. The products good; Very fine mulberries. A journal, which is here also about an English acre, of rich land in the vale not watered, sells for 500 *livres* [£21 17s. 6d.]; watered for 1,000 [£43 15s.]. They plough with mules abreast without a driver, having a line for reins as in England; the beam of the plough is long enough to reach to the circular iron, about 9 inches under the yoke, to which the mules are collared. The yokes are like those in which oxen are worked, only with collars instead of bows. This method, which is very common in France also, has both its advantages and disadvantages; it will be a light draught, when the pitch of the beam is proportioned to the height of the mules, but if the share must be raised or lowered according to their height, it will be bad both for the land and the animals. To have the line of traction from the draught to the body of the plough is not quite correct, but it is much better than the common plough beams made either too long or too short: in this case, the length of the beam is ascertained; but the chief origin and intention of it is cheapness. The mould-board of the plough here has no iron on it and is fixed to the left side, the share is double, as if to work with a mould-board on either side; this is a great fault. Only one handle. It did its work tolerably. The wheat in sheaves is yet in the field, but the stubbles all ploughed, a narrow slip only left on which the wheat remained: this shows good attention to the succession of crops.

Ibid., 224–5, 232–4 (July 1787)

(c) Barcelona

Barcelona was the one major city reached by Young during his brief Spanish tour. At Barcelona he found the excellence of his hotel in strange contrast to the Spanish inns he had encountered on his way. Barcelona, too, presented its own contrasts. Some of the streets were broad, with great houses and magnificent public buildings, while other streets were so thick in dust that it was difficult to tell whether or not they were paved. The theatre was an impressive one and larger than Covent Garden, but the most remarkable feature of Barcelona was the quay, some half a mile long, and built on two levels, the lower level opening on to warehouses, and the upper built at the same height as the neighbouring street with connecting carriageways and stairs. Although large numbers of people were employed in making silk stockings and handkerchiefs, trade was Barcelona's chief activity, and when Young was there as many as 140 ships could be found in the harbour. The city, however, was subject to heavy taxation, and Young was surprised to find that the Inquisition had powers to enquire into offences against public morals and not merely matters appertaining to faith, so greatly extending its authority. There were thought to be, he noted without comment, as many as 1,200 to 1,500 monks and nuns in the city:

(5) Approach Barcelona: buildings many and good; numerous villas, and within 2 or 3 miles. They spread to the right and left, and are seen all over the country. The first view of the town is very fine; the situation beautiful, and the road so great and well made as to add much to the general scene; indeed there can nowhere be a finer; it is carried in an even line over all narrow vales, so that you have none of the inconveniences which otherwise, are the effect of hills and declivities. A few palm-trees add to the novelty of the prospect to northern eyes. The last half-mile we were in great haste to be in time for the gates, as they are shut at nine o'clock; we

had had a most burning sun for 40 miles, were a good deal fatigued, yet forced to undergo a strict search at the gate, as everything pays an entrée to government that goes into the town. When this was over, we went to the *French Crown*. but all full, then to *La Fonde*, where we found good quarters.

My friend thought this the most fatiguing day he had ever experienced; the heat being excessive, oppressed him much. The contrast of this inn, which is a very great one, with many waiters, active and alert, as in England; a good supper, with some excellent Mediterranean fish, ripe peaches, good wine, the most delicious lemonade in the world, good beds, &c., &c., contrasted most powerfully with the dreadful starving or stinking fare we had everywhere else met with.

The 17th view the town, which is large, and to the eye in every street remarkably populous; many of the streets are narrow, as may be expected in an old town, but there are also many others of a good breadth, and with good houses. Yet one cannot, upon the whole, consider it as well built, except in what relates to the public edifices, which are erected in a magnificent style. There are some considerable openings, which though not regular squares, are highly ornamental, and have a good effect in setting off the new buildings to the best advantage. One quarter of the city, called Barcelonetta, is entirely new and perfectly regular, the streets all cutting each other at right angles; it is true the houses are all small, being meant for the residence of sailors, little shop-keepers, and artisans, but it is at the same time no inconsiderable ornament to the city. One front of this new town faces the quay. The streets are well lighted; but the dust so deep in some of them, especially the broader ones, that I know not whether they are all paved or not. The governor's house and the new fountain are on a scale and in a style which shows that there are no mean ideas of embellishment here. The royal foundry for cannon is very great. The buildings spacious, and nothing wanting to show that no expense is spared. The guns cast are chiefly brass; they were boring several 24 pounders, which had been cast solid, and which is an operation so truly curious that one can never view it without paying some homage to the genius that first invented it. In time of war 300 men are employed, but at present the number is not considerable. The theatre is very large, and the seats on the two sides of the pit (for the centre is at a lower price) extremely commodious; there are elbows to separate the places, so that you sit as in an elbow chair; we were present at the representation of a Spanish comedy, and an Italian opera after it, and were surprised to find clergymen in their habits in every part of the house. This, which is never seen in France, shows a relaxation in points of religion that may by and by have its effect. They have an Italian opera twice a week, and plays the other evenings. I saw a blacksmith, hot from the anvil, come in and seat himself in the pit, with his shirt-sleeves tucked above his elbows. The house is larger than ours at Covent-Garden. Every well-dressed person was in the French fashion; but there were many others that still retained the Spanish mode of wearing their hair, without powder, in a thick black net which hangs down the back; nothing can have a worse effect, or be, in idea, more offensive in so hot a climate. But the object at Barcelona which is the most striking, and which has hardly anywhere a rival, is the quay; the design and execution are equally good. It is about half a mile long, as I guessed by my eye. A low platform is built but a few feet above the level of the water, of stone, close to which the ships are moored; this is of breadth sufficient for goods, and packages of all sorts in loading and unloading the vessels; a row of arched warehouses open on this platform, above and over which is the upper part of the quay, which is on a level with the street; and, for the convenience of going up or down from one to the other, there are ways for carriages and also staircases. The whole is most solidly erected in hewn stone, and finished in a manner that shows a true spirit of magnificence in the most useful sort of public works. It does credit to the kingdom. The road by which we travelled for several miles to Barcelona, the bridge which we passed the river, and this quay, are all works which will reflect a lasting honour on the present king of Spain. They are truly great. There are now about 140 ships in the harbour, but the number is often many more.

The manufactories at Barcelona are considerable. There is every appearance as you walk the streets of great and active industry; you move nowhere without hearing the creak of stocking-engines. Silk is manufactured into stockings, handkerchiefs (but these are not on so great a scale as at Valencia), laces, and various stuffs. They have also some woollen fabrics, but not considerable. The great business of the place is that of commission; there are not many ships belonging to the town, but the amount of the trade transacted here is very considerable.

The industry and trade, however, which have taken root and prospered in this city have withstood the continued system of the court to deal severely with the whole province of Catalonia. The famous efforts which the Catalans made in the beginning of this century to place a Prince of the house of Austria upon the throne of Spain, were not soon forgotten by the Princes of the House of Bourbon. Heavy taxes are paid in Barcelona; nothing comes into the town without paying an entrée; a load of 220 bottles of wine pays 12 pesettos, which is about 12s. English: even wheat is not exempted. Houses pay a heavy proportional tax, which is levied with such strictness that the least addition or improvement is sure to be attended with an increase of the tax. Nor is taxation the only instance of severity, the whole province continues to this day disarmed, so that a nobleman cannot wear a sword unless privileged to do it by grace or office, and this goes so far, that they are known, in order to be able to exhibit this mark of distinction, to get themselves enrolled as familiars of the inquisition, an office which carries with it that licence. I note this correctly, as the information was given me; but I hope the person who gave it was mistaken, and that no such double dishonour is in question: in a court to drive men fourscore years after their offence, and which offence was only fidelity to the Prince they esteemed their sovereign – to so unworthy a means of personal distinction. The mention of the inquisition made us enquire into the present state of that *holy* office, and we were informed that it was now formidable only to persons very notorious in ill-fame; and that when it does act against offenders an inquisitor comes from Madrid to conduct the process. From the expressions, however, which were used, and the instances given, it appeared that they take cognisance of cases not at all connected with faith in religion; and that if men or women were guilty of vices which made them notoriously offensive, this was the power which interposed: an account by no means favourable, for the circumstance which was supposed most to limit their power was the explicit nature of the offence, that it was against the catholic faith, and by no means against public morals, to secure which is an object of very different judicatures in every country.

There are reckoned to be from 1,200 to 1,500 monks and nuns in the city.

Price of Provisions

Bread, 4 *sous* and a fraction [2*d.*] per lb. of 12-oz. } that of the poor people, very little less; but they buy the soldier's bread, which comes cheaper; they live very much on stock-fish, &c.

Mutton, 22½ *sous* [1*s.*] the lb. of 36 oz.

Pork, 45 *sous* [2*s.*] the lb. of 12 oz.

Hams sometimes three or four pesettos or shillings the lb. of 12 oz., wine four to five *sous* [2½*d.*] the bottle.

The markets are now full of ripe figs, peaches, melons, and more common sorts of fruit, in great profusion. I bought three large peaches for a penny, and our *laquais de place* said that I gave too much, and paid like a foreigner. Noble orange trees are in the gardens in the town full of fruit: and all sorts of garden vegetables in the greatest plenty and perfection. The climate in winter may be conjectured from their having green peas every month in the year.

Labour. Common day wages are 25 *sous* French [1*s.* 1*d.*], sometimes rise 33 *sous* [1*s.* 5*d.*], the very lowest 22½ [1*s.*]. Stocking weavers earn 33 *sous*.

Ibid., 234–41 (July 1787)

4. ITALY

Young's three-month tour of Italy came as a major extension of his third and final visit to France. He entered Italy through Antibes on the Mediterranean coast on 16 September 1789, returning to France via Chambéry, east of Lyons, on 25 December. His tour was an extensive one, embracing many of the major cities of northern Italy, including Turin, Milan, Venice and Florence. Indeed, his account is more concerned with the great Italian cities, their buildings and antiquities, than with agriculture, which for once seems relegated to second place. It is true, however, that Young found it difficult to make contact with leading agriculturists, and he was often unimpressed by the farms which he saw. Ever a critical observer, he found much to praise and perhaps rather more to condemn in the country, and among his particular disappointments were the weather and the modes of transport. Let us begin with his account of travelling conditions.

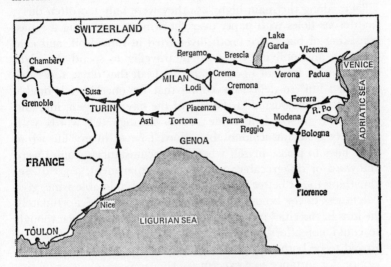

Map 3 *Young's Tour in Italy*, 1789
(Contemporary international boundaries shown)

(a) Travel in Italy

A traveller of vast experience, Young for the most part found little that was pleasing in the public carriages, roads and wayside inns of Italy. At Toulon, on the eve of leaving France, he had been advised to sell his one-horse chaise that had carried him the many miles from Paris. Italy, he was told, was dangerous for the solitary traveller, the roads infested with robbers, and the innkeepers ready to steal even the hay and oats from one's horse. The *vetturini*, or hired coachmen, he was informed, were cheap and were to be found everywhere. Young's experience, however, was that these hired coachmen were dishonest and unreliable, and their vehicles dirty and uncomfortable (excerpt (1)). Even worse was the covered barge which conveyed him from Venice to Bologna in an area where the roads were too bad to permit the use of coaches. The nauseating state of the barge's cabin caused Young to walk most of the way, following the barge along the banks of the Po. As he remarked, the barge was surely too cheap to be good, the journey of 125 miles costing only the equivalent of 17s. 6d., including food and accommodation (excerpt (2)).

The inns, he found, varied greatly. In the smaller towns and villages along the main highways they were only too often dirty, pestiferous holes with paper over the windows, offering a repast consisting of black rice broth, liver fried in rancid oil, and cold cabbage, and obliging the prudent traveller to spend the night in his clothes for fear of 'the itch'. At Lodi the 'dirty, miserable wretched inn' so depressed Young that for once he felt unable to write up his journal at the end of the day: 'my pen, ink, and tablets are useless before me ... to arrange ten words with propriety is an unsurmountable effort. I never in my life wrote three lines to please myself when the circumstances around were untoward or disagreeable; a clean, neat apartment, a good fire, something to eat better than paste-soup, with tolerable wine, give a lightness to the bosom and a facility to the ideas.' Fortunately the inns in the cities proved to be highly satisfactory, even though he could not afford to stay in the best of them. Some indeed proved to be both very good and very cheap, as did Petrillo's at Venice, for instance (see excerpt (9)).

Young thought that the poor state of many of the roads, and the swarms of robbers which endangered the lives and property of those who travelled them, cast a sad reflection on the standards of Italian government. He was favourably impressed, however, by the remarkably large number of opera houses, some of them new and magnificent, which enhanced such small and unimportant places as Lodi, situated only twenty miles from the two great theatres of Milan; and within some ten or fifteen miles of Lodi there were others to be found at Codogno, Crema and Piacenza. As a keen theatre-goer and enthusiast for opera, Young was inclined to criticise the taste of Italian audiences. What disgusted him most, however, was not the artistic standards but an extraordinary example of the Italian theatre's sanitary arrangements which he came across in Venice (excerpt (3)):

(1) Yesterday I agreed with a *vetturino* to take me this morning at six o'clock to Brescia; but not being perfectly well, insisted

that he should not come for me without his *vettura*, nor
before the time. The rascal knocked me up at five, and then
without the carriage; it was only four steps, he said, and
wanted to hurry away my trunk. I begin to know them, and
therefore steadily refused to stir: after much vain persuasion
away they went, and in three quarters of an hour returned.
The dog drove me a full mile and half on the road to Brescia
to an inn, where there was another *vetturino*, to whom he
had sold me; and there I found myself packed with three
other persons in the worst place; to the contrary of all which,
the scoundrel had signed an agreement. My expressions of
anger only got me laughed at. The world has not such a set
of villains as these *vetturini*. I have read guides and direc-
tories and travels that speak of this way of journeying as
passable: – if not good, very bearable; but they must be very
partial or very careless if they mention them without indigna-
tion. Their carriages are wretched, open, crazy, jolting,
dirty dung-carts; and as to their horses, I thought, till I
saw them, that the Irish garrans had no rivals on the globe;
but the *cavalli di vetturini* convinced me of the error. My
company were two merchant-like people and a young man
going to the university of Padua; the two first, repeating
prayers and counting beads. How the country came to be
well irrigated is a question. Paternosters will neither dig
canals nor make cheese.

(2) My last day at Venice. I made, therefore, a gleaning of
some sights I had before neglected, and called once more on
my friend ——, asssuring him truly that it would give me
pleasure to see him in England or to be of any service to him
there. The *Corriere di Bologna*, a covered barge, the only
conveyance, sets off tonight at eleven o'clock. I have taken
my place, paid my money, and delivered my baggage; and
as the quay from which the barge departs is conveniently
near the opera house, and *Il Burbero di buon Cuore* acted
for the first night, I took my leave of Signor Petrillo's
excellent inn, which deserves every commendation, and went
to the opera. I found it equal to what the *prova* had indicated; it is an inimitable performance; not only abounding
with many very pleasing airs, but the whole piece is agreeable: and does honour to the genius and taste of Signor

Martini. Swift, in one of his letters to Stella, after dining
with Lords Oxford and Bolingbroke, and going in the
evening to some scrub [mean, insignificant person], says he
hates to be a prince and a scoundrel the same day. I had
tonight all this feeling with a vengeance. From the representation of a pleasing and elegant performance, the music
of which was well adapted to string one's feelings to a
certain pitch, in clear unison with the pleasure that sparkled
in so many eyes and sounded from so many hands – I
stepped at once in full contrast into the bark *detto Corriere
di Bologna*; a cabin about ten feet square, round which sat
in silence and the darkness visible of a wretched lamp, a
company whose rolling eyes examined, without one word of
reception, each passenger that entered. The wind howled
and the rain beat in at the hole left for entering. My feelings
that thrilled during the evening were dissipated in a moment,
and the gloom of my bosom was soon in unison with that of
the scene.

Of this voyage from Venice to Bologna all the powers of
language would fail me to give the idea I would wish to
impress. The time I passed in it I rank among the most
disagreeable days I ever experienced, and by a thousand
degrees the worst since I left England; yet I had no choice:
the roads are so infamously bad, or rather so impracticable,
that there are no *vetturini*; even those whose fortune admits
posting make this passage by water, and when I found that
Monsieur de la Lande, secretary to the French ambassador
at Turin, had made the same journey, in the same conveyance, and yet in his books says not a word against the accommodation, how was I to have divined that it could prove so
execrable? A little more thought, however, would have told
me that it was too cheap to be good – the price for the whole
voyage of 125 miles is only 30 *pauls* [17s. 6d.], for which you
are boarded. After a day's spitting of a dozen people in 10
feet square (enough to make a dog sick), mattresses are
spread on the ground, and you rest on them as you can,
packed almost like herrings in a barrel; they are then rolled
up and tumbled under a bulk [framework], without the
least attention which side is given you the night after; add
to this the odours of various sorts, easy to imagine. At dinner,
the cabin is the kitchen, and the *padrone* the cook; he takes

snuff, wipes his nose with his fingers, and the knife with his handkerchief, while he prepares the victuals, which he handles before you till you are sick of the idea of eating. But on changing the bark to one whose cabin was too small to admit any cookery, he brought his steaks and sausage rolled up in paper, and that in his flag of abomination (as Smollett calls a continental handkerchief), which he spreads on his knees as he sat opening the greasy treasure for those to eat out of his lap with their fingers, whose stomachs could bear such a repast. Will an English reader believe that there were persons present who submitted, without a murmur, to such a voyage, and who were beyond the common mercantile crews one meets with in a *vetturini*? – some well dressed, with an appearance and conversation that spoke nothing of the blackguard. I draw conclusions operating strongly against the private and domestic comforts of life from such public vehicles: this is the only one for those who pass to and from Venice, Bologna, Florence, Rome, and Naples, and of course must be exceedingly frequented; and there are no *voitures* by land to rival it. If these people were clean, decent, and comfortable at home is it credible that they would submit to such a mode of travelling? The contrast would shock them as it would Englishmen, who would move heaven and earth to establish a better convey-ance at a higher price. The people who travel thus form the great mass of a nation, if we except the poor; it is of little consequence how the Cornari and the Morosini live; they live probably like great lords in other countries; but the public and national prosperity is intimately connected with the comforts and accommodation of the lower classes, which appear in Italy to be, on comparison with England, miserably inferior. Their excellencies, the *aristocrats* of Venice, do not travel thus; and as to *the people*, whether they go on their heads, in the mud, or to the devil, is all one to the spirit of their government. For myself I walked much of the journey, and especially on the banks of the Po for the better view of that great river, now rendered immense by the late dreadful floods which have deluged so much of the country. Along the banks, which are high dykes, raised many feet against its depredations, there are matted huts at every 100 or 200 yards, with men stationed called *guardia di Po*, ready to assemble with their tools at a moment's warning in case of a breach; they have fires all night. Soldiers also make the rounds night and day to see that the men are at their stations, and to give assistance if wanted. There is a known and curious piece of roguery against which much of this caution is bent: the mischief of a breach is so great that when the danger becomes very imminent the farmers in the night cross the river in boats in order to bore holes in the banks to enable the water the easier to make a breach, that by giving it a direction contrary to that of their own lands they may render themselves secure. For this reason the guards permit no navigation, except by privileged barks, like the *corrieri*, firing at all others that are seen on the river. It is now an immense body of water, twice and in some places perhaps even thrice as broad as the Thames at London. As to the face of the country, from the Lagunes to Ferrara it is everywhere nearly the same as what I have so often described; whether grass or arable, laid out into rows of pollards, with vines trained to them at various distances, but always near enough to give the whole the appearance of a wood when viewed from the least distance. It does not seem to want people, towns and villages being numerous; and there are all the signs of a considerable navigation, every village being a port with abundance of barges, barks, boats, etc. Coffee-houses remarkably abound in the Venetian dominions; at all towns, and even villages, where we passed they are to be found, fortunately for me, as they were my resource to make amends for the dirty fingers and beastly handkerchief of our Signor Padrone.

(3) There is nothing more striking in the manners of different nations than in the idea of shame annexed to certain necessities of nature. In England a man makes water (if I may use such an expression) with a degree of privacy, and a woman never in sight of our sex. In France and Italy there is no such feeling, so that Sterne's Madame Rambouillet was no exaggeration. In Otaheite to eat in company is shameful and indecent; but there is no immodesty in performing the rites of love before as many spectators as chance may assemble. There is between the front row of chairs in the pit and the orchestra, in the Venetian theatre,

a space of five or six feet without floor: a well-dressed man, sitting almost under a row of ladies in the side boxes, stepped into this place, and made water with as much indifference as if he had been in the street, and nobody regarded him with any degree of wonder but myself. It is, however, a beastly trick: shame may be ideal, but not cleanliness; for the want of it is a solid and undoubted evil. For a city of not more than 150,000 people, Venice is wonderfully provided with theatres; there are seven; and all of them are said to be full in the carnival. The cheapness of admission, except at the serious opera, undoubtedly does much to fill them.

> *Travels in France and Italy during the Years 1787, 1788 and 1789*, ed. Thomas Okey (Everyman, ed., 1915) 244–5, 259–60, 261–4 (Oct–Nov 1789)

(b) Agriculture in Italy

Though Young began his Italian tour with the object of seeing as much of the farming as possible, he found it difficult to obtain detailed information of individual farms and practices. Many of the persons to whom he had letters of introduction were away from home, and others proved not to be knowledgeable or helpful, being often theorists rather then practical farmers. A visit to the agricultural society in Milan was a fiasco (excerpt (4)), and the unusually brief accounts which Young gave of the farms he managed to view indicate that he saw little remarkable, and in general found them as disappointing as the weather was unfriendly (excerpt (5)). November in northern Italy seemed a more severe season than at home, and he began to long for 'our BLESSED ISLE, from which no one will ever travel but to return with feelings fresh strung for pleasure and a capacity renovated by a thousand comparisons for the enjoyment of it'.

(4) In the morning, deliver letters to Signor Vassari and the Messieurs Zappas, gentlemen in commerce, from whom I might receive information relative to the exports, etc., of the Milanese. At noon to the society of agriculture (called the Patriotic Society), which, fortunately for me who am a member, had a meeting today: the Marchese di Visconti in

the chair, with ten or a dozen members present, to all of whom Signor Amoretti introduced me. I never expect much from societies of this sort; but this of Milan was today employed on a button and a pair of scissors: it seems they want at this city to make the finer sorts of hardware, in order to rival those of England and lessen the import which, in spite of every obstacle, is very great: the idea originates with the government and is worthy of its little ideas; a true peddling spirit at present throughout Europe. An artist in the town had made a button and half a pair of scissors, one half English and the other half of his own manufacture, for which he claimed and had a reward. Similar are the employments of societies everywhere! In England, busied about rhubarb, silk, and drill-ploughs; – at Paris with fleas and butterflies; – and at Milan with buttons and scissors! I hope I shall find the *Georgofili* at Florence employed on a top-knot. I looked about to see a practical farmer enter the room, but looked in vain. A goodly company of i Marchesi, i Conti, i Cavalieri, i Abati, but not one close-clipped wig, or a dirty pair of breeches, to give authority to their proceedings.

(5) Early in the morning with Signor Amoretti to Magna, seven miles to the south of Florence, to Signor Paoletti. This gentleman, *curé* of that parish, had been mentioned to me as the most practical writer on agriculture in this part of Italy, having resided always in the country, and with the reputation of being an excellent farmer. We found him at home and passed a very instructive day, viewing his farm and receiving much information. But I must note, that to this expression, *farm*, must not be annexed the English idea; for Signor Paoletti's consist of three *poderi*, that is, of three houses, each with a farmer and his family, *alla Meta*, who cultivates the ground and has half the produce. It is unnecessary to observe that whenever this is the case the common husbandry, good or bad, must be pursued. It will surprise my English readers to find that the most practical writer at Florence of great reputation, and very deservedly so, has no other than a *métayer* farm. But let it not be thought the least reflection on Signor Paoletti, since he classes in this respect with his sovereign, whose farms are

in the same regimen. Signor Paoletti's maples for vines appeared to be trained with much more attention than common in Tuscany, and his olives were in good order. This day has given me a specimen of the winter climate of Italy; I never felt such a cold piercing wind in England. Some snow fell; and I could scarcely keep myself from freezing by walking four or five miles an hour. All water not in motion from its current or the wind was ice; and the icicles from the dripping springs in the hills were two feet long. In England when a fierce N.E. wind blows in a sharp frost we have such weather; but for the month of November I believe such a day has not been felt in England since its creation. The provision of the Florentines against such weather is truly ridiculous: they have not chimneys in more than half the rooms of common houses; and those they do not use, not because they are not cold, for they go shivering about with chattering teeth with an idea of warmth from a few wood ashes or embers in an earthen pan and another contrivance for their feet to rest upon. Wood is very dear, therefore this miserable succedaneum is for economy. Thank God for the coal fires of England, with a climate less severe by half than that of Italy. I would have all nations love their country; but there are few more worthy of such affection than our BLESSED ISLE, from which no one will ever travel but to return with feelings fresh strung for pleasure and a capacity renovated by a thousand comparisons for the enjoyment of it.

Ibid., 235, 280–1 (Oct–Nov 1789)

(c) Italian cities

With rather little to be achieved in the agricultural sphere, Young spent much of his time in Italy touring the famous palaces, churches and galleries of the cities. Sometimes he was disappointed, as at Turin (excerpt (6)), which he found ugly and dirty, and not to be compared with London, and also at Vicenza (excerpt (7)), where Palladio's celebrated buildings were in a poor state of repair. However, the opera house at Milan (excerpt (8)) was impressive, though the famous cathedral seemed inferior to St Paul's, and he thought that the ancient documents treasured in the Abbey of St Ambrose would have possessed greater interest had they referred to ploughs rather than religious benefactions. The many pleasures of Venice, and its cheapness, both delighted him, but at this point in his journey he began to tire of so much brick and stone and wish for the fields of the countryside (excerpt (9)). In Florence Young divided his time between visits to the galleries, meetings with agriculturists, excursions to farms, and *conversazioni* of high society (excerpt (10)).

Turin, SEPT. 26TH 1789

(6) This being the first Italian city of renown for beauty that I have seen, I have been all eyes today. Some travellers have represented it as the prettiest town in Europe, and the Strada di Po the finest street. I hurried to it with eagerness. I was in the middle of it, asking for it. *Questa, questa!* replied an officer, holding up his hands as if to point out an object of great beauty which I did not see, and in truth I saw it not. It is straight and broad and nearly regular. Two rows of brick barns might be so equally. The houses are of an ugly obfuscated brick; a few have stucco, and that old and dirty; the scaffold holes in the walls of the rest are left unfilled; some of them are enlarged by time, and several courses of bricks between those holes not pointed, which has as bad an effect; the windows are narrow and poor; some with iron balconies – some without; the arcades, for there is a row on each side of the street, would be destructive of beauty, if it was here: the arches are plastered, which patches the line with white: and through them are exhibited nothing but poor shops that encumber their spans with all sorts of lumber; the lamps are fifty or sixty yards asunder. In a word, there are fifty streets at London to which this cannot be compared. If those who have travelled in Italy think this street fine, what am I to meet with in other towns? – The Strada della Dora Grossa is by far a finer street than that of the Po, but the houses are greatly too high. There is a beautiful arcade entrance to the herb-market, which seems to have furnished the idea of that at the new buildings of Somerset House. The streets are almost all quite regular and at right angles. I expected that this circumstance would have been attended with much more beauty than it is. It gives too great a sameness; the constant return of the same angles tires the eye; and I am convinced that a city would

be much more striking and more admired that had varied lines instead of uniform ones. Circles, semi-circles, crescents, semi-ellipses, squares, semi-squares, and compounds composed of these, mixed with the common oblongs, would give a greater air of grandeur and magnificence. The most splendid object I have seen at Turin is the staircase and saloon in the château contiguous to the royal palace. There is nothing at Versailles, except the gallery, to be compared with it. The front of this edifice is fine, and the whole does honour to Juvara. This morning I should have delivered my letters, but am unlucky. The Marchese de Palavicino, president of the agrarian society, and Signor Bissatti, the secretary of it, are both in the country. Signor Capriata, the *président en second*, I met with, but he is no practical farmer; he has been obliging enough, however, to promise me an introduction to some persons who are conversant with agriculture. Meeting with these disappointments I began to fear I might want the intelligence that was necessary to my design; and be in that ineligible situation of seeing only the outsides of houses, and knowing nothings of the persons within. With time thus on my hands I inquired for a bookseller, and was directed to Signor Briolo, who prints the memoirs of all the learned bodies here; among others, those of the agrarian society, which I bought, and afterwards turning over found that I made a pretty conspicuous figure in one written by the Cavaliere di Capra, colonel of the regiment of Tortona, on the size of farms. He is a bitter enemy to large ones: not content with strictures on Piedmont, he presses England into his service, and finds it necessary to refute me as I appear in the translation of Monsieur Freville, from which he quotes passages which I never wrote. I wished to assure the author that it was the French translator and not the English farmer that he had refuted. I laughed very hearty with Signor Capriata at this adventure of the memoirs. In the evening to the opera; the theatre is a fine one, though not the principal; the house nearly full, yet all the world is in the country.

(7) Vicenza, OCT. 26TH 1789
My friendly Abbate, continuing his obliging offices, had the goodness to accompany me this morning to a very

famous woollen fabric, at present under the direction of an Englishman, and to a magazine of earthenware in imitation of Mr Wedgwood. It is surely a triumph of the arts in England to see in Italy Etruscan forms copied from English models. It is a better imitation than many I have seen in France. View the Olympic theatre of Palladio, which pleases all the world; nothing can be more beautiful than the form, or more elegant than the colonnade that surrounds it. Of all his works here I like the Palazzo Barbarana least. I am sorry to see that most of Palladio's edifices are of bricks stuccoed, except the Palazzo Raggione, which is of durable stone; and that there is hardly one of them which is not out of repair. The roof of the Palazzo di Raggione, which must offend every eye, is not of Palladio; only the case of arcades that surround the building, which is one vast room of 200 feet by 80 used for the courts of justice, and also as a common *jakes* by the mob, and dreadfully garnished. A pretty use to which to apply an edifice of Palladio. The brick columns of this great architect are of the finest work I ever saw; and some of the stucco only now failing, after 200 years. At Verona and Vicenza there are very few new houses, and no signs that I could see of the wealth and prosperity of the present age. There are exceptions, but they are few. A silk merchant here has built a good house; and Signor Cordelina, an advocate at Venice, a large and handsome one that cost 100,000 ducats, without being finished: he made his fortune by pleading.

(8) Milan, OCT. 4TH 1789

Reach Milan in the forenoon. This great city stands in the midst of a dead level country, so thickly planted that you see nothing of it till you are in the streets. To the *Albergo del Pozzo* in time to wait on the Abbate Amoretti, secretary of the patriotic society, to whom I had letters from Monsieur Broussonet and Signor Songa of London: I found him admirably well lodged in the *palazzo* of the Marquis de Cusina: this, said I to myself, looks well to find a man of letters in a splendid apartment, and not poked, like a piece of lumber, into a garret: it is a good feature in the Italian nobility. I entered his apartment, which is a cube of about thirty feet, from a great saloon of forty or fifty. He received

me with easy and agreeable politeness which impresses one at
first sight in his favour. Soon after he returned my visit. I
find him an agreeable, well-informed, and interesting character. Waited also on the Abbate Oriani, astronomer royal,
who expressed every wish to be of use to me. At night to the
opera; a most noble theatre; the largest as well as hand-
somest I have seen; the scenes and decorations beautiful.
Though it is Sunday I look with amazement at the house,
for it is three parts full, even while much of the world are
in the country: – how can such a town as Milan do this?
Here are six rows of boxes, thirty-six in a row; the three
best rows let at 40 *louis d'or* a box. This is marvellous for an
inland town without commerce or great manufactures. It
is the PLOUGH alone that can do it. I am delighted with the
accommodation of the pit; one sits on broad easy sofas,
with a good space to stir one's legs in; young persons may
bear being trussed and pinioned on a row of narrow benches,
but I am old and lazy, and if I do not sit at my ease would
not give a fig to sit there at all. . . .

OCT. 9TH. This day was appointed for visiting a few
objects at Milan, for which Signor Beecken had the goodness to desire to be my *cicerone*; his chariot was ready after
breakfast, and we went from sight to sight till five o'clock.
Buildings and pictures have been so often and so well
described that for modern travellers nothing is left, if they
expatiate, but to talk of themselves as much as of the objects.
I shall note in a few words the things that struck me most.
I had read so much of the cathedral and came to it with
such expectation that its effect was nothing. There are
comparative measurements given of it with St Paul's and St
Peter's that seem to rank it in the same class for magnitude:
to the eye it is a child's plaything compared to St Paul's.
Of the innumerable statues that of St Laurence flayed is
the finest. The architecture of the church of St Fedele, by
Pellegrino, is pleasing; it contains six columns of granite; and
there are other fine ones also in that of St Alesandro. But I
found Padre Pini, professor of natural history, a better object
than his church; he has made a great and valuable collection
of fossils, and has taken the means necessary for self-
instruction, much travel and much experiment. [At] St Celso
there are two statues of Adam and Eve, by Lorenzi, that

cannot be too much admired; and a Madonna, by Fontana. Here also are pictures that will detain your steps by the two Procacinis. The great hospital is a vast building, once the palace of the Sforzas, dukes of Milan, and given by Duke Francis for this use. It has a net revenue of a million of *livres*, and has at present above one thousand three hundred patients. At the Abbey of St Ambrose, built in the ninth century, and which has round arches, anterior to gothic ones, they showed us a MS. of Luitprandus, dated 721, and another of Lothaire, before Charlemagne. If they contained the register of their ploughs they would have been interesting; but what to me are the records of gifts to convents for saving souls that wanted probably too much cleaning for all the scrubbing-brushes of the monks to brighten? But unquestionably the most famous production of human genius at Milan is the last supper of Leonardo da Vinci, which should be studied by artists who understand its merit, as it is not a picture for those who, with unlearned eyes, have only their feelings to direct them. View the Ambrosian library.

(9) Venice, NOV. 1ST 1789

The cheapness of Italy is remarkable, and puzzles me not a little to account for; yet it is a point of too much importance to be neglected. I have, at Petrillo's, a clean good room that looks on the grand canal and to the Rialto, which, by the way, is a fine arch, but an ugly bridge; an excellent bed, with neat furniture, very rare in Italian inns, for the bedstead is usually four forms like trussels set together; fine sheets, which I have not met with before in this country; and my dinner and supper provided at the old price of 8 *pauls* a day, or 3s. 4d. including the chamber. I am very well served at dinner with many and good dishes, and some of them *solids*; two bottles of wine, neither good nor bad, but certainly cheap; for though they see I drink scarcely half of it in my negus at supper, yet a bottle is brought every night. I have been assured by two or three persons that the price at Venice, *à la mercantile*, is only 4 to 6 *pauls*; but I suppose they serve a foreigner better. To these 8 *pauls* I add 6 more for a *gondola*; breakfast 10 *soldi*; if I go to the opera it adds 3 *pauls*; thus, for about 7s. 3d. a day, a man lives at Venice, keeps his servant, his coach, and goes every night to a public entertainment. To dine well at a London coffee-house, with a pint of bad port, and a very poor dessert, cost as much as the whole day here. There is no question but a man may live better at Venice for £100 a year than at London for £500; and yet the difference of the price of the common necessaries of life, such as bread, meat, etc., is trifling. Several causes contribute to this effect at Venice; its situation on the Adriatic, at the very extremity of civilised Europe, in the vicinity of many poor countries; the use of gondolas, instead of horses, is an article perhaps of equal importance. But the manners of the inhabitants, the modes of living, and the very moderate incomes of the mass of people, have perhaps more weight than either of those causes. Luxury here takes a turn much more towards enjoyment than consumption; the sobriety of the people does much, the nature of their food more; pastes, macaroni, and vegetables are much easier provided than beef and mutton. Cookery, as in France, enables them to spread a table for half the expense of an English one. If cheapness of living, *spectacles*, and pretty women are a man's objects in fixing his residence, let him live at Venice: for myself I think I would not be an inhabitant to be Doge, with the power of the Grand Turk. Brick and stone, and sky and water, and not a field nor a bush even for fancy to pluck a rose from! My heart cannot expand in such a place: an admirable monument of human industry, but not a theatre for the feelings of a farmer! – Give me the fields, and let others take the tide of human life at Charing Cross and Fleet Ditch.

(10) Florence, NOV. 22ND 1789

In the forenoon to the *conversazione* of the senator Marchese Ginori, where were assembled some of the *literati*, etc., of Florence; the Cavaliere Fontana, so well known in England for his eudiometrical experiments [experiments to test quantity of oxygen in air], Zucchino, Lastri, Amoretti, the Marchese Pacci, who has a reputation here for his knowledge of rural affairs, Signore Pella, etc. The *conversazioni* are commonly in an evening, but the Marchese Ginori's is regularly once a week in a morning. This nobleman received me very politely: indeed he is famous for his attention to

every object that is really of importance; converses rationally
on agriculture and has himself, many years ago, established
in the neighbourhood of Florence one of the most considerable manufactories of porcelain that is to be found in
Italy. Dine with his majesty's envoy extraordinary, Lord
Hervey, with a great party of English; among whom were
Lord and Lady Elcho, and Mr and Miss Charteris, Lord
Hume, Mr and Mrs Beckford, Mr Digby, Mr Tempest, Dr
Cleghorn, professor of history at St Andrews, who travels
with Lord Hume, with ten or a dozen others. I had the
honour of being known to Lord and Lady Hervey in
Suffolk, so they were not new faces to me; of the others I
had never seen anything: the company was too numerous
for a conversation from which much was to be gained. I sat
by the fellow of an English college, and my heels had more
conversation with his sword than I had with its owner:
when a man begins every sentence with a cardinal, a prince,
or a celebrated beauty, I generally find myself in too good
company; but Miss Charteris, who seems a natural character,
and was at her ease, consoled me on the other side. At this
dinner (which by the way was a splendid one), I was,
according to a custom that rarely fails, the worst dressed
man in the company; but I was clean, and as quietly in
repose on that head as if I had been either fine or elegant.
The time was when this single circumstance would have
made me out of countenance and uneasy. Thank my stars
I have buried that folly. I have but a poor opinion of Quin
for declaring that he could not afford to go plain: he was
rich enough in wit to have worn his breeches on his head,
if he had pleased; but a man like myself, without the talent
of conversation, before he has well arranged his feelings
finds relief in a good coat or a diamond ring. Lord Hervey,
in the most friendly manner, desired I would make his table
my own while I was at Florence – that I should always
find a cover at three o'clock, *for dinners are not the custom
here, and you will very rarely find me from home*. This
explains the Florentine mode of living; at Milan great
dinners are perpetual, here the nobility never give them. I
have no idea of a society worth a farthing where it is not the
custom to dine with one another. Their *conversazioni* are
good ideas when there are no cards – but much inferior to

what one has at dinner for a select party. In England, without this, there would be no conversation; and the French custom of rising immediately after it, which is that also of Italy, destroys, relatively to this object, the best hour in the whole day.

Ibid., 229–30, 234, 238–9, 249, 254–5, 278–9

Appendix: The Works of Arthur Young

(Dates of first editions only are given; later editions were often considerably extended and revised.)

The Theatre of the Present War in North America: With Candid Reflections on the Great Importance of the War in that Part of the World (1758).

Reflections on the Present State of Affairs at Home and Abroad (1759).

The Universal Museum, or Gentlemen's and Ladies' Polite Magazine of History, Politicks and Literature for 1762, vol. I (1762).

Museum Rusticum et Commerciale: or, Select Papers on Agriculture, Commerce, Arts and Manufactures (1764–6): vol. III, no. 45, 'Common Farmers vindicated from the Charges of being universally ignorant and obstinate'; no. 46, 'On the Mowing Wheat, and Cultivation of Lucerne'; no. 47, 'Of Manuring Land at a Large Expense'; no. 63, 'Of the Improvement of Wet Pastures'; no. 74, 'The Profit attending Arable and Pasture Land compared, as found by Experience, near Bury, in Suffolk'; vol. IV, no. 8, 'Of the Usefulness of Acquiring a Knowledge of Foreign Practices in Husbandry'; no. 9, 'An Enquiry respecting the Prices of the Implements used in the New Husbandry'; no. 10, 'Some Errata in Number 74, vol. 3, corrected'; no. 38, 'The Use of Broad-Wheel Waggons recommended to Farmers'; no. 62, 'Reasons why Farming so often proves unprofitable'; no. 63, 'An Answer to Ruricola Glocestris in which is contained an Estimate of the Expenses and Profits of a Dairy of Four Cows'.

A Letter to Lord Clive, on the Great Benefits which may result to the Public from patriotically expending a small part of a large private fortune: Particularly in promoting the Interests of Agriculture by Forming an Experimental Farm (1767).

The Farmer's Letters to the People of England: containing the Sentiments of a Practical Husbandman, on Various Subjects of the Utmost Importance: To which is added, Sylvae: or, Occasional Tracts on Husbandry and Rural Oeconomics (1767).

A Six Weeks' Tour through the Southern Counties of England and Wales (1768).

Letters concerning the Present State of the French Nation (1769).

An Essay on the Management of Hogs; Including Experiments on Rearing and Fattening them (1769).

A Six Months' Tour through the North of England (1770).

The Expediency of a Free Exportation of Corn at this time, with Some Observations on the Bounty and its Effects (1770).

The Farmer's Guide in Hiring and Stocking Farms (1770).

A Course of Experimental Agriculture (1770).

Rural Economy; or, Essays on the Practical Parts of Husbandry (1770).

Proposals to the Legislature for Numbering the People; Containing Some Observations on the Population of Great Britain, and a Sketch of the Advantages that would probably accrue from an exact Knowledge of its Present State (1771).

The Farmer's Tour through the East of England (1771).

The Farmer's Kalendar: or, Monthly Directory for all Sorts of Country Business (1771).

Political Essays concerning the Present State of the British Empire (1772).

Essays on the Spirit of Legislation, in the Encouragement of Agriculture, Population, Manufactures, and Commerce (1772).

Observations on the Present State of the Waste Lands of Great Britain (1773).

Political Arithmetic. Containing Observations on the Present

State of Great Britain and the Principles of her Policy in the Encouragement of Agriculture (1774).

Political Arithmetic, Part II. Containing Considerations on the means of Raising the Supplies within the Year. Occasioned by Mr Pulteney's Pamphlet on that Subject (1779).

A Tour in Ireland: with General Observations on the Present State of that Kingdom: Made in the Years 1776, 1777 and 1778, and brought down to the end of 1779 (1780).

An Enquiry into the Legality and Expediency of Increasing the Royal Navy by Subscriptions for Building County Ships (1783).

Annals of Agriculture and other Useful Arts, vols. I–XLVI (1784–1815).

The Question of Wool Truly Stated. In which the Facts are Examined for and against the Bill now depending in Parliament (1788).

A speech on the Wool Bill, that might have been spoken in the House of Commons (1788).

A Letter on Tithes to Arthur Young with his remarks on it: and a Second Letter in answer to those remarks (1792).

Travels during the Years 1787, 1788 and 1789. Undertaken more particularly with a view of ascertaining the Cultivation, Wealth, Resources and National Prosperity of the Kingdom of France (1792).

The Example of France, a warning to Britain (1793).

Postscript to the Survey of Hampshire. In a letter to Sir John Sinclair (1794).

General View of the Agriculture of the County of Suffolk (1794).

An Idea of the Present State of France, and of the Consequences of the Events passing in that Kingdom (1795).

The Constitution Safe without Reform: Containing some Remarks on a Book, entitled 'The Commonwealth in Danger', by J. Cartwright (1795).

National Danger and the Means of Safety (1797).

An Enquiry into the State of the Public Mind amongst the Lower

Classes: and on the Means of Turning it to the Welfare of the State (1798).

General View of the Agriculture of the County of Lincoln (1799).

The Question of Scarcity Plainly Stated, and Remedies Considered. With Observations on Permanent Measures to keep Wheat at a more Regular Price (1800).

An Inquiry into the Propriety of Applying Wastes to the Better Maintenance and Support of the Poor (1801).

Letters from his Excellency George Washington to Arthur Young, containing an Account of his Husbandry with a Map of his Farm, his Opinions on Various Questions in Agriculture; and many Particulars of the Rural Economy of the United States (1801).

Georgical Essays: by A. Hunter (1803–4): vol. I, essay 8, 'On Top-Dressings'; vol. IV, essay 27, 'On the Size of Farms'; vol. V, essay 4, 'On Hogs and their Management'; vol. V, essay 27, 'On Carrots'; vol. VI, essay 8, 'On Summer Fallowing'.

General View of the Agriculture of Hertfordshire (1804).

General View of the Agriculture of the County of Norfolk (1804).

'An Essay on Manures', *Bath and West of England Society, Letters and Papers*, vol. X (1805) p. 97.

General View of the Agriculture of the County of Essex (1807).

General Report on Enclosures. Drawn up by order of the Board of Agriculture (1808).

On the Advantages that have resulted from the Establishment of the Board of Agriculture (1809).

General View of the Agriculture of the County of Oxford (1809).

On the Husbandry of Three Celebrated British Farmers, Messrs Bakewell, Arbuthnot and Ducket (1811).

An Enquiry into the Progressive Value of Money in England, as marked by the price of Agricultural products (1812).

Baxteriana: Containing a Selection from the Writings of Baxter (1815).

An Enquiry into the Rise of Prices in Europe, during the last twenty-five years, compared with that which has taken place in England; with Observations on the Effects of high and low prices (1815).

Oweniana: or, Select Passages from the Works of Owen (1817).

Communications to the Board of Agriculture, new series, vol. 1, 'On the Culture of Carrots' (1819).

Index